WANDF

Other "Burning Issues" Titles from Solid Ground

In addition to *Wandering Stars* which you hold in your hand, Solid Ground is proud to introduce several of our books in our "Burning Issues" Series –

YEARNING TO BREATHE FREE? *Thoughts on Immigration, Islam & Freedom*
by David Dykstra

PULPIT CRIMES: *The Criminal Mishandling of God's Word*
by James R. White

THE TRUTH SET US FREE: *Twenty Former Nuns Tell Their Stories of God's Amazing Grace,* Edited by Richard Bennett with Mary Hertel

FROM TORONTO TO EMMAUS: *The Empty Tomb and the Journey from Skepticism to Faith, A Rational and Scriptural Response to "The Lost Tomb of Jesus"*
by James R. White

LETTERS TO A MORMON ELDER by James R. White

IS THE MORMON MY BROTHER? By James R. White

COMMON FAITH, COMMON CULTURE: *How Christianity Defeats Paganism*
by Joseph M. Bianchi

TWO MEN FROM MALTA: *A Shipwrecked Apostle and a Toronto Newspaperman Challenge Thoughtful Roman Catholics to Examine their Faith*
by Joe Serge with Joel Nederhood

JESUS LOVES THE CHURCH AND SO SHOULD YOU
By Earl M. Blackburn

BE CAREFUL HOW YOU LISTEN: *How to Get the Most out of a Sermon*
by Jay Adams

Call us at **205-443-0311**
Visit us on the web at **solid-ground-books.com**
Email us at **mike.sgcb@gmail.com**

WANDERING STARS

Contending for the Faith
with
The New Apostles and Prophets

KEITH GIBSON

SOLID GROUND CHRISTIAN BOOKS
Birmingham, Alabama USA

Solid Ground Christian Books
PO Box 660132
Vestavia Hills AL 35266
205-443-0311
sgcb@charter.net
www.solid-ground-books.com

WANDERING STARS
Contending for the Faith with the New Apostles and Prophets

Keith Gibson

First Solid Ground Edition – December 2011

Cover design by Borgo Design
Contact them at borgogirl@bellsouth.net

ISBN- 978-159925-317-6

Dedication

To my wife and my children and their families,
may your passion for Jesus always include a passion for the truth.

Acknowledgements

I first need to thank my wife and my children for encouraging me in the process of writing and for helping with the editing of the manuscript but most of all for putting up with me when I was struggling with the content.

Thank you to my church family for standing beside me in the gospel and loving the truth. Thank you for not being afraid of controversy.

I owe a great debt of gratitude to my former blogging partner on "The Sign of Jonah" blog, Drew. Drew, I owe much inspiration to you.

Many thanks to those who regularly read and commented on the blog. Thank you for encouraging me to write. Thank you for helping me clarify my thoughts.

Most of all, I want to give praise to God. Thank you for the great salvation that is ours. Thank you for the gift of your Word.

TABLE OF CONTENTS

FOREWORD
By Craig Branch

The author of "Wandering Stars", Keith Gibson is both a pastor and a staff-member with us at the Apologetics Resource Center, where I am the director. These two callings provide Keith with a healthy blend of sound doctrine (and correcting heresy, 1 Tim. 1:3-7), and its application in shepherding the flock.

Our ministry works closely, arm and arm, cross denominationally so we have a working knowledge of flexibility within the symphonic theology of the Church. As the expression goes, "we major on the majors and minor on the minors."

But there are lines of heresy and the closer one gets to those lines, more damage occurs. This book addresses a growing movement that brings serious error inside the church.

Jesus warns concerning these last days that "fake prophets will arise and will show great signs and wonders so as to mislead, if possible, even the elects" (Mt. 24:24). The New Apostolic and Prophetic Movement and Five-Fold Ministry does bring serious error into the church.

Keith and I have collaborated on this book somewhat for some time and I know he has done extensive research and consultations with individuals involved and with well respected theologians across the theological spectrum. Living in the Kansas City area gives Keith much first-hand knowledge from the International House of Prayer and the Kansas City Prophet Movement which has been the breeding ground for the Apostolic and Prophetic Movement.

Early on in the book Keith addresses the first hurdle of the opposing views on whether miraculous spiritual gifts continue today or have ceased. Keith explains the positions but moves past that to the fact that even non-cessationists should be of great concern for them as well.

We want Christians to better understand the reality of the miraculous power of the Holy Spirit in and through His church and that we don't only have academic head knowledge of Biblical principles to follow. But the Church must understand the dangers of false doctrines. Keith addresses the numerous errors and practices that flow out of the basic Apostolic and Prophetic error as well.

The Scripture instructs us to "be diligent to present yourself approved to God as a workman who does not need to be ashamed, handling accurately the word of truth" (2 Tim. 2:15). I strongly commend studying through this book carefully as it corrects the errors and presents the truth. Jesus said, "abide in My word and you shall know the truth and the truth shall set you free" (Jn. 8:31-31).

INTRODUCTION

Don't Skip This Section

"I heard what I call the internal audible voice of the Lord...It was as clear as crystal. I heard the actual words. There was no guess-work. It was not impressions. It was the word of the Lord came to me. And the Lord said this, 'I am going to change the understanding and expression of Christianity in the whole world in one generation.'"-Mike Bickle

It is a serious thing to claim to speak for God. So serious, in fact, that a prophet who claimed to speak for God and whose words did not come to pass was to be put to death according to the Old Testament. God takes both His Name and His word so seriously that He gave some of the harshest rebukes in all the Old Testament to those who were claiming to bring revelation from Him that He had not sent. Consider His words through the prophet Jeremiah:

> Jeremiah 23:9-12,15,16,22 (ESV) 9 Concerning the prophets: My heart is broken within me; all my bones shake; I am like a drunken man, like a man overcome by wine, because of the LORD and because of his holy words. 10 For the land is full of adulterers; because of the curse the land mourns, and the pastures of the wilderness are dried up. Their course is evil, and their might is not right. 11 "Both prophet and priest are ungodly; even in my house I have found their evil, declares the LORD. 12 Therefore their way shall be to them like slippery paths in the darkness, into which they shall be driven and fall, for I will bring disaster upon them in the year of their punishment, declares the LORD..... 15 Therefore thus says the LORD of hosts concerning the prophets: "Behold, I will feed them with bitter food and give them poisoned water to drink, for from the prophets of Jerusalem ungodliness has gone out into all the land."

[16] Thus says the LORD of hosts: "Do not listen to the words of the prophets who prophesy to you, filling you with vain hopes. They speak visions of their own minds, not from the mouth of the LORD........[22] But if they had stood in my council, then they would have proclaimed my words to my people, and they would have turned them from their evil way, and from the evil of their deeds."

It would appear today that many within the apostolic and prophetic movement do not understand the seriousness of the words, "God said" or "Thus saith the Lord".

For example, in his book, *Growing in the Prophetic*, Mike Bickle, one of the key leaders in the movement, demonstrates this lack of understanding. He writes:

"For the most part, the same New Testament prophetic gift can operate in very different packages. Usually people have no problem with the woman in the prayer group who feels a burden to pray for someone, who senses the Holy Spirit leading her prayer, and who states that God is 'impressing' something on her heart. All of this is in a package that most people are familiar with and understand.

"But if she speaks up during the Sunday morning service in her non-charismatic church and loudly proclaims her revelation interspersed with 'Thus saith the Lord', she could get a significantly different response. Here are the same words and the same message, but delivered in a very different package."[1]

Bickle's last sentence is telling...and wrong. It is far different to claim an impression than it is to loudly pronounce, "Thus saith the Lord". The former is the hesitant expression of a thought, something that may or may not be completely true. The latter is a claim to divine revelation that by definition cannot contain anything but truth and which carries divine authority and must be obeyed.

The words, "Thus saith the Lord", change everything. A higher level of authority is being claimed. One should be extremely careful before one puts words in the mouth of God.

From the time of Montanus in the mid-second century to the present there have always been those within the church who have claimed to be prophets.

That is nothing new. Even in the modern era, there have been a number of people who claimed prophetic gifts since the Azusa Street Revival in 1905. A few of these gathered substantial followings based largely on their perceived abilities to heal. However beginning in the early 1980's a significant change began to occur. An explosion in the number of independent ministries based around the prophetic gifting began. Many of these new prophetic ministers have now achieved superstar status within segments of the body of Christ. Schools to train prophets have been established and the church is witnessing a veritable explosion of prophetic activity. New doctrines are being written on an almost daily basis. Teachings and practices which the church has never held in all of her 2,000 year history are now commonplace.

Though no specific date can be given for the beginning of the prophetic movement, it began to emerge on a world-wide level in the 1980's. In 1982, Mike Bickle began Kansas City Fellowship, the home of the controversial Kansas City Prophets. At the same time, other prophetic ministries were gaining prominence throughout the Church. On October 23, 1987, Bill Hamon hosted and sponsored the first "National Prophet's Conference" with over 700 people in attendance.[2] Today the movement has literally hundreds of thousands of adherents. At the time of this writing, the Elijah List, an email newsletter publishing the words of many of today's new prophets, is received daily by over 130,000 people worldwide.[3] The Indentity Network, a similar prophetic email list is even larger, boasting a daily readership of over 150,000 people.

Emerging out of the Prophetic Movement, the Apostolic Movement began in earnest in the 1990's. In 1999, in Singapore, a group of apostles gathered and laid the foundation for what has become the International Coalition of Apostles (ICA). Shortly thereafter, C. Peter Wagner was asked to lead the group.[4] This organization, which is perhaps the most visible arm of the New Apostolic Reformation, now boasts a membership of nearly 500 individuals all claiming apostolic status.[5] These apostles claim to have been given their office, not merely on grace alone, but in response to their works for God. The ICA official definition states the following,

> "However an office, such as the office of apostle, is not given by grace alone, but given as a result of works that have demonstrated faithfulness in stewarding the gift."[6]

Compare these words with those of the apostle Paul who stated:

> "For I am the least of all the apostles, unworthy to be called an apostle, because I persecuted the church of God. But by the grace of God I am what I am." 1 Cor. 15:9-10

These new apostles do not claim to merely be in the apostolic succession and the guardians of apostolic truth. No, these new apostles claim to be even greater than the former apostles. As this book will demonstrate, they are claiming that the church cannot come to maturity and fulfill its mission apart from them. They are claiming authority over geographic regions and various marketplaces. They are mutually appointed and mutually affirming.

The issues occurring within the apostolic and prophetic movements are not peripheral. They affect nearly every central doctrine of the Christian faith. This is not by accident. Mike Bickle has stated that he had an encounter with God while in Egypt where he heard the "internal audible voice of God",

> "Suddenly the Lord gave me this sentence: 'I am going to change the understanding and expression of Christianity in the whole earth in one generation.' "[7]

Rick Joyner, in his book, *A Prophetic Vision for the 21st Century,* has made very similar statements as have C. Peter Wagner and Bill Hamon. We will examine their claims throughout the book. But they are demanding a change, a new paradigm, new wineskins.

The majority of the Church has not taken seriously the claims of the modern apostles and prophets to be introducing a new paradigm into the Body of Christ. These claims are far more than idle boasts. Indeed the paradigm shifts have already begun in many segments of Christianity. To say that the movement has grown rapidly would be a gross understatement. The issues raised go far deeper than a mere debate over the cessation or continuation of spiritual gifts. Without intending to be alarmist, it is the contention of this book that many of the statements and teachings of leaders within this movement strike at the very heart of essential Christian doctrine and the nature of Christianity.

If the church does not respond to these issues, the Christian faith that we pass on to our children and grandchildren will bear little resemblance doctrinally to the historic faith.

Those within the prophetic movement are ready to battle the established church. Many have prophesied a coming Civil War within the Body of Christ. We will examine this in detail in later chapters but consider the words of Bickle as indicative of the milder form of this pronouncement,

> "The Lord says: 'I will change.' And I understood the emphasis of *I*, it will be sovereignly initiated. The King of Kings is orchestrating it, he says, 'I will change.' And when the Lord says, 'I'm gonna change the synagogue system to an early church with fishermen...' I'm telling you when power bases shift, if it happens in political arenas they call it Revolution. It's called a Revolution. If it happens in the Spiritual arena, Conflict."[8]

Bickle continues in this vein by saying,

> "I've cared enough about that word *change* to study political and spiritual changes thru history, and I'm telling you they are bloody, they are hurtful, it is not a pretty sight to the flesh. But the Lord says, 'I am changing.' And the word *changing* is the scary part."[9]

The purpose of this book will be to examine this new movement and many of the associated teachings and phenomena in the light of Biblical revelation. When this is done we believe the readers will agree that the new apostolic and prophetic movement poses a serious threat to the doctrinal integrity of the Church.

It is vital to understand that this is not a "Charismatic vs. Non-Charismatic" issue. The issues involved are more central than that. I believe, when the issues are carefully examined, that all members of the Church, regardless of their stripe or their particular view of spiritual gifts, will find cause for concern. Because it is my sincere desire that this book not be perceived as merely an attack on the Charismatic community, I have taken great pains to use a number of noted Charismatic and Pentecostal theologians' writings in order to point out the errors in the apostolic and prophetic movements. Pentecostal and Charismatic authors who have reputations for Biblical orthodoxy such as Gordon Fee and Wayne Grudem, as well as doctrinal statements and position papers from Pentecostal denominations such as the Assemblies of God are used to demonstrate that the modern apostolic and prophetic movement must be considered heretical even by believers who believe in the continuation of the sign gifts.

The question often arises as to whether I have spoken with the individuals with whom I am taking issue. The fact is that extended conversations and contacts with people who could be considered leaders in the apostolic and prophetic movement have been held. Additionally, because the prophetic movement tends to have its own unique vocabulary, I have interviewed those within the movement to insure that the problem was not one of miscommunication. At every point I have tried to make sure that I could honestly say, "I understand", before saying, "I disagree". I have not, however, met with all the individuals concerned, as there are literally hundreds of people operating independent prophetic ministries within the Church today. It would simply be impossible to meet with them all. Nor is this required. Doctrine is a public issue and is open to public correction. We are not dealing with a private offense between two individuals (as in Matthew 18) but rather with the proclamation of false doctrines striking at the very core of what it means to be Christian. In discussions with those in the prophetic community I have raised the issues that will be the substance of this book. I have appealed to those who are more Biblically oriented within this branch of Christianity to speak out on the subject and attempt to impact the movement of which they are a part. It was my hope that this correction would come from those inside the movement itself. To date, none of them have been willing to do so. Therefore the time has come that I have felt compelled to address the issues.

All of the ministries to which this book will refer are national in scale. This is important because these ministries influence literally thousands of people. Influence of this level must bring with it an accompanying level of accountability. I have attempted to reference a large variety of the teachers within the apostolic/prophetic community in order to demonstrate that the issues of concern do not center around one or two errant ministries but rather span the gamut of the movement. However, having said that, certain ministries are definitely more prominent than others and therefore warrant fuller inspection.

I want to state at the outset that I am not questioning the sincerity or Christianity of many of those involved in the movement but rather their doctrines and practices. Doctrines are being espoused by a number of high profile, highly influential ministries that directly undermine many essential Christian teachings.

Nor am I saying that the modern apostles and prophets are completely wrong in everything that they say or teach. It is virtually impossible for a movement to be wrong about everything. But I am saying that the problems are significant enough to demand a response.

While a book of this kind is by its very nature polemical, I will attempt to be even-handed and charitable in dealing with the matter, though it is doubtful that any of the ministries critiqued will believe that this objective has been accomplished.

A word must be said about our process of evaluation. Countless hours have been spent reading the writings and listening to the sermons of the prophets themselves. I have read literally thousands of prophetic messages. For the most part, the formal doctrinal statements of the individual ministries have been bypassed. This may at first be disturbing to some. However, there are several reasons for this approach. First, a doctrinal statement only has value insofar as it is actually used to govern the teaching produced by a particular ministry. Most doctrinal statements are never referred to again once they are written and approved. Therefore the doctrinal statement tells very little about what is actually taught and believed within any given ministry. A better understanding will be gained by listening to what is taught day after day. It is the contention of this book that many of the messages of these prophetic ministries actually introduce doctrines that are contrary to their official statements. Secondly, by virtue of their brevity, many doctrinal statements are ambiguous and open to interpretation. For instance, the doctrinal statements of most modalists (those who deny the Trinity by teaching that the Father, Son and Spirit are one in person) are vague enough to slip past many believers. The reality is that many doctrinal statements lack the specificity necessary to make a fair assessment of the positions held by a particular ministry. Finally, a doctrinal statement may be copied from a book or other ministry site and may not actually be the product of the teacher in question. Years of working with cults have taught the necessity of looking beyond the doctrinal statement when evaluating a movement, ministry or individual teacher.

One final note. There is always the temptation when dealing with a subject of this nature, to pull out the most outlandish quotes in an attempt to make one's point more forcefully. Though it is certain that some will feel that this is exactly what has been done, I have attempted to resist this temptation. While an extreme example has occasionally been used in order to demonstrate how heretical the movement is at its fringes, for the most part, I have attempted to use quotes from those considered more "mainstream" within the apostolic and prophetic movement. It is my desire to demonstrate that the issues addressed in this book are rampant within the community and not isolated in one or two marginal teachers.

It is my sincere prayer that this book will be used in some small measure to awaken the church to the seriousness of the errors being propagated within the apostolic/prophetic movement and to call the church back to the truth.

CHAPTER ONE

Are These the Days of Elijah?
Cessassionism vs Continualism

"These are the days of Elijah, declaring the word of the Lord. And these are the days of your servant, Moses, righteousness being restored." From the song, "Days of Elijah" by Robin Mark

It would seem remiss to have a discussion concerning the prophetic and apostolic movements without first taking at least a cursory look at the larger issue of spiritual gifts. Perhaps no issue so divides the church today as this issue.

It is nearly impossible to come to this discussion from a neutral perspective, unless one has never considered the subject at all. All of us have a bias. All have been influenced by previous study of the Scripture, church background and experience. To fail to acknowledge this is to be truly blind.

However, this is not to say that the truth cannot be found. One must be open to having one's own biases challenged in the light of Biblical revelation.

This chapter will take a brief overview of the dominant positions within the body of Christ today. This will necessarily involve a great deal of generalization. Within each of the major camps there are a number of nuances and variations. It is beyond the scope of this book to look at each of them. The author will also lay his own cards on the table so that the reader may understand the bias that he brings to the discussion as well.

Additionally, we will take a closer look at a very influential book published by the esteemed theologian Wayne Grudem on the subject of New Testament prophecy, as his views have been widely accepted and quoted by the prophets themselves, though it is my contention that the modern prophets have taken Grudem's premise far beyond the boundaries that he himself would find acceptable.

In our next chapter we will also consider the office of the apostle. What is this office? Are there apostles today? We will consider this question particularly in the light of the popular teaching of the five-fold ministry. What is this teaching and is it consistent with Biblical revelation?

Further, we will attempt to explain why this subject is truly not a concern only to those in the cessationist camp. In fact, it is the contention of this book that Charismatics should be particularly concerned as the prophetic movement has the potential to undermine the credibility of the Charismatic movement as a whole and further because it is the Charismatic community that is particularly vulnerable to accepting these prophets because of their acceptance of the continuation of the sign gifts.

Four Views on Miraculous Spiritual Gifts

One's position on spiritual gifts in general has obvious impact on one's initial reaction to the subject of the gifts of apostle and prophet in particular. One's view of spiritual gifts as a whole will form the frame of reference for one's approach to the modern day apostles and prophets. Therefore it is necessary to gain at least a basic understanding of how the subject of spiritual gifts is viewed within the larger Christian community.

In an excellent book entitled, *Are Miraculous Gifts for Today?*, four Biblically committed scholars outline, support and critique the four most common positions on the continuation or cessation of the miraculous or sign gifts within the church today. Each of these positions falls within the pale of orthodoxy. Each of these positions is held by a large segment of the Body of Christ and is believed by Christians committed to the authority of Scripture. On pages 10-13, the authors give a brief description of the major positions. These may be summarized as follows:[10]

Cessationist position- As the name implies, this view holds that all the miraculous gifts have ceased. This would include gifts such as healing and miracles as well as the revelatory or word gifts such as prophecy, tongues, interpretation of tongues, word of wisdom and word of knowledge. This position is straightforward and those holding this position would obviously have serious theological problems with the modern apostolic/prophetic movement, even before examining the particular doctrines being taught.

Pentecostal/Charismatic position- Pentecostal would refer to anyone associated with official Pentecostal denominations such as Foursquare Full Gospel or the Assemblies of God. Charismatic would refer to those giving contemporary expression to the miraculous gifts within more mainline or established denominations as well as in Independent, non-denominational churches. While there are differences within the two groups, they share in common a belief that all of the gifts are in existence today. They also share in common a belief that the "baptism of the Holy Spirit" is a separate event, subsequent to salvation and is evidenced by speaking in tongues. This group would largely be open to the idea of modern day prophets, though as we will see, many are not as open to the idea of a continuation of the apostolic office.

Third Wave Position- This position might be typified by persons such as C. Peter Wagner and Jack Deere. This group agrees with the Pentecostal/ Charismatic position that all of the miraculous gifts exist today but disagrees with them concerning the baptism of the Holy Spirit and the necessity of speaking in tongues. Third Wavers in general believe that the baptism of the Holy Spirit occurs at salvation and identify speaking in tongues as one gift but not the initial or essential sign of the baptism. Third Wave churches are frequently non-denominational. As with Pentecostals and Charismatics, this movement is open to the idea of modern day apostles and prophets, and, in fact, both Wagner and Deere would be classified as leaders within the Apostolic and Prophetic Movement.

Open but Cautious Position- This position, which is not normally represented within theological discussion, represents a large number of Evangelicals. These believers are not convinced by the cessationist arguments that the miraculous gifts have completely ceased. However, while they are appreciative of many aspects of the Charismatic movement such as expressive worship and the challenge to renewal in prayer, they are very concerned about what they perceive as doctrinal excesses and abuses within the Pentecostal/Charismatic and Third Wave Movements. While they may believe that the gifts are possible, they are unconvinced that what is happening today within the Pentecostal/Charismatic/Third Wave movement represents a true biblical expression of these gifts.

It is within this final broad category that the author of this book approaches the subject of spiritual gifts. I do not classify myself as a cessationist in the sense that this is commonly meant. I believe that the gifts of the Spirit are given to the church for the church age. I do however strongly insist that these gifts must be regulated according to the boundaries set out for their use within the pages of Scripture. Therefore, there is much that is being done within the name of spiritual gifts with which I cannot agree.

Having looked momentarily at the subject of spiritual gifts in general, and having attempted to make my own bias known, we will now turn our attention to the subjects of the prophetic and apostolic specifically as these are the real issues this book attempts to address. We begin with a key book written by a highly respected Evangelical scholar that has that has been co-opted by many within the prophetic movement to support their practices and justify the egregious amount of false prophecy occurring in their circles. The book is *The Gif of Prophecy in the New Testament and Today*.

Evaluation of Wayne Grudem's, *The Gift of Prophecy in the New Testament and Today*

Professor and eminent theologian Wayne Grudem has written a widely popular book on the subject of New Testament prophecy. His views have been lauded by a number of Evangelical theologians including J.I. Packer and D. A. Carson. His view is well-reasoned and contains a very serious treatment of the subject. His book is of critical importance for anyone seeking to understand the modern prophetic movement because his reasoning is used by many of the modern prophets to establish their credibility as well as to provide cover when their prophecies prove to be false. It is not my purpose to either defend or critique Grudem's work. To do so, would require another book in and of itself. My purpose is merely to succinctly articulate Grudem's central points and then to demonstrate their impact upon the modern apostolic and prophetic movement.

In the book, Grudem argues for a closed canon and a cessation of the office of apostle but for a continuance of New Testament prophecy, which he defines as a lower form of revelation where one expresses in human words impressions that "God brings to mind."[11]

According to Grudem, the New Testament equivalent of the Old Testament prophet is the Apostle. Old Testament prophets spoke the "very words of God". They wrote Scripture. New Testament apostles also spoke the "very words of God" and wrote Scripture.[12]

These gifts functioned with 100% accuracy. According to Grudem, there are no prophets or apostles in this sense in existence today. He writes,

> "Now it must be admitted that some confusion arises when charismatics call prophecy the 'word of the Lord' but then say it is not exactly the word of the Lord, but that confusion seems to come from the lack of distinction between Old Testament and New Testament prophecy. In actual practice **no responsible charismatic leader says that prophecy today is equal in authority to Scripture, or should be treated as such.**"[13] (emphasis added)

According to Grudem's thesis, New Testament prophecy, such as what was occurring at Corinth or what Philip's daughters practiced, is of a much lower nature. It is speaking from impressions that God brings to mind. It might be likened to a sort of spontaneous preaching although Grudem himself does not make that analogy. It could include impressions of direction that the individual believes are coming from God. In many church circles phrases like, "the Lord spoke to my heart", or "I sense the Lord leading us", are relatively common and would constitute a form of what Grudem calls New Testament prophecy.

These prophets and their prophecies are to be judged for appropriateness and truthfulness in the light of God's unchanging and inerrant revelation which is to be found in the pages of Scripture but these prophets are not required to meet the standards for judging a prophet given by God in Deuteronomy 13 and 18 which would require death if the prophecies do not come to pass because they are not claiming that level of revelatory authority. Instead they are to be judged much as one would evaluate a sermon. When one hears a sermon, one understands that the pastor is not claiming to be speaking with inerrant authority. A critical point is that, for Grudem, the Old Testament tests of a prophet do not apply to New Testament prophecy.

Let's briefly consider these two key passages.

Deuteronomy 13:1-5 states,

> "If a prophet or one who foretells by dreams appears among you and announces to you a miraculous sign or wonder, and if the sign or wonder

of which he has spoken takes place, and he says, 'Let us follow other gods' (gods you have not known) 'and let us worship them', you must not listen to the words of that prophet or dreamer. The Lord your God is testing you to find out whether you love him with all your heart and with all your soul. It is the Lord your God you must follow, and him you must revere. Keep his commands and obey him; serve him and hold fast to him. That prophet or dreamer must be put to death , because he preached rebellion against the Lord your God, who brought you out of Egypt and redeemed you from the land of slavery; he has tried to turn you from the way the Lord your God commanded you to follow. You must purge the evil from among you."

The other key text is Deuteronomy 18:20-22 which states,

"But a prophet who presumes to speak in my name anything I have not commanded him to say, or a prophet who speaks in the name of other gods, must be put to death. You may say to yourselves, 'How can we know when a message has not been spoken by the Lord?' If what a prophet proclaims in the name of the Lord does not take place or come true, that is a message the Lord has not spoken. That prophet has spoken presumptuously. Do not be afraid of him."

It is important to note that God gave both a doctrinal and practical test for establishing a prophet. In the doctrinal test of Deuteronomy 13, the prophet must point to the one true God and lead people in His way. In the practical test of Deuteronomy 18, the prophet's predictions must come to pass. Those claiming to be prophets who failed these tests were to be executed. These two texts provide the foundational principles for differentiating between a true and false prophet.

In arguing that the New Testament gift of prophecy is of a different nature, Grudem points out that in the New Testament, in passages like 1 Corinthians 14, Paul says that the prophets are to speak and the rest are to judge but there is no attempt to gather up and preserve their words and add them to the Canon nor is there any admonition to execute the prophets for speaking incorrectly. For instance, while Paul acknowledges the presence of prophets within the Corinthian church, there remains no record of anything any of these prophets ever spoke. Similarly, while the book of Acts record that Philip's daughters prophesied, there is no record of their prophecies. Further there is no indication that the prophets are to be put to death or even excommunicated. This is, in Grudem's estimation, because the level of revelation, and therefore the *accountability*, is much lower. In fact, Grudem argues that it is really the prophecy and not the prophet that is normally being judged. Speaking of 1 Thessalonians 5:19-21 he writes:

> "There it is the *prophecies* (vs 20) that are evaluated or judged, not the prophets. This Pauline passage is much closer to 1 Corinthians 14:29 than the other non-Pauline passages, which may be speaking to situations which are quite dissimilar. In fact, in both 1 Thessalonians 5:19-21 and 1 Corinthians 14:29ff. there is an absence of any warning about false prophets, a lack of criteria for judging them and an absence of any hint of strangers coming from the outside and pretending to be prophets. While other passages speak of tests to reveal false prophets, 1 Corinthians 14:29 and 1 Thessalonians 5:19-21 speak rather of a different sort of evaluation, the *evaluation of the actual prophecies* of those who are already accepted by the congregation."[14]

It is this idea of a lower level of accountability more than any other that has been seized upon by members of the modern apostolic and prophetic movement and used by them to deflect any objective evaluation of their prophetic status. **It should be noted that, unlike Grudem, these modern prophets demand an accountability that is lower while arguing for a revelatory status that is equal to or even higher than the New Testament Apostles.** As this book will demonstrate, members of this new movement claim to be the greatest apostles and prophets who have ever lived while at the same time demanding to be given a pass when their prophecies fail and their doctrines prove to be unbiblical.

In Grudem's opinion, New Testament prophets should refrain from "thus saith the Lord" declarations and instead offer their words in a more humble, "I think the Lord is suggesting something like...." fashion.[15] Grudem would further assert that these words do not write new doctrines or practices for the church. These words are to bring edification, exhortation and comfort as Paul wrote in 1 Corinthians 14.[16]

It should be noted that if all today's apostles and prophets were claiming was this low form of revelation, a book of this nature would not be necessary. If all they were doing was bringing personal words of encouragement or comfort to local church bodies with a humble, "I sense that the Lord might be saying", then there would be no need to address the things being said in the way that this book will seek to do. The local pastors and elders, as well as the members of each congregation would evaluate these words based on their conformity to the inerrant standard of God's revelation given in Scripture and accept or reject them.

But this is not all that is happening with the modern apostolic and prophetic movement. Instead however, these modern prophets are rewriting Christian theology, establishing new doctrines unknown in the history of the church. Today's prophets move well beyond the modest position outlined in Dr. Grudem's work. They make dogmatic pronouncements of what God is doing in the world, even declaring how Christians across the globe are to pray and seek God. They boldly declare the destinies of nations. They brashly declare that the church cannot fulfill its mission on earth without them. Consider, for example, merely the titles of the following prophecies published to over 130,000 believers worldwide on the Elijah List:

"North Korea: The Lord Said He is Going to 'Tear Down That Wall'"[17]

"Spain: This Next Move of My Spirit
Will Crush Terrorism and Religious Facades"[18]

"Great Composers Coming, the Spirit of the Renaissance,
Terrorism Defeated by the Kingdom of God"[19]

"New Intercessory Assignment: Judicial Intercession"[20]

As these titles would indicate and as the rest of the book will demonstrate, the activity and claims of the prophets of today are a far cry from the humble local church ministry Dr. Grudem addresses in his book.

These new apostles and prophets have been given virtual rock star status in much of the church. Most alarmingly, as will be demonstrated in chapter five, today's prophets claim authority equal to or even in some cases greater than the Old Testament prophets and New Testament apostles… that is, until they miss. When they give an errant prophecy (and this is a very frequent occurrence as we will also demonstrate) they quickly run back under Grudem's umbrella and claim that New Testament prophets cannot be judged by Old Testament standards.

In short, they want the authority of the prophets and apostles of Scripture but not the accountability.

But they simply cannot have it both ways. Whether one agrees with Dr. Grudem or not, his position upholds a closed canon and the sufficiency of Scripture to guide the life of the believer. If today's prophets are going to operate under one of his principles they should accept them all.

If on the other hand, they want to claim the status of prophets and apostles equivalent to those in the Bible, then the church has every right to demand that they pass the same test as those prophets of old. If what they are doing is of the same or an even higher caliber than the authors of Scripture then surely accuracy ought to be expected. If they claim this status then they fall under the standards of Deuteronomy 13 and 18. Simply put, if these are the days of Elijah, as the popular song claims, then today's prophets must be expected to meet the same standards that Elijah met. However, not one of them even comes close.

Modern prophets and apostles should be consistent. Either step up to the plate and speak with the accuracy demanded of the prophets and apostles in Scripture or admit that what is being done is radically different and of a much lower character. Either modern apostles must stop making "thus saith the Lord" pronouncements predicting the destinies of nations and giving instructions and assignments to the universal church, or they must be ready to be judged by Deuteronomy 18 and similar passages. If they are speaking words that God gave them via open heaven visitations, face-to-face encounters and other forms of direct, unmistakable communication then these words must come to pass because the Lord is never wrong.

Are only Cessationists concerned?

It will be easy for those who are so inclined to perceive this book as anti-Charismatic, just one more fundamentalist tirade against spiritual gifts. Such a perception would be very unfortunate.

As I indicated earlier in the book, these issues should not be seen as Charismatic vs. Non-Charismatic. The issues that will be dealt with in the body of this book have bearing on the central doctrines of the Christian faith. In this regard, the substance of this book should be the concern of every believer. These are the issues where the Body of Christ historically has found common ground. That ground is being eroded and taken away.

Secondly, there is every reason for those in the Charismatic community to be particularly concerned. First, because these teachers are most closely identified with the Charismatic branch of Christianity. Therefore, the aberrant teachings that they are proposing have the potential to discredit the entire movement unless leaders within the Charismatic community begin to make firm distinctions between themselves and members of the apostolic/prophetic movement.

There is always the tendency among people to paint those of another group with a broad brush. Many people will not distinguish between these teachers that are on the theological fringe of the Charismatic movement from solid, Biblically-based and theologically sound scholars like Wayne Grudem or Gordon Fee. Therefore it is imperative that leaders within the Charismatic movement at large take these issues seriously and sound an alarm.

Additionally, it is those within the Charismatic movement who are the most predisposed to be influenced by these teachers. Few who are deeply convinced that gifts such as prophecy have ceased will spend much time listening to or reading the works of today's prophets. The followers of the modern apostles and prophets are drawn primarily from the Charismatic community.

We appreciate those within the Charismatic community who do attempt to bring a corrective word. But these voices seem few and far between. It is imperative that a broader chorus of voices begin to speak out and demand accountability and an adherence to the fundamental doctrines of the faith, including the sufficiency and authority of Scripture.

With this then as an introduction, let us further examine the specific doctrines and issues to be found within the movement.

CHAPTER TWO

Did Jesus Fail?
The Five-fold Ministry
and Christian Restorationism

"Ever since the dark ages, God has been restoring Truth to the Church in order to get us back to the place of fullness where we can actually rule and reign in the world rather than be dominated by the very things we are to have victory over." - Ryan Wyatt

In the previous chapter we discussed the issue of the continuation of miraculous gifts in the church today and gave special attention to the subject of the prophetic gift. Now we move to the subject of the apostolic and a specific teaching within this movement that has come to be known as the "five-fold ministry doctrine".

What about apostles today?

In order to approach this question, we must first say that the answer will largely be determined by what one means by an apostle. This may at first seem like an obvious answer but in reality it is not quite so simple. The word apostle means one who is sent, a delegate or an ambassador. Contrary to popular belief, the Bible does not always use the word "apostle" in a technical sense referring to those who exercised authority over the church and laid the doctrinal foundation for the body of Christ. At times the word is used merely to indicate someone who is a church representative. Therefore, if by apostle, one means those who represent the church or those who plant churches or those who exercise administrative authority over more than one church, such as in a denominational setting, then certainly there are apostles today, though most of those occupying such positions would never choose such a term for themselves and it seems counterproductive and confusing to use the term "apostle" in this way today. At other times the word is used to indicate those uniquely chosen by Christ to lay the foundation for the church. It is in this sense that the word is normally used and it is in this sense that it will be considered here. It is the contention of this book that there are no apostles of this nature within the church today nor should we expect to see any.

Within the majority of those claiming to be Christians, continualists as well as cessationists, there has historically been a consensus that the apostolic office has ceased. That consensus no longer exists today. Today, the International Coalition of Apostles (ICA) founded by C. Peter Wagner boasts a membership of nearly 500 individuals all claiming some level of apostolic authority. Many within the Charismatic wing of the church now believe that the apostolic ministry was intended by God to continue throughout the history of the church. Chuck Pierce, who is considered by many to be an apostle, represents this new view when he writes,

> "The apostle John was probably the last of the original apostles who walked on Earth. These apostles were responsible to pass their mantle of revelation from generation to generation."[21]

It is interesting that Pierce offers no evidence Biblically or historically to support his assertion that the twelve apostles were responsible to pass their mantle of revelation on to succeeding generations and indeed there is no evidence within the pages of Scripture of any attempt to do so. With the exception of Matthias, who was chosen to replace Judas as a member of the original twelve, the apostles made no effort to replace their number as they passed away. Apparently, they were unaware of their mandate to pass on their revelatory mantle.

Many continualists now affirm that the office of the apostle is being restored to the church through what has commonly become known as the "five-fold ministry" teaching. This teaching, which has its roots in the Latter Rain movement of the 1940's-1960's and William Branham, has become so common among some segments of the Charismatic community that it is accepted by most followers without serious reflection. This teaching, which is based loosely on Ephesians 4:11-13, states that there are five ministries that are essential to the building up of the body: apostles, prophets, evangelists, pastors and teachers. The teaching further states that the first two offices ceased to function at some time in the past history of the church but are now being restored in these last days by the Holy Spirit as the bride of Christ is being prepared to meet the Bridegroom. This teaching has become dogma among many believers. It should be noted that while the five-fold ministry teaching mentions evangelists, pastors and teachers, those who hold to this view of ministry give very little attention to the last three giftings. Without question, the emphasis of the teaching is on the apostolic and prophetic.

Robert Bowman offers an excellent commentary on the subject of the five-fold ministry when he writes,

"The sole proof-text used to support this concept is *Ephesians 4:11-13*, which states that Christ gave 'some as apostles, and some as prophets, and some as evangelists, and some as pastors and teachers,...until we all attain to the unity of the faith and the full knowledge of the Son of God.' The word 'until,' it is argued, proves that the church today needs apostles and prophets as much as evangelists, pastors, and teachers. However, it is the 'building up' of the church (v.12) which must continue until the church is mature, not all five of the offices listed in verse 11. This is clear when the whole text is read as follows: 'And He gave some as apostles, and some as prophets, and some as evangelists, and some as pastors and teachers; [these offices were given] to equip the saints for the work of service, [which work has as its goal] to build up the body of Christ until we all attain to the unity of the faith...' The offices of apostle and prophet would naturally cease in the church once their role in 'equipping the saints' was completed; that is, once the New Testament canon was completed.

Some have objected that there is no reason to bracket off the apostles and prophets from the other three offices listed in verse 11. However, in the very same epistle, Paul states that the church has 'been built upon the foundation of the apostles and prophets' (*Eph. 2:20*) and that Christ's mystery concerning the church was 'revealed to His holy apostles and prophets in the Spirit' (3:5). These statements indicate that the role of apostles and prophets was fulfilled in the first century.

The New Testament is particularly clear about the temporary role of the apostles, since they were chosen to give eyewitness testimony of the risen Christ (Acts 1:21-26; 5:32; Luke 1:1-4; 1 Cor. 9:1). Paul indicated that he was the last person to see the risen Christ and receive an apostolic commission (1 Cor. 15:8). The epistles of 2 Peter and Jude, among the very last New Testament writings to be penned, exhort the readers to avoid false doctrines by recalling the teachings of the apostles (2 Pet. 1:12-15; 2:1; 3:2, 14-16; Jude 3-4, 17). Peter and Jude did not say, 'Listen to the apostles living today,' but instead urged believers to 'remember what the apostles said.'"

Bowman concludes his article with the following assessment:

"Therefore, in the usual biblical sense of the term, there are no apostles today. Nor are there any prophets in the usual sense, as they were part of the 'foundation' laid in the first-century church. This is not to deny the continuing validity of the gift of 'prophecy,' since Paul does refer to prophesying as a basic activity in which all Christians are urged to participate to the extent God gifts them (Rom. 12:6; 1 Cor. 11:4-5; 12:10; 13:2, 8-9; 14:1-6, 20-33; 1 Thess. 5:20), and in a general functional sense persons exercising this gift are even called 'prophets' (1 Cor. 14:32, 37). Yet Paul also speaks of specific persons who occupied an office of 'prophet' which was second in authority only to apostle (1 Cor. 12:28-29). It is this office of 'prophet,' not all prophecy, which I am arguing passed away around the end of the first century."[22]

Some Pentecostal denominations have taken a similar position as Bowman in response to the modern apostles and prophets. In 2000 the Assemblies of God published a position paper concerned with the so-called revival manifestations rampant at the time. This paper also addressed the claim of the restoration of the apostolic. It states,

"The leadership of the local church, according to the Pastoral Epistles, is in the hands of elders/presbyters and deacons. These are the last of Paul's epistles. There is no indication in these last writings of continuing offices of apostles and prophets, though the ministry functions still continue."[23]

In counter-point to this position, Charismatic author Sam Storms argues for a continuation of the apostolic office. Storms does a very nice job outlining the qualifications for an apostle and in stating that this is an ecclesiastical position, not a particular spiritual gift. However, after conceding that one must be a personal witness to the resurrected Christ and must be taught by Him in order to qualify as an apostle, Storms surprisingly leaves the door open to apostles existing today. In fact he states that he expects to see them functioning in the Church before the return of Christ. Storms writes,

"Are there apostles today? I certainly believe that it is the agenda of the Holy Spirit to bring them forth before the coming of the Lord.

However, there is considerable debate as to whether those with an "apostolic anointing" today are in the office of an apostle. I am open to the possibility that they are. But if so, they must meet the criteria set forth above and display the characteristics portrayed in the [New Testament]."[24]

Of course this would entail personal training and encounters on the scale of the apostle Paul, and indeed many of the modern apostles and prophets claim to have had personal encounters with the risen Christ. But this seems unconvincing since Paul considered himself an apostle born out of due time. There is no indication in any of the writings of the New Testament of any thought of apostolic continuance. Further, Storms fails to give a convincing explanation as to how he knows that bringing forth apostles is "the agenda of the Holy Spirit" in this day. Nor does Storms give a convincing argument as to the necessity of modern apostles.

Charismatic theologian Wayne Grudem notes this problem as well. He writes,

"Yet is seems quite certain that there were none [apostles] appointed after Paul. When Paul lists the resurrection appearances of Christ, he emphasizes the unusual way in which Christ appeared to him, and connects that with the statement that this was the 'last' appearance of all, and that he himself is indeed 'the least of all the apostles, unfit to be called an apostle'."[25]

Grudem concludes,

"It seems that no apostles were appointed after Paul, and certainly, since no one today can meet the qualification of having seen the risen Christ with his own eyes, there are no apostles today. In place of living apostles present in the church to teach and govern it, we have instead the writings of the apostles in the books of the New Testament. Those New Testament Scriptures fulfill for the church today the absolutely authoritative teaching and governing functions which were fulfilled by the apostles themselves during the early years of the church."[26]

This last point is significant. In a very real sense the apostles of Christ are still leading the church today and performing their foundational role through the teachings that they left the church in the New Testament. In arguing for the need for a continuation of apostles, those within the movement have taken an approach similar to the Mormon Church by claiming that without the presence of living apostles, the foundation has been eroded. These apostles are necessary they believe, in order to keep the church functioning properly and in order to settle doctrinal issues. However, when one looks at those claiming the office of apostle today, not only do they fail to meet the central biblical qualifications, the practical outworking has only been increased disorder and doctrinal confusion as will be demonstrated in the rest of this book. In fact, a consistent result that may be seen in those who are following these new apostles and prophets is an abandonment of the teachings of the apostles and prophets contained in Holy Scripture.

Furthermore, it is simply mistaken to assume that physical presence is essential in order for the apostles to fulfill their foundational role. In several passages the apostle Paul speaks of Christ as the head of the church (see for example, Eph. 1:22; 4:15 and Col. 1:18). Yet it is certain that we no longer have Christ physically present among believers today. Christ does not have to be physically present in order to fulfill His role as the head of the church. In a similar vein, we do not require the physical presence of apostles within the church today for apostles to fulfill their role as a foundation for the church.

It also seems significant that no attempt was made by the apostles to replace themselves once they began to pass away. If this office is essential to the proper functioning of the church, why did these men not seek to have others put in place to carry this out? Surely this was gross negligence at best. They appointed bishops and elders but not apostles. Though the early church fathers may have seen themselves as standing in the apostolic succession, they did so in the sense of guarding and preserving the truths that had been deposited with them from the New Testament apostles, not in the sense of establishing new truths and new doctrines.

Grudem notes this very pointedly in his Systematic Theology. He writes,

> "It is noteworthy that no major leader in the history of the church—not Athanasius or Augustine, not Luther or Calvin, not Wesley or Whitefield—has taken to himself the title of 'apostle' or let himself be called an apostle. If any in modern times want to take the title 'apostle' to themselves, they immediately raise the suspicion that they may be motivated by inappropriate pride and desires for self-exaltation, along with excessive ambition and a desire for much more authority in the church than any one person should rightfully have."[27]

It is interesting also to note that teachers of the five-fold ministry doctrine routinely disagree on when the gift temporarily stopped and when it began to be restored.

Those who seek to establish a continuance of the New Testament apostle and of a prophetic gift equal to or greater than that exercised by those in the pages of Scripture fail to make any distinction between the period in which the canon was still being written and the period in which we currently live.

Jude, who wrote one of the last books in our New Testament, gives no indication of a continuation of the apostolic office. Instead, he points his readers BACK to the words of the apostles they had already received. In Jude 3, he speaks of contending for the faith "once for all delivered [past tense] to the saints". But an even stronger case can be made from Jude 17 where he states, "But you, beloved, ought to remember the words that were spoken beforehand by the apostles of our Lord Jesus Christ." There is no support in this passage for any notion of apostolic continuance of the type suggested by Wagner and those in his coalition of "apostles".

Restorationism vs Reformation

Jesus stated that He would build His church. Jesus promised that the gates of hell would not prevail against the church. Was Jesus wrong? What happened to the church during the Middle Ages? Did the church need to be restored or simply reformed? What do these two terms even mean? How one answers these questions has a tremendous impact on one's understanding of the church and the present debate.

In the view of the reformation, serious error had crept into the church and the church needed cleansing and a return to the pure message of the gospel. The cry was, "to the source!" indicating a need to return to Scriptures and the doctrines that had originally been given. The Reformers did not believe that any central doctrine had been lost. Therefore they did not see themselves as restoring the church because the church itself had not been lost but rather corrupted.

The restorationist view is that central truths as well as Divine activity had been lost. Since the time of the Reformation, God has been restoring these truths to the church. Dr. Orrel Steinkamp, a Pentecostal minister, summarizes this teaching well in his article on the New Apostolic Reformation.

> "To Latter Rain teachers it seemed obvious that if there was to be a repeated apostolic Pentecost then apostles and prophets must be restored as well. These teachers then devised a historical scheme of restoration. Church history was understood as a succession of recoveries of lost or neglected truths. Luther recovered justification by faith, Baptists believers' baptism, Wesley holiness, A.B. Simpson healing and the early Pentecostal pioneers the gifts of the Spirit. The recovery process was now extended further. The end time body of Christ must go on to maturity and restore the apostles and prophets and these restored ministries must lead the church to a new and final dimension of power and authority not only bringing in the final harvest but establishing the Kingdom of God upon the earth."[28]

Modern "prophet" Ryan Wyatt gives us the classic expression of this teaching when he writes:

> "The sad thing is that not too long after Jesus arose from the dead, man took the things of Heaven and locked them up in a box only to release the things that fit their man-made religion of Christianity. Jesus came to give us Heaven on earth and man turned around and boxed it all up into a nice, tidy religion that lacks the power of Heaven to truly transform our world. Ever since the dark ages, God has been restoring Truth to the Church in **order to get us back to the place of fullness where we can actually rule and reign in the world rather than be dominated by the very things we are to have victory over.**"[29]

The difference between reformation and restoration may seem subtle but it is actually very significant. The reformers believed that the truth still resided within the doctrines of the church but had been clouded by error. Their efforts then were aimed at stripping away the doctrines added by the Roman Catholic church and returning to the source, the Scriptures. In the view of the Reformers the truth had not been lost but rather covered up and mixed with error.

In the Restorationist view (especially Charismatic Restorationism) key items were lost for a time to the church. The history of the Reformation and beyond, therefore, has been the restoring of these vital truths to the church. The latest restoration is that of the apostle and prophet.

It must be noted that cultists and aberrant Christian groups since the time of Alexander Campbell have been making this same claim, all with disastrous results. Groups with as divergent beliefs as Mormons, Jehovah's Witnesses and Unity School of Christianity all claim in some way to be the restoration of original or primitive Christianity which was lost at some point in church history.

If the Restorationist view is correct, Christ was unable to preserve His church. The truth could not be found for generations. Essentially Jesus failed in His mission and had to start over. Without intending to, this restorationist view undermines the ability of Christ to keep His promises.

Bill Randles, a Pentecostal pastor and outspoken critic of the restorationist movement, writes the following,

> "How could the church lose justification? Justification by faith is the whole basis for the church, the church has always had it as well as sanctification, healing and the baptism of the Holy Spirit. There has always been the true church which has been equipped by Jesus Himself, the Shepherd and Bishop of our souls. What Luther, Wesley, and the others did is what other true Christians have done down through time. They took what God gave them and introduced it to others. But they couldn't have 'restored' it to the church. The church has always been complete in Christ! If you buy into the restoration concept, it inevitably sets you up for the evolutionary church concept, a deluding, intoxicating idea that makes the current expression of the church feel that she is the ultimate center of God's purposes, over and above all previous expressions of the church. Let's not flatter ourselves."[30]

Randles' point is well taken. The church cannot exist without doctrines like justification. To lose the idea of justification by grace would mean that the church temporarily ceased to exist. This would make Jesus a failure since He said that the gates of hell would not prevail against the church. Randles is further correct in his statements about the future implications of these teachings. Once one accepts the restorationist foundation one is inevitably led to a belief that today's church is the highest expression of what God is doing and has ever done in the world. This teaching is man-centered and prideful.

But the problems do not stop here. Modern apostles and prophets have created an entire series of new doctrines that are part of the restorationist package. These doctrines also should be carefully examined to determine whether they truly line up with God's revelation.

Evaluation of the Restoration of David's Tabernacle

> "On that day I will raise up the tabernacle of David which has fallen down, and repair its damages; I will raise up its ruins, and rebuild it as in the days of old; That they may possess the remnant of Edom, and all the Gentiles who are called by My name, " says the Lord who does this thing." Amos 9:10-11

One of the most common restorationist teachings within the prophetic/apostolic community is the doctrine that God is right now, through these anointed leaders and through the worship and prayer movement of our day, rebuilding David's tabernacle. It is believed that David's tabernacle and Davidic-style worship then are the example for the modern church. This teaching, which is supposedly based on the passage cited above, then becomes the mandate for the 24 hour prayer and praise ministries such as IHOP, the reinstitution of Jewish worship practices, teachings such as the Zadok priesthood, Christian Nazirites and even that the church is the Melchizedek priesthood as well as a host of other items including much of the dominionist teachings within the movement. This teaching is a good example of how a seemingly minor deviation from Scripture can, when carried to its ultimate conclusions, lead to serious error. Therefore it behooves us to carefully examine this passage and its usage to understand what the Lord is truly saying here.

Word meaning and usage: The first thing to note is that the word translated (inappropriately) as "tabernacle" in both the KJV and NKJV in Amos 9:11 is the word "cukkah". This word is most commonly translated "booth" and is the word used to describe the booths that the Jews were to make out of cut boughs and live in during the Feast of Booths commemorating their wilderness wandering. The word itself, therefore, is more in line with a lean-to type of structure than the tent that David erected to cover the ark in 2 Samuel 6:17 where the word is "ohel" and indicates a structure that can be seen from a distance. Had the translators of the King James used the word "booth" (which incidentally appears as a footnote in the NKJV) much of the confusion could have been avoided.

The word is used elsewhere in the Old Testament in a metaphoric sense much like it is in the Amos passage. Notice its usage by Isaiah in chapter 1 verses 7-8.

> "Your country is desolate, your cities are burned with fire: Strangers devour your land in your presence; And it is desolate, as overthrown by strangers. So the daughter of Zion is left as a **booth** (cukkah) in a vineyard, as a hut in a garden of cucumbers, as a beseiged city."

Notice that the word is used of a structure that is small and insignificant. Isaiah, speaking to Israel of God's impending judgment, is stating that Israel will be reduced to something insignificant and shabby instead of the great nation that they have been.

The overall message of the book of Amos is similar. The verses prior to the passage in question have been speaking of God's impending judgment upon the nation. Yet in the midst of this message of judgment is a ray of hope, a time of restoration is coming. The booth of David will be rebuilt. Yet this is not a prophecy of the rebuilding of Davidic worship but of the Davidic royal line which was left in ruins after the judgment. This is a prophecy of the coming of Christ and the restoration that He will bring. David is frequently used in prophetic Scripture as a type of Christ. It is no different here. This prophecy is fulfilled in Jesus and His kingdom.

New Testament Usage. Note how the New Testament believers understood the message of this passage. Look at Acts 15:13-19.

> "And after they had become silent, James answered saying, 'Men and brethren, listen to me: Simon has declared how God at first visited the Gentiles to take out of them a people for His name. And with this the words of the prophets agree, just as it is written,
>
> *After this I will return and will rebuild the tabernacle of David, which has fallen down; I will rebuild its ruins, and I will set it up; So that the rest of mankind may seek the Lord, even all the Gentiles who are called by my name, Says the Lord who does all these things."*
> Known unto God from eternity are all His works. Therefore I judge that we should not trouble those from among the Gentiles who are turning to God."

The logic of James is clear. There is no need for the Gentiles to convert to Judaism because God has already demonstrated that He accepted them apart from the law and because this is in agreement with what the prophets indicated would happen after Christ came, for the prophets clearly wrote that the rest of mankind would seek the Lord. Notice that there is no hint in James' understanding of this passage of any rebuilding of Davidic worship or priesthood, despite the many creative attempts by leaders with the apostolic movement to teach otherwise.

Jesus is the Branch that comes from the root of Jesse who becomes the King who rebuilds the booth of his father David that has fallen down and who will reign on David's throne. Exactly how and when this is understood to occur depends on one's eschatology but the message clearly has nothing to do with Davidic-style worship being restored in the last days.

And one must ask, "If restoring the Tabernacle of David and Davidic worship is so important, why didn't anyone in the New Testament or the writings of the church fathers ever talk about it? Why has no one ever taught this until now?" These are truly bothersome questions. The restoration of the Tabernacle of David is just one more piece of the restorationist mythology.

There is one more restorationist doctrine that should be considered at this point.

Evaulation of Establishing God's Throne Through Worship

Another of the more popular restorationist teachings to come out of the prophetic movement is the idea that God's throne is established through the worship of his people. This teaching is based exclusively on one verse of Scripture, Psalm 22:3

> "Yet thou art holy, O Thou who art enthroned upon the praises of Israel" (NASB).

It is important to note that this idea goes well beyond the belief that God simply manifests His presence during worship, which, while still not specifically found in this passage, is a much more Biblical concept overall. Instead, this teaching is that the rule of God on earth is somehow established as His people worship.

CHAPTER TWO: *Did Jesus Fail?*

Some comments by Dick Eastman should make this particular teaching clear. He writes:

> "Today's growing harp and bowl intercessory worship movement is precisely this, possibly taken to new heights in the pursuit of God. And you can join this movement daily. It's simple: Declare in song (worship) and prayer (intercession) that God dwells, or is enthroned, in every situation. **This is the result of all this intercessory worship: God is being enthroned BECAUSE His people are pursuing him in passionate worship as never before. THRONE ZONES ARE BEING ESTABLISHED through the earth where God can dwell in all His fullness.**"[31]

Now before we discuss the passage in question and before we analyze Eastman's comments in detail, let's notice a couple of things. First notice that, according to Eastman, God's throne is established on the earth as a result of the pursuit and worship of His people. Man is responsible for establishing the rule of God. Second notice that there are supposedly "throne zones" or geographic areas where God can "dwell in all His fullness" and these are also established by man. Eastman begins with a dubious interpretation of one verse and then theologizes into an entire superstructure of doctrines such as "throne zones" which cannot be found anywhere in the pages of Holy Scripture. These doctrines exalt man and leave God on the outside waiting for His people to act.

It must be noted that the verse itself is somewhat ambiguous especially in the Hebrew. This is why the verse is translated very differently depending on which translation one reads. For instance, the NIV reads, "Yet you are enthroned as the Holy One; You are the praise of Israel." Obviously, this translation lends little support to the idea that God's throne is somehow established by the activity of man.

How can one determine what is actually meant? As usual, context provides the key. David begins by declaring his own despair and feeling that he has been forsaken by God (vs 1). Jesus quoted these verses verbatim while on the cross and scholars have long recognized the Messianic implication of the passage. But that is not the primary emphasis in this particular discussion. David then makes a definite statement of confidence in the sovereignty of the Holy God, the one worshipped by the nation of Israel. (vs 3) David reminds himself that this God is the God of his fathers and that God was faithful to deliver them. (vs 4-5) He then moves back into a declaration of his own emotional state in vs 6-8. This is followed by another declaration of his trust in God (vs 9-10) Then David once again declares the agony of his own situation (vs 11-18) followed by another profound statement of his faith in God and his determination to worship (vs 19-31).

In this poem, David consistently confronts his own immediate situation of despair and anxiety with what he knows to be eternally true about God i.e. his sovereign faithfulness. David is not teaching us that our worship establishes God's throne but rather that God's throne is eternally established and therefore God is to be worshipped regardless of our present circumstances and in the knowledge that God's sovereignty will prevail. Our worship does not establish God's throne in the earth for David declares in this very passage in verse 28 "for dominion belongs (present tense) to the Lord and He rules (also present tense) over the nations."

Not only is this teaching that our worship establishes God's throne over certain geographic regions to free up evangelism and transformation another classic example of bad Bible study and prophetic Scripture twisting, it is once again decidedly man-centered. As in so many of the teachings of this movement, once again we see God waiting for man to act. Man is responsible for establishing God's rule. Man clears the heavenlies so that God can act. Man is the key to the puzzle. Man opens the way for God. There is little here but the exaltation of the flesh.

This teaching may be very popular but it is obviously false. God is the sovereign Lord of the universe who rules over all nations. As Nebuchadnezzar learned, "the Most High rules the kingdom of men and gives it to whom he will" (Daniel 4:25). We add nothing to the establishment of His throne since it has already been established for all of eternity. Nor do we create "throne zones" where God CAN dwell in His fullness. We worship BECAUSE God's throne is established not in order to make it so. God's rule is not established by our worship.

Conclusion

There is no biblical justification for a belief that apostles exist today of the same stature as the Biblical apostles. Such apostles are unnecessary since the Biblical apostles still provide leadership to the church through their writings in the New Testament. Apostles do not have to be physically present in order to provide a foundation for the church anymore than Christ must be present physically in order to lead His church. The New Testament apostles give no indication that they felt a continuation of their office was necessary and indeed made no provision for any such continuation. Additionally, we have seen that the five-fold ministry doctrine and other restorationist teachings fail biblically and undermine the character of Christ instead placing an undue emphasis on the activity of man.

The church today does not need new apostles. The church today needs to return to the teachings given to us by the true apostles of Christ found in the New Testament.

CHAPTER THREE

Catch Me if You Can
The Need to Test Prophets

The God of the Bible is a God of Truth. Consistent with His nature, He calls His people to distinguish truth from error. He warns them of the existence of and the damage caused by false prophets. Further the Lord gives guidelines in His Word for the testing and evaluation of prophets and prophetic messages.

In this chapter we will consider the subject of the testing of prophets and prophecies. Consideration will be given to the tests proposed by those within the prophetic community. It is the contention of this chapter that the vast majority of those claiming to be prophets within the Body of Christ today, at least those with a national platform, fail to meet the criteria set forth by God in His Word and must therefore be rejected. In fact, today's prophets consistently fail to meet the criteria they themselves advocate for testing prophets.

Because it is my earnest desire to move past the discussion of the cessation or continuation of spiritual gifts in the hope of writing something that may prove useful to the entire Church, I will be addressing this subject from the perspective allowing for the possibility of prophetic utterances today. The question I hope to address is, "If prophetic utterances are for today, how would they be tested and either validated or invalidated?"

Additionally, I want to ask the sticky question that seems to be avoided by nearly every writer associated with the modern apostolic and prophetic movement, "At what point must the church declare that a particular minister is not a prophet at all or is a false prophet?" Again, it is the premise of the rest of the book that the vast majority of those claiming prophetic status today must be rejected regardless of one's position on the gifts.

The Supporters Speak

Even the most ardent supporters of and participants in the modern prophetic movement agree that prophecy must be tested.

Michael Sullivant, in discussing predictive prophecies that fail to occur, writes,

> "If someone gives an errant predictive prophecy, his or her credibility has to be reexamined. It could be that they simply spoke out of their own heart or mind....If such an errant utterance has been given publicly, then some kind of public statement needs to be made to clear up the matter."[32]

Obviously, testing had to occur in order to determine that the prophecy did not come to pass. Further, testing would have to occur in order to determine why the failed prophecy was given and to examine the credibility of the one claiming to be speaking prophetically. Then, according to Sullivant, the leadership of the church is responsible for correcting any damage caused by the failed prophecy by issuing a public statement, assuming the prophecy was made public.

Jack Deere, one of the leading advocates of the modern prophetic movement, in a chapter entitled, "Recognizing the Voice", states emphatically,

> "All private revelation in any form ought to be checked against the Scriptures. I do not believe that God will ever contradict the Bible. He may contradict our *interpretation* of the Bible, just as he did Peter's interpretation of the Levitical food laws (Acts 10), but he will never contradict the actual teaching of the Bible. All prophetic words, impressions, dreams, visions and supernatural experiences of any sort ought to be tested in light of the teaching of the Bible."[33] (italics in the original)

Deere's understanding that an omniscient God of truth will not contradict Himself is dead on. Since God knows all things, He cannot be wrong about anything He states. Since God is utterly without sin, He will not lie and in fact the Scriptures state that it is impossible for Him to do so.

Deere's caveat that the Lord may contradict our interpretation of Scripture also has merit. Few if any teachers would be so bold to presume that their understanding or interpretation of Scripture is perfect on all points. One should be open to the idea that one has not properly understood some aspects of Scripture. However, while acknowledging this fact, there are certain tenets of the Christian faith which have been agreed upon by the vast majority of believers down through the ages. These constitute the main and plain truths of Scripture. These teachings are truly no longer up for debate. There are some things the church knows with certainty. Prophetic utterances that contradict these core truths must be rejected immediately.

One issue that Deere does not address is the question of prophecies that add to the revelation of Scripture. By this I mean, a prophecy may not contradict a teaching of Scripture but may bring revelation of a doctrinal nature that is not explicitly taught in Scripture or supported as a logical deduction from Scripture. Deere is silent on this subject.

Fortunately, other prophets have addressed this matter and they are universal in their claim that modern prophecy should not establish doctrine. We will discuss modern revelation and the establishing of doctrine in detail later in the book. For now, this quote by Rick Joyner is representative of the consensus of the modern prophets on this issue. Joyner writes,

> **"Prophetic revelation is for revealing the strategic or tactical will of the Lord, not for imparting doctrine.** The written Word, which is our doctrine, is finished and no revelation will come from God to add to it or take away from it. Any that would presume to do this we should immediately judge as false prophecy, and reject it regardless of how it comes. About this, we can have no doubt."[34] (emphasis in the original)

Notice that Joyner is emphatic. Any prophecy that presumes to impart doctrine is to immediately be judged as false prophecy. Joyner indicates this is something, about which, there can be no doubt.

It must be noted at this point that, based on the criteria given by Deere and Joyner alone, as will be demonstrated repeatedly throughout this book, one must reject the overwhelming majority of prophetic words being delivered by the new apostles and prophets. This cannot be stressed enough. The modern prophets fail to meet their own tests for authentification.

One of the best works on the subject of testing prophecy, written by an advocate of the modern prophetic movement, is by Ernest B. Gentile. After citing the warnings of Jesus concerning the coming of false prophets (which will be considered in this chapter momentarily) Gentile summarizes the message thusly,

> "Jesus was deliberately alerting the future leaders of the Church to the need of testing prophecy. He even supplied them with several basic principles that would later be amplified to handle the full range of prophetic activities."[35]

Gentile then gives twenty-six different questions that should be used to test a prophetic word covering such topics as; the source of the prophecy, the objective of the prophecy, the message given, the person who prophesies, the delivery used, and the effect on the recipient of the message.[36] Gentile advises that prophets be weighed for their Christ-likeness and demeanor. The message should be evaluated to see if it is, among other things, Christ-exalting. Gentile agrees that the message must be consistent with Scripture writing,

> "*Is the prophecy in accord with the letter and spirit of Scripture?* Does it contradict the Bible? John Blattner comments: 'The principle here is simple: the Holy Spirit does not contradict himself. We can trust that any message that is authentically inspired will be in accord with previous revelation.'"[37] (Italics in the original)

Gentile's list is extremely thorough. What is amazing to this author is that Gentile can apply this list with any consistency to the major prophetic ministries in the church today and come away with the conclusion that any of them are truly speaking from God.

But the point remains that even the prophets themselves admit that prophecy is to be tested. We now turn our attention to the teaching of the Scriptures themselves to see the counsel of the Lord in this area.

Testing Prophets in the Old Testament

Without a doubt the foundational passage for the testing of a prophet in the Old Testament is Deuteronomy 18:19-22. We will reference this passage several times throughout this book. Here God states,

"And whoever will not listen to my words that he shall speak in my name, I myself will require it of him. But the prophet who presumes to speak a word in my name that I have not commanded him to speak, or who speaks in the name of other gods, that same prophet shall die. And if you say in your heart, 'How may we know the word that the LORD has not spoken?'—when a prophet speaks in the name of the LORD, if the word does not come to pass or come true, that is a word that LORD has not spoken; the prophet has spoken it presumptuously. You need not be afraid of him." (ESV)

Notice that the words of the prophet who speaks in the name of the Lord carry the authority of God Himself. Therefore God Himself will judge the person who disobeys a word spoken by one of God's prophets. But there is an exception. If it is determined that the prophet spoke in the name of the Lord without actually hearing from the Lord, not only is his word to be rejected, the prophet himself is to be put to death.

This raises a very natural question. "How can one distinguish between words spoken by the inspiration of the Lord and those that are spoken by a prophet presumptuously?" The answer is that the word of the Lord will come to pass. If the prophetic word does not come to be, the prophet has spoken without the commandment of the Lord.

This test is grounded in two essential aspects of God's nature. First, as a God who is holy, God would never lie. Second, as a God who is omniscient—including possessing an omniscient knowledge of the future—God can never be mistaken. (Some leaders in the modern prophetic movement have moved to the heretical position of Open Theism in order to cover for the many failed prophecies occurring today. This will be discussed in the chapter on the nature of God.)

Another issue at the heart of this test concerns the nature of prophecy itself. The prophet spoke the very words of God. There is an immediacy to the revelation. In philosophical terms, immediacy is the idea that knowledge is given to the mind in such a way as to prevent distortion or interpretation. This passage assumes that the prophetic word is given to the prophet in such as way that the prophet can relay the word to the people without distortion or even faulty interpretation. There is no hint in this passage or any other in the Bible that a prophet may receive a true word but deliver a faulty message because the prophet's interpretation of the revelation was incorrect. The same God who delivers the revelation superintends the delivery of the revelation by the prophet.

Another key passage related to the testing of a prophet can be found in Deuteronomy 13:1-5 which states,

> "If a prophet or a dreamer of dreams arises among you and gives you a sign or a wonder, and the sign or wonder that he tells you comes to pass, and if he says, 'Let us go after other gods,' which you have not known, 'and let us serve them,' you shall not listen to the words of that prophet or that dreamer of dreams. For the LORD your God is testing you, to know whether you love the LORD your God with all your heart and with all your soul. You shall walk after the LORD your God and fear him and keep his commandments and obey his voice, and you shall serve him and hold fast to him. But that prophet or that dreamer of dreams shall be put to death, because he has taught rebellion against the LORD your God, who brought you out of the land of Egypt and redeemed you out of the house of slavery, to make you leave the way in which the LORD your God commanded you to walk. So you shall purge the evil from your midst."

Here the prophet gives a sign that actually does come to pass. So should the prophet automatically be accepted because of the display of supernatural power and knowledge? Not necessarily. In this case the prophet teaches the people to follow after a different God from the God of the covenant. In such an event, the people are to understand that God has allowed the sign to come to pass in order to test the hearts of His people. The people are to understand that God does not contradict Himself. They are to test prophets by their adherence to what God has already revealed. They are to follow the true God and not chase after the false god of the prophet even if a supernatural sign occurs.

It should be noted that this commandment covers more than just prophesying in the name of a different god or pointing to a different god by name but also a different god by nature. In other words, the prophet may speak in the name of Yahweh but bring a revelation that is inconsistent with how Yahweh has revealed Himself or in contradiction to what Yahweh has commanded. This prophet would still be leading the people in rebellion against the true God and in that sense leading them to follow a different god. O. Palmer Robertson states the point well,

"Over against the deliverances of the false prophets are set the commands, ordinances and statutes that have been revealed through Moses and his true successors. The most basic test of the prophet is his adherence to the 'forth-telling' that has already come by divine revelation."[38]

So it is not enough for a prophet to claim that his or her revelation came by the God of the Scripture. The prophet's message must be consistent with the truth already revealed in Scripture.

Testing Prophets in the New Testament

The testing of prophets and prophecy was not merely an Old Testament concern. Both Jesus and the apostles were very concerned with the potential for God's children to be led astray. Warnings about false prophets abound in the New Testament. There is no better place to begin than with the words of Jesus Himself. In Matthew 7:15-23 we read,

"Beware of false prophets, who come to you in sheep's clothing but inwardly are ravenous wolves. You will recognize them by their fruits. Are grapes gathered from thorn-bushes, or figs from thistles? So, every healthy tree bears good fruit, but the diseased tree bears bad fruit. A healthy tree cannot bear bad fruit, nor can a diseased tree bear good fruit. Every tree that does not bear good fruit is cut down and thrown into the fire. Thus you will recognize them by their fruits. Not everyone who says to me, 'Lord, Lord,' will enter the kingdom of heaven, but the one who does the will of my Father who is in heaven. On that day many will say to me, 'Lord, Lord, did we not cast out demons in your name, and do many mighty works in your name?' And then will I declare to them, 'I never knew you: depart from me, you workers of lawlessness.'"

Nearly everyone in Christian circles is familiar with Jesus' statement that we would know false prophets, "by their fruit". However familiar the church may be with the words of this passage, the understanding of many Christians concerning the application of this passage is limited at best. Far too many Christians assume that the fruit of the ministry includes only things like its temporal success and size (too many people assume that a big ministry automatically indicates God's blessing) or whether or not the people involved subjectively seem sincere, happy, peaceful or perceive themselves to be closer to God. Good works such as giving to the poor are seen as fruit. Additionally, in today's sign-seeking culture, the presence of supernatural manifestations is often taken to be an undeniable evidence of the blessing of God.

Certainly some of these things are fruits and should be considered when evaluating a ministry. But I have seen Mormons justify the truth of the LDS church using these very arguments. "Look at all that we give to the poor and how we care for people. Look at how happy, peaceful and moral our people are. Look at the prophecies of Joseph Smith and the healings he performed."

What is rarely recognized is that doctrine is also a fruit. The teachings of a movement must also be examined in the light of Biblical revelation as a part of the fruit inspection. For regardless of whether or not a person claims to feel closer to God, false doctrine cannot do anything but take them further away from the one true God. Activities and practices that are not condoned in Scripture, at a minimum, take people away from those practices of true discipleship that bring lasting health and growth.

Another fruit that is rarely considered is the impact on the lives of those who have been damaged by false prophecy. What about those who have uprooted families, sold homes and moved to different states or even countries in response to a word by a prophet promising a ministry that awaited them only to see the prophecy fail? What is the impact in the lives of those who sought a prophet about a sick loved one and received assurance of God's healing only to see the loved one die? What is the impact on their faith and walk with God? Is this not a fruit? These stories are real and they are numerous. I have looked into the eyes of many people who have been devastated in one way or another because they acted in faith on a word they believed came from a true prophet of God only to see that word fail. I have never heard of the prophet coming back to the individual either to apologize or to help pick up the pieces of their lives. And what of those who have become completely burnt out after living for years on the hype of the next big thing, the next coming wave of the Spirit, the next manifestation etc.? Is not this also a fruit?

My point is that our evaluation must go deeper.

This passage also contains a sober warning concerning manifestations of the miraculous. These are not necessarily an indication of the presence of the Lord. Jesus' words to those who held up their own miraculous activities as proof of their discipleship, "I never knew you", should at least help every Christian to understand that supernatural power is not the final proof.

Another passage along these same lines is Matthew 24:24 where Jesus states,

> "For false christs and false prophets will arise and perform great signs and wonders, so as to lead astray, if possible, even the elect."

Here again we see that Jesus warns that there will come prophets who will be accompanied by great supernatural activity but who are false. Power is not the test.

The overwhelming emphasis of the New Testament is on testing the message or in other words the doctrine of the prophet. 1 Thessalonians 5:19-22 is indicative of this type of this type of warning.

> "Do not quench the Spirit. Do not despise prophecies, but test everything; hold fast what is good. Abstain from every form of evil."

Much could be said about this passage but for the purposes of this book only a couple of points will be said. All prophecies are to be tested. The purpose of the testing is to weed out the bad from the good. While verse 22 is often used out of context by those wishing to dictate areas of conscience like appropriate musical styles, in reality it has to do with prophecy. Those prophecies that do not pass the test are to be rejected. Believers are to hold fast to those things that are tested and found to be true.

The question then arises, "What is the basis for the test in the apostle's mind?" I believe Gordon Fee is correct when he asserts the answer to this question can be found in the second letter to the same congregation. In 2 Thessalonians 2:15 Paul writes,

> "So then, brothers, stand firm and hold to the traditions that you were taught by us, either by our spoken word or by our letter."

This admonition comes virtually on the heels of Paul's correction of a prophecy circulating that the Day of the Lord had already come (2 Thess. 2:2). Fee summarizes the impact of this discussion well,

> "Paul's point seems clear: they are to weigh all such 'Spirit' utterances in light of his own apostolic teaching. I would assume that the same holds true for all believers in all generations."[39]

So we see that Paul applies a doctrinal test to those who would claim to speak for God. The other writers of the New Testament concur. For instance John writes,

> "Beloved, do not believe every spirit, but test the spirits to see whether they are from God, for many false prophets have gone out into the world. By this you know the Spirit of God: every spirit that confesses that Jesus Christ has come in the flesh is from God, and every spirit that does not confess Jesus is not from God. This is the spirit of the antichrist, which you heard was coming and now is in the world already." (1 John 4:1-3)

John is concerned to warn his readers of the many false prophets who have gone out into the world. In teaching his flock how to recognize these false prophets John does not appeal to any of the standard "fruit" tests given by many in the church today. Instead, John applies a doctrinal test. In John's day, the church was already combating an early Christian heresy known as Docetism which denied the full humanity of Jesus asserting that He merely appeared to be human. John pulls no punches but calls these teachers false prophets having the same spirit as the antichrist.

The form that heresy takes may change over time but it is no less serious. Those who bring a Christology different from that of the apostles are false prophets. We will examine the Christology of many of the modern prophets in chapter eight and weigh their teachings against the message of Scripture.

Peter likewise warns his readers of the danger of false prophets and applies both a doctrinal test and a character test. He writes,

> "But false prophets also arose among the people, just as there will be false teachers among you, who will secretly bring in

destructive heresies, even denying the Master who bought them bringing upon themselves swift destruction. And many will follow their sensuality, and because of them the way of truth will be blasphemed. And in their greed they will exploit you with false words. Their condemnation from long ago is not idle, and their destruction is not asleep." (2 Pet. 2:1-3)

Peter indicates that it is to be expected that false teachers will creep into the church for false prophets have always troubled the people of God. Satan is ever attempting to lead the people of God astray. He further indicates that they will introduce destructive heresies by stealth. No one has ever attempted to garner a following by announcing himself to be a heretic. Instead these teachers claim to be a part of the fellowship.

When Peter states that they even deny the Master who bought them, he almost certainly does not have in mind something as blatant as an outright denial of Jesus Christ. Remember that in context these men are acting in secret. Instead, what Peter is indicating is that these men, while professing Christ adamantly, introduce teachings and conduct that in practice deny their claim. Peter highlights lifestyles of sensuality and greed which are inconsistent with a relationship with Jesus Christ.

But the heresies are also a denial of the Master who bought them. Because of the lack of emphasis on doctrine in too many churches today, this concept may be unfamiliar to many readers. Please allow an illustration.

Suppose someone claims to be a close personal friend of the author of this book. However upon discussion he relates that Keith Gibson is a former professional athlete, who has a full head of blonde hair, loves country music and has nineteen children. Since none of these things are true of the author of this book, the person's closeness to the author is denied by the truths he claims to know.

In the same way, a teacher may claim great intimacy with Jesus. But if the doctrines or truths that he claims to know about Jesus are different than what Jesus has revealed about Himself in the pages of Scripture, that teacher's profession is called into question. His doctrines are a denial of the Master. Many of today's prophets claim great intimacy with Jesus. They speak as though they have an immediate hotline to God. They receive revelations on a regular basis. They make great claims. One even claims that God shares with him the secrets of other's hearts and lives, not so that he can minister to them, but just because God is his friend and delights to share these things. But these same teachers bring doctrines about God that are contrary to what is true about Him. My friends, this is inconsistent! True intimacy both requires and leads to a true knowledge. My wife and I are intimate because we know each other truly and we know each other truly because we are intimate. Once again the modern prophets cannot continue to have it both ways. It is impossible that they are truly as intimate with God as they claim while continuing to spout untruths about His nature and ways.

There are a great number of other Biblical passages that one could consider on the importance of testing prophets and prophecies. In fact, despite the lack of importance that the modern prophets place on doctrinal truth, virtually every book in the New Testament contains warnings about false apostles, false prophets and false teachers. The Bible just doesn't have the same attitude about doctrine as much of today's church. But it is hoped that the passages discussed above will be sufficient to make the case.

The Consistently Wrong Prophet

We have seen that prophets and prophecies are to be tested. Both the Old Testament and the New Testament are clear on this point. In the Old Testament a prophet who prophesied falsely or who gave a message in contradiction with the revealed truth of God was to be put to death. In the New Testament, the church is consistently and repeatedly warned against following those who bring doctrines contrary to that of the apostles.

Even those within the apostolic and prophetic community, with only a few exceptions, recognize and admit the need to test prophecies. They will concede that prophecies that are false should be corrected though there are few examples of this actually occurring in a public way and a multitude of examples of prophets attempting to justify one another...but that's another discussion.

The issue that no one in the modern apostolic and prophetic movement seems to address is the prophet that is consistently wrong, either in doctrine, prophetic fulfillment or both. What is to be done with this person? At what point should they be called a false prophet? At what point should the church stop giving them a public arena? At what point should they be publicly denounced as Paul did with false teachers in the Pastoral Epistles?

One suspects, though it would be impossible to prove, that the hesitancy of the modern prophets to engage in this discussion stems from their knowledge that none of them would pass the test. Even by their own admission, modern prophets are only 66% right. While it is highly questionable that any of the men and women claiming prophetic status today actually achieves that modest number, using their own figures, this means that one in every three prophecies given by today's prophets is false. Factoring in the thousands of prophecies being given worldwide by the modern prophets, that leaves the church drowning in a virtual ocean of false prophecy. At what point does the church cry, "Enough!"?

Fortunately, the Scriptures hold the key. Consider the following passages written by the apostle Paul.

"But avoid foolish controversies, genealogies, dissensions, and quarrels about the law, for they are unprofitable and worthless. As for a person who stirs up division, after warning him once and then twice, have nothing more to do with him, knowing that such a person is warped and sinful; he is self-condemned." (Titus 3:9-11)

The word for the person who "stirs up division" or, as other translations say is, "a factious man" is the word from which we get our word, "heretic". The King James Version translates verse 10 thusly,

"A man that is an heretick after the first and second admonition reject;"

It is evident from the context that Paul is speaking of doctrinal division because he warns Titus to avoid, among other things, foolish controversies and quarrels about the law. The entire tenor of the passage is doctrinal in nature. And what is Paul's instruction? Those who bring false doctrine are to be given two warnings and then rejected if they refuse to repent.

Another passage with a similar instruction is Romans 16:17 which states,

"I appeal to you brothers, to watch out for those who cause divisions and create obstacles contrary to the doctrine that you have been taught; avoid them"

Once again, it is patently obvious that Paul has in mind false doctrine because he states that the divisions are "contrary to the doctrine that you have been taught". His answer here is completely consistent with that in Titus. These teachers are to be avoided.

The fact is, despite the assertions of those in the prophetic movement to the contrary, there is no justification for allowing a prophet who consistently prophesies incorrectly or who brings false doctrine to continue in ministry. These people are to be called into account, confronted and, if unrepentant, rejected. The New Testament considers the truth too precious and error too harmful for false prophecy and false doctrine to be perpetually tolerated.

It is time for all of God's people, regardless of their view on spiritual gifts, to demand that the modern prophets either adhere to the timeless truths of the faith, and conform to the parameters given in Scripture or be silent! It is time the church call these teachers what they are; false teachers, false prophets and false apostles. It is time that the church stop giving national platforms to teachers spouting the impressions of their own minds.

Unfortunately, however, the modern apostles and prophets have made it very clear they have no intention of listening. That is the subject of our next chapter.

CHAPTER FOUR

We're Not Listening and You Can't Make Us
Answering the Objections of Modern Apostles, Prophets and Their Defenders.

"I'm not going to listen to people I think aren't legitimate leaders in the body of Christ" - Rick Joyner

In dealing with the new apostles and prophets as well as their followers, one quickly encounters a problem. They do not wish to listen. In fact, the prophetic movement has developed an entire series of pat answers and knee-jerk reactions to those raising concerns about their teachings which make any substantive dialogue on the actual issues themselves virtually impossible. Not only have modern prophets filled the church with extra-Biblical and unbiblical revelations and doctrines, leading many away from the pure faith, they have also insulated themselves from any correction by the larger body of Christ. These straw-men arguments and red herrings are essentially thought terminators and must be refuted before any significant progress can be made on the larger issues.

In this chapter we will address the most common arguments raised by the apostles, prophets and their defenders. It is hoped that dealing with these early, those in the prophetic movement who might take the time to actually read this book will be open to seriously consider the information found on the subsequent pages. It is also hoped that those reading this book in order to inform themselves of the dangers of the movement or to reach a friend or loved one currently in the movement will be better equipped to scale the walls that will immediately be erected in defense of the modern apostles and their false doctrines.

The Martyr Complex

Martyrdom is a powerful symbol in religion. The person claiming martyr status becomes untouchable, unquestionable. Further, it immediately positions the one doing the challenging as evil, a Nazi, or worse. It is why Mormons talk of the martyrdom of Joseph Smith (despite the fact that he had a gun, fired into the mob coming up the stairs and killed a young man before being shot himself) and position their detractors as "anti-Mormons".

I have noticed a similar trend among many within the prophetic movement. I am not saying that these people are cult leaders or that the prophetic movement is a cult. I am only saying that in this instance they frequently employ similar tactics. To confront them, is to persecute them.

Prophetess Victoria Boyson does this repeatedly. In two different prophetic words ("The Religious Spirit that Seeks to Convince Us It is God" and "Warriors of Truth") she claims that those who "speak against" other Christians release demonic activity against their lives. Or consider the words of Rick Joyner:

> "Two ministries go on continually before God's throne: One is the ministry of *intercession*, the other is *accusation*....Satan, however, is called "the accuser of our brethren", and we are told that his ministry goes on "day and night" before the throne of God (Rev. 12:10) How can Satan continue to accuse the saints before God if he has been thrown out of heaven and no longer has access to the throne? The answer: Satan uses the saints, who do have access to the throne, to do this diabolical work for him."[40]

Moving past Joyner's interesting speculation that it is actually through the words of Christians that Satan accuses the brethren before the throne, the central point is obvious, any form of criticism is the devil's work.

This tactic seems to be Joyner's modus operandi. In a number of his writings he deflects any and all criticism by attributing it to satanically inspired persecution.

In his most popular book, "The Final Quest", upon seeing a vast army of Christians under the control of the devil, Joyner hears the voice of the Lord state,

"This is Satan's ultimate deception. His ultimate power of destruction is released when he uses Christians to attack one another."[41]

Later, in the same book, Joyner has an experience where he is allegedly in heaven and is approached by a man there. This man according to Joyner had a great ministry that Joyner had respected but he is one of the lowest in the kingdom of heaven. This man tells Joyner why his position is so low,

> "We sowed fear and division throughout the church, all in the name of protecting the truth. In my self-righteousness I was headed for perdition."[42]

Notice that the defense of the truth is equated with sowing division among the brethren. Notice also that the one involved was headed to perdition. We will deal with the divisiveness argument momentarily.

It is possible to supply a virtually endless number of examples of today's prophets teaching the same thing. But the point is that no meaningful dialogue can take place when one of the parties is playing the victim. Even in the culture at large, victims get a pass.

The New Testament however does not support this assumption that disagreeing with a teacher's doctrine is tantamount to persecuting them. There are numerous examples of the apostles warning again false teachers and even at times calling them out by name in order to protect the rest of the body and this is never equated with persecution. For instance, Paul mentions that Phygelus and Hermogenes were among those who turned away from him (2 Tim. 1:15). He calls out Hymenaeus and Philetus for teaching that the resurrection was already passed and upsetting the faith of some (2 Tim. 2:17-18). He says that Demas has loved the present world (2 Tim. 4:9). He warns Timothy to beware of Alexander the coppersmith because he did great harm to Paul (2 Tim. 4:14-15). Paul mentions those in Corinth who denied the bodily resurrection of the saints (1 Cor. 15). It is presumable that the body of believers in Corinth would have known who these men were. Similarly, Paul confronts those stressing circumcision and conformity to the law in his letter to the Galatians. Likewise the apostle John openly exposes Diotrephes for not recognizing John's authority (3 John 9). In fact, virtually all of the New Testament epistles contain some warning about false teaching and false teachers. Paul even commands the church at Rome to mark or note those who are bringing doctrinal error into the church and to avoid these teachers (Romans 16:17).

Apparently the apostles didn't realize that they were persecuting these men, engaging in the devil's work and releasing demonic activity when they confronted false doctrine.

So we need to understand:

1. Calling attention to what someone is teaching is not persecuting them.

2. Pointing out what one believes to be the logical conclusions of another's teachings and practices is not persecuting them.

3. Taking strong objection, even to the point of demonstrating emotion and using forceful language and occasional rhetorical devices, to another's teachings is not persecuting them.

4. Warning others that they may be better off avoiding the teachings of certain ministers is not persecuting these ministers.

The Appeal to Unity

Another common tactic employed by today's prophets and apostles is to accuse those who attempt to correct false doctrine of being divisive, of sowing discord among the brothers. We have already seen one such instance in the writings of Rick Joyner. There are many others.

In his book, "Overcoming Evil in the Last Days", Joyner impugns the motives of those who would dare to be concerned about false teaching creeping into the church and writes, "Although this spirit usually comes in the guise of protecting the sheep, the truth, or the Lord's glory, it is an evil, critical spirit that will always end up causing division and destruction."[43]

Unity within the body is very important. Jesus prayed that we may be one just as He and the Father are one. Paul makes a powerful appeal for unity in Ephesians 4. It is a serious issue.

But Biblical unity is a unity based on truth not in opposition to it. The Bible does not advocate peace at any price. There are lines of no compromise. We are not to join hands with false teachers.

Romans 16:17 indicates that it is those bringing the new and different doctrines who are responsible for creating the division. Similarly the apostle John declared that those who went out from us did so that it might be manifest that they were not of us (1 John 2:19). 1 Cor. 11 indicates that it is necessary that divisions come so that it may be obvious who those are who are approved of God.

It is the new apostles and prophets who are the true schismatics. They have chosen a course that takes them away from the rest of the body. Consider it this way, if the church is continuing to teach the historic doctrines of the faith and a particular teacher moves away from these doctrines to teach something else, who moved? Who created the separation? Who is really causing the division? Pointing out that a division exists by exposing the new, false doctrines is not the cause of the division. The fault here does not lie with those concerned with biblical truth but with those who have abandoned it.

You are a Pharisee

In his book "Overcoming Evil in the Last Days", Joyner devotes an entire third of the book to the subject of the "religious spirit". (Interestingly, the book only deals with three evils, racism, witchcraft and the religious spirit. The obvious implication is that the religious spirit is one of the three most serious evils to be overcome in the last days.) Joyner writes,

> "The Lord had little trouble with demons while He walked on earth. They quickly recognized His authority and begged for mercy. It was the conservative, zealous, religious community that immediately became His greatest enemy. Those who were the most zealous for the Word of God crucified the Word Himself when He became flesh to walk among them. The same is still true."[44]

Joyner's point is easy to see. His backhanded slap at the conservative Evangelical community is obvious, although because Joyner mentions no names specifically, he can feel that he is staying above the fray and is not guilty of the very thing that he is condemning. In Joyner's system, to stand squarely on the truth of God's Word is to be a Pharisee and a potential enemy of God, even worse trouble than a demon. We deal in depth with the nature of the Pharisees momentarily. Suffice it for now to say that the problem Jesus had with them was not that they were Biblically oriented.

Joyner continues with the seriousness of this spirit. "All of the cults and false religions combined have not done as much damage to the moves of God as the opposition, or infiltration, of the religious spirit in the Church. Cults and false religions are easily discerned, but the religious spirit has thwarted or diverted possibly every revival or movement to date, and it still retains a seat of honor throughout most of the visible Church."[45]

Joyner's absolute ignorance is evident when he says that cults and false religions are easy to discern. Would that this were so but the over 180,000,000 people involved in cults and the billions involved in false religions testify differently. And Joyner continues his assault on the vast majority of the Body of Christ when he states that the religious spirit "retains a seat of honor throughout most of the visible Church." His hypocrisy is evident as he engages in the very activity he condemns. But of course we are not supposed to notice that.

The charge of being a Pharisee is extremely emotionally powerful for the Pharisees stand among the worst of the bad guys in the New Testament. This is doubly true when it is combined with the rhetoric that it was the Pharisees who killed Christ. Mike Bickle demonstrates this attack well when he states,

> "It was the ones pressing into Biblical orthodoxy that murdered Christ."[46]

So to be passionate about the truth is to be a Pharisee and a Christ-killer.

However, I would like to consider whether or not the charge itself has any merit. Were the Pharisees those who were biblically orthodox? I first began to think about this after hearing a presentation in which the speaker made a passing comment that "the Pharisees were not biblicists." A careful study of Scripture bears this out. The problem with the Pharisees is not that they held the Scriptures in too high esteem but rather that they were perfectly willing to cancel them out in favor of their own doctrines. Consider the following examples:

Matthew 15:1-9 (ESV) 1 Then Pharisees and scribes came to Jesus from Jerusalem and said, 2 "Why do your disciples break the tradition of the elders? For they do not wash their hands when they eat." 3 He answered them, "And why do you break the commandment of God for the sake of your tradition? 4 For God commanded, 'Honor your father and your mother,' and, 'Whoever reviles father or mother must surely die.' 5 But you say, 'If anyone tells his father or his mother, What you would have gained from me is given to God, 6 he need not honor his father.' So for the sake of your tradition you have made void the word of God. 7 You hypocrites! Well did Isaiah prophesy of you, when he said: 8 " 'This people honors me with their lips, but their heart is far from me; 9 in vain do they worship me, teaching as doctrines the commandments of men.' "

Notice clearly that the problem was not their adherence to the Bible but rather their adherence to their own doctrines devised by men.

Another example:

John 5:45-47 (ESV) 45 Do not think that I will accuse you to the Father. There is one who accuses you: Moses, on whom you have set your hope. 46 If you believed Moses, you would believe me; for he wrote of me. 47 But if you do not believe his writings, how will you believe my words?"

Once again, notice that the problem is not their adherence to the Scriptures.

Multiple other examples could be cited. Now here is the point. Among the many errors of the Pharisees, was their tendency to place their own doctrines, invented by men, above the Scriptures. What the Bible had to say could be cancelled out in favor of what they said.

I would submit that we see much the same thing happening in the prophetic movement. We see a host of teachers inventing new doctrines that are completely unsubstantiated by Scripture and then presenting them as fact even if they contradict the direct teachings of the Word of God. This will be demonstrated in the succeeding chapters of this book.

It is not those who cling to the revealed truth of God found in the Scripture who are the true spiritual descendants of the Pharisees.

Selective Listening

Of course, another way to refuse to deal with those who raise concern about the teachings of the new prophets and apostles is simply to ignore them. In an interview with Charisma magazine, when asked about those who have concerns about his false prophecies, doctrines and involvement with the Knights of Malta, Rick Joyner replied, "I'm not going to listen to people I think aren't legitimate leaders in the body of Christ"[47]

Given Joyner's attitude toward those involved in discernment ministries it is doubtful that anyone who would dare to attempt to correct him would be found on his list of "legitimate leaders" in the Body of Christ. Joyner has thus positioned himself largely above correction.

Other prophets have taught that a prophet can only be corrected by someone who also has the status of a prophet or a greater status (i.e apostle). Since most of the teachers in the Evangelical and Protestant world would never claim to be prophets or apostles, this essentially means that modern prophets are completely uncorrectable by the vast majority of the church! Additionally, since the only ones who would claim to be prophets or apostles are those who already agree with many of the same premises as these prophetic teachers, the chance that they would ever be challenged or corrected is exceedingly small. One only needs to spend a little time reading prophetic newsletters like Elijah List or the Identity Network to see that this is certainly the case. All manner of aberrant doctrines are readily available and the prophets are very careful not to bring corrective words against one another.

Demonize the Opposition

Another common strategy employed by the modern prophets to deflect scrutiny away from their unbiblical teaching is to begin to discuss some kind of demonic influence in the person raising the concern. We have already seen hints of this in some of the quotes used previously. This usually comes in the form of a discussion of the Jezebel spirit, the religious spirit and the accuser of the brethren (I have also been told that I have a Judas spirit, Saul spirit and Eli spirit. Let the reader be warned). All of these entities are defined differently by the various prophets but it is certain that they are very bad. The religious spirit is generally applied to anyone who attempts to ask questions like, "Why hasn't the church ever believed this before?" or "Where is the doctrinal basis for these new practices?" The person is immediately painted as someone who is stuck in the old wineskins and is not responding to the new things that God is doing. Rick Joyner speaks of the activity of the religious spirit in the following manner:

> "A religious spirit will usually give a counterfeit gift of discernment of spirits. This counterfeit gift thrives on seeing what is wrong with others rather than seeing what God is doing so that we can help them along. This is how a religious spirit does some of its greatest damage to the church. Its ministry will almost always leave more damage and division than healing and reconciliation. It's wisdom is rooted in the Tree of the knowledge of Good and Evil and though the truth may be accurate, it is ministered in a spirit that kills."[48]

It must be pointed out that Joyner offers no Biblical support for his declaration that a religious spirit even exists and that it gives a counterfeit gift of discernment of spirits. But then again, to ask for a scriptural basis is merely to prove that one HAS a religious spirit. Once again Joyner appeals to his mystical understanding of the poisonous Tree of Knowledge. What is fascinating is that Joyner admits that the person may be accurate in their discernment of error. But of course, that doesn't really matter. Remember that we have already seen that the religious spirit has done more damage to the moves of God than all the cults and false religions combined.

The religious spirit is one terrible entity but so is the accuser of the brethren, a name reserved in the Bible for Satan himself. In a similar vein to Joyner, Francis Frangipane writes:

> "More churches have been destroyed by the accuser of the brethren and its faultfinding than by either immorality or misuse of church funds. So prevalent is this influence in our society that, among many, faultfinding has been elevated to the status of a 'ministry'".[49]

These are truly ominous words. Certainly no one would wish to be accused of being possessed by something so destructive. It's enough to make anyone consider shutting down their thinking capacities and merely towing the line. Better to just drink the kool-aid than risk such demonic infestation.

But far and away the most common demon one can anticipate being accused of carrying is the Jezebel spirit. The Jezebel spirit is generally, though not universally, applied to those who will not respond to the authority of these new apostles and prophets. After all, as one prophetic disciple expressed to me, Jezebel sought to control the king and she attacked the prophets of God. Joyner states,

> "Basically, the spirit of the Jezebel is a combination of the religious spirit and the spirit of witchcraft that is the spirit of manipulation and control....This spirit attacks the prophetic ministry because that has always been the primary way in which the Lord gives timely, strategic direction to His people."[50]

We already saw how destructive the religious spirit was but the Jezebel spirit is worse because it adds the spirit of witchcraft. This spirit is also associated with sensuality by some of the modern prophetic teachers.

Emotionally these are powerful weapons, especially for those who are biblically untrained. Who wants to believe that they might be the instrument of a demon intent on stopping the move of God and destroying the church? The effect of this argument is generally exactly what the prophet desired, a fear among God's people to examine the revelations of the prophet in the light of God's revealed Word and silence when the new teachings fail to pass the test.

God in a Box

So you think that manifestations like spiritual drunkenness, jerking, roaring, barking and crawling around like an animal doesn't seem consistent with God's revelation of Himself and His instructions to the church given in Scripture? You are concerned that *Ekstasis* worship seems more like the trance states induced in pagan worship practices? Well this is the answer for you. You are trying to put God in a box. You are trying to dictate and limit what God can and can't do.

The power of this argument stems from the fact that the Scriptures portray God as an awesome Being who does amazing and unexpected things, who is not formulaic in His ways.

The net result of the argument though is an "anything goes" approach to divine activity. As long as the worshipper herself feels good about what is happening, the source is assumed to be God and no one can state differently.

64

But the question is not one of trying to box God in but rather one of taking God at His word. If God has said that He is not the author of confusion in the worship service but of peace (1Cor. 14) can we believe that or not? If it is true then doesn't that give us guidelines for determining that some manifestations are contrary to God's nature as He has revealed it Himself? Are the Scriptures truly sufficient as they claim? If this is so, then won't they give us the parameters for the activities of the Holy Spirit? Shouldn't we apply these parameters in evaluating the modern manifestations? Taking God at His word is the essence of faith. It is not limiting God to accept what He has declared to be true about Himself. It is not limiting God to seek to live and worship according to the boundaries He established. God has given these boundaries and warnings for the protection of His people. He has done this precisely so that we can determine what is and is not from Him.

God Offends the Mind to Reveal the Heart

Once again, emotionally powerful because it implies that if you are not willing to shelve your brain and follow along, you have a heart problem. But the Bible never once says this. The Bible does not treat the intellect as a problem. The heart and mind are frequently used interchangeably in Scripture. This is a doctrine written by modern apostles and repeated so frequently that is has gained acceptance among the Biblically illiterate. It has become a maxim. In reality, this is just the modern apostle/prophet's way of saying, "You think too much. Just go with the flow and see where it leads." Once again, the underlying message is crystal clear. Don't think. Don't question. This approach to Christianity is both unbiblical and unwise.

God Will Judge You

If the attempt at silencing their critics through guilt doesn't work, the modern prophets will move to intimidation. God will judge you.

Look at the words of Apostolic Pastor Dutch Sheets in a prophecy about the "Shift in 2006".

> "Opposition to the apostolic and prophetic will also be the greatest this year.

- He is going to expose wineskins (new or old), and religious spirits, taking off the masks of those who oppose His move. Those who refuse to move in current truth will begin to openly criticize leaders in the Body of Christ that are moving in the flow of the apostolic and the prophetic. Some have been doing so in a very subtle way but this year it will become obvious. When they do, God is going to begin to judge them."[51]

This warning by Dutch Sheets would actually make sense if these modern apostles and prophets were truly in the mold of the Old Testament prophets or New Testament apostles. These men spoke with God's authority. To reject their word was to reject the Word of God.

But since today's apostles and prophets are frequently wrong and will not subject themselves to the Biblical tests, they are engaged in something far different.

By attacking anyone who expresses concern based on doctrinal issues, the modern prophets have created an environment of passive acceptance. They place themselves above rebuke and correction, even from the Word of God. This may truly lead to a case of the blind leading the blind.

CHAPTER FIVE

What if it Means What it Says?
Modern Apostles and the Bible

"For the Word alone is yesterday's manna... it is no longer enough to feed my people" - Wendy Alec supposedly quoting Jesus

The Bible unwaveringly claims to be from the very mouth of God. The phrase, "the Lord said" or its equivalent is the most common statement in all the Scriptures. Only the Word of God is said to be able to make one wise unto salvation, to be profitable for doctrine, reproof, correction and instruction in righteousness. Only the Word of God is said to possess the power to pierce to the division of soul and spirit and joint and marrow and to discern the thoughts and intents of the heart. Jesus indicated that while even heaven and earth may pass away, His words would never pass away.

Therefore, the Bible is the fundamental place to start in our discussion of the central doctrines of the faith being impacted by the apostolic and prophetic movements because it is our sole infallible source for faith and practice. It is in the Scriptures that we find the revelation of God. It is within the pages of the written word that we learn of the Living Word, Jesus Christ. Therefore, how one views the Scriptures will have a definitive bearing on how one's theology develops. Scripture is a watershed issue. Subtle deviations from orthodoxy at this point can lead to extreme problems as one progresses farther along. In a very real sense, one's view of Scripture is a fork in the road.

No doctrine is under more regular assault from within the prophetic community than the doctrines relating to the Scriptures. The orthodox church has long held that the canon of Scripture is inerrant in its original form, that the canon is complete and that it is the sole infallible authority for faith and practice. The church has believed that the Scriptures contained all the information needed to live a godly life. In other words that God did not leave any information out of the Word that would be essential for "life and godliness". Further, the church has believed that the Scriptures could be understood by the normal person, a doctrine sometimes referred to as the perspicuity of Scripture. In other words, that God meant what He said and that He has made the main issues of Christianity plain enough that they can be apprehended by the one who seeks Him with a receptive heart. *The teachings of the modern prophets are undermining all of these beliefs.*

The Westminster Confession, one of the greatest expressions of Protestant orthodoxy ever written, states the following in chapter one, section 6 on the sufficiency of Scripture:

> "The whole counsel of God concerning all things necessary for His own glory, man's salvation, faith and life, is either expressly set down in Scripture, or by good and necessary consequence may be deduced from Scripture: unto which nothing at any time is to be added, whether by new revelations of the Spirit, or traditions of men."

The confession continues with this statement is section 7 on the perspicuity of Scripture:

> "All things in Scripture are not alike plain in themselves, nor alike clear unto all: yet those things which are necessary to be known, believed, and observed for salvation are so clearly propounded, and opened in some place of Scripture or other, that not only the learned, but the unlearned, in a due use of the ordinary means, may attain unto a sufficient understanding of them."

This chapter will examine the modern prophets' handling of Scripture, their understanding of the role, inspiration, inerrancy, authority and sufficiency of Scripture and their direct claims about their own words in relation to Scripture.

Prophetic Hermeneutics- Making it up as you go.

God has chosen to reveal Himself through the vehicle of Scripture. At the risk of being overly simple, this means that God has chosen to reveal

Himself through words. This brings up a fundamental question, "How are the words of Scripture meant to be understood?" The way one answers this question will have a dramatic impact on how one approaches the Bible. Does the Bible mean what it says in plain language or is there a meaning behind the words that only the initiated can see? One of the foundational differences between orthodox Christianity and the cults is the approach to Scripture. For instance cults like Unity School of Christianity spiritualize the words of the Bible. Every word has a supposedly "deeper" meaning that brings out the true message. In this way, Unity teachers can claim to follow the Bible while at the same time denying every orthodox doctrine believed by Christians.

For example, consider how the Metaphysical Bible Dictionary discusses the character, Eve.

> "Love, or feeling, in individual consciousness. The I AM (wisdom) puts feeling into what it thinks and so 'Eve' (feeling) becomes the 'mother of all living'"[52]

It should be obvious that when the Bible is handled in this way, verses can be interpreted to mean whatever the individual interpreter wishes them to mean. The Bible is no longer a rule or standard but is more akin to silly putty which can be molded according to the wishes of the reader. If the Bible is to serve in any real way as the rule for faith and practice, it must have some objective meaning that stands outside of the individual and which can be ascertained by the average believer.

The Word of God is the only thing that God says has been exalted alongside of His Name. Psalm 138:2 declares, "...for You have exalted above all things Your Name and Your word." Therefore, Scripture should command the utmost respect. Since it is in fact the Word of God and not the word of men, it should be handled with care. Peter instructs us that the Word of God should not be subjected to private interpretations.

> "Knowing this first that no prophecy is of any private interpretation for prophecy never came from man but holy men of God wrote as they were born along by the Holy Spirit". 2 Pet. 1:20-21

Hermeneutics has been described as the art and science of Biblical interpretation. In handling the Bible properly one should consider such things as context, history, grammar, and the genre of the literature among other things. The goal of hermeneutics is to understand the passage according to the original intent of the author, as inspired by the Holy Spirit.

Historically Christianity, especially Protestant Christianity has followed the grammatical/historical approach to hermeneutics. An overly simplified explanation of this approach is to say that the Bible should be studied in its historical and grammatical context and with the normal understanding of the words used. The intent is to discover the meaning intended by the author of the particular passage.

The historical/grammatical approach takes into account the use of literary devices such as metaphor, simile, hyperbole and even allegory. But it does not spiritualize the Bible if the plain meaning of the text makes sense. It is essentially a belief that God meant the Bible to be understood by the normal believer within the community of faith. This is sometimes referred to as the "plain sense" principle of interpretation. Professor Steve Lemke states this principle well when he writes,

> "We should assume that the 'plain sense' meaning of a word is what is intended unless we have reasons to believe otherwise...In some cases Scripture is clearly using hyperbole, metaphor, or poetic language to communicate a point. For example, when Jesus said, 'I am the door', (John 10:9), it would be silly to suggest that Jesus was saying that He is a literal door that swings on hinges! But unless we have such clear signals in the text that a symbolic meaning is intended, we should assume that the plain sense or literal meaning is the primary meaning. We should not impose mystical or symbolic interpretations on a text that was not intended in this way."[53]

Lemke's statement is directly in line with the words of the apostle Paul. In 2 Corinthians 1:13 Paul stated, "For we are not writing any other things to you than what you read or understand." The implication of this statement in Pauline theology is that his words were meant to be understood by the common reader. His words did not contain hidden meanings or interpretations that could only be understood by super-anointed individuals.

Many times poor theology can be traced directly to the way a person approaches the Bible. It has been said that the Bible can be made to support anything and this is certainly true if verses are taken out of context.

An improper approach to interpreting the Word of God will invariably lead to faulty conclusions and poor doctrine.

The result is that those who are regularly ingesting a steady diet of such teachings remain largely biblically illiterate with regard to what the Bible truly teaches. Kevin Reeves discusses this condition when he writes,

> "This will no doubt spark a barrage of protests, as the Bible is cited profusely in defense of everything from the current contrived spiritual warfare to false prophecy. But a real test for spiritual maturity is not how many individual Scriptures a person may know, but how they understand those same Scriptures in context. Removed from the rest of a passage, one text can become the gateway into a limitless variety of counterfeit doctrines."[54]

Today's prophets, and consequently their followers as well, are consistently sloppy in their approach to Scripture, frequently ignoring context, history and grammar. They can even be seen redefining words when necessary to force verses to fit their preconceived ideas. The intent of the author of the text is rarely considered. The Bible is left to mean whatever the prophets say it means today.

The following examples are given to demonstrate that this is not an occasional problem within the prophetic community. Indeed a negligent handling of the Scripture is rampant within the movement. It is hoped that the following examples, drawn from multiple sources will establish the truth of this statement beyond reasonable doubt.

In his message, "Contending for the Power of God", Mike Bickle urges his followers to press forward for the Christian experience he believes that should typify the end-time church.

> "[Jude says] I want you to contend. I want you to fight. I want you to *press into God* for the type of experience that was left you by the early apostles."[55] (Emphasis on the CD itself)

Here Bickle performs a classic bait and switch with the words of Scripture. He begins with the verse and gives the impression that he is interpreting the passage but then quickly changes the meaning of significant words in the verse. No reputable Greek lexicon translates the word "contend" as "press into God" (whatever that means). Secondly, the context of the passage indicates that Jude was not asking his readers to contend for some kind of apostolic experience of power but rather for the central tenants of the Christian faith and life against false teachers who had risen up within the midst of the church. Jude writes, "For certain people have crept in unnoticed who long ago were designated for condemnation, ungodly people, who pervert the grace of our God into sensuality and deny our only Master and Lord, Jesus Christ." (Jude 4) Thus, while Bickle gives the impression that he is basing his teaching upon the Bible, he has actually manipulated the Bible to justify his own belief.

Only moments later in the same message Bickle urges his listeners to ask God for the "breaker anointing" which he will ultimately define as a "catalytic deposit of the Holy Spirit that allows heaven to invade earth for the purposes of God to go forward in new dimensions."[56] Bickle states it like this:

> "Ask God for the Breaker Anointing which is something we link back to Micah chapter 2 verses 12 and 13....Micah chapter 2 verses 12 and 13, which speaks about an anointing to break open to allow the work of God to go forward in new dimensions."[57]

Here is what the passage actually states:

> I will surely assemble all of you, O Jacob;
> I will gather the remnant of Israel;
> I will set them together like sheep in a fold,
> like a flock in its pasture,
> a noisy multitude of men.
> He who opens the breach goes up before them;
> they break through and pass the gate,
> going out by it.
> Their king passes on before them,
> the Lord at their head.

Any careful reading of Micah 2:12-13 will see that the passage is relating to the re-gathering of Israel. The passage has strong Messianic implications. However, nowhere in the passage is any indication of an anointing to be received by individuals that is necessary for the purposes of God to advance in some supposed new dimension. Bickle's interpretation is simply unfounded and no one in the history of the church has ever understood this passage in such a way. It might also be beneficial at this point to mention how man-centered this particular teaching is, though this will be discussed more fully in subsequent chapters. God's purposes must wait for men to break through in prayer to receive an anointing. In the prophetic theology, man is the ultimate mover, the decision-maker. God is always waiting on man.

Kirk Bennett on his teaching "Prophecy and the Arts" follows a similar, make-it-up-as-you-go, approach to Scripture when commenting on Matthew 8:20. In speaking to a man who had just claimed that he would follow Jesus wherever he goes, Jesus replies, "Foxes have holes and birds have nests. But the Son of Man has nowhere to lay His head." Any reasonable reader of the text will understand that Jesus is warning this would-be follower of the hardship that he should be prepared to endure in following Christ.

But Bennett offers the following, startling interpretation:

"When Jesus said this I think He was speaking about us. I think he was speaking about us because He didn't have a people in which to dwell yet."[58]

Once again notice that Bennett has gone well outside of the boundaries of normal word usage and completely ignored the immediate context in giving His interpretation.

In speaking about Jesus' lovesickness and longing for His bride, (a subject that will be examined in detail in our chapter on "Modern Prophets and Jesus") Allen Hood gave the following colorful commentary on Galatians 4:4.

"Jesus was born of a woman in the fullness of time, **when he couldn't take it any longer.** Jesus was saying 'Father is it time? Father is it time?'....[the Father answering] 'Almost'...[Jesus] 'Father is it time?' 'Almost'.. [Jesus] Father, [Jesus screaming] Faaatheeeeeeer' The angels are saying, 'Just let Him go. He's driving us all crazy. He's lovesick. Send him!!' [Hood chuckles on tape] Jesus is saying, 'Father is it time?' And the moment the Father says, 'Now!'" (Emphasis added)[59]

In the series, "Thunder from Heaven", Bickle finds in Revelation 10, in John's experience eating the little book and hearing the seven thunders, justification for a belief that in these last days God is going to raise up 10,000 apostolic preachers who will fulfill Amos 3:7, will declare what the seven thunders spoke, participate with God in His end-time judgments and whose declarations will literally change things on the earth and in the spirit.[60]

While certainly the book of Revelation is open to a variety of interpretations depending on one's eschatological position, no one in the history of the church has ever seen this mandate anywhere in Revelation 10. The fact of the matter is that such an idea cannot be found in the passage.

Shawn Bolz, one of the younger prophets and a young man who came up under Mike Bickle at Metro Vineyard makes some striking comments regarding Proverbs 6:31, "Yet if he is caught, he must pay sevenfold, though it costs him all the wealth of his house." Bolz indicates that this Scripture is "rightfully used many times to break off a poverty spirit."[61]

Nowhere does this verse say anything about a poverty spirit (nor does the rest of the Bible for that matter) nor does it say anything about breaking one off.

Bolz provides another example of the prophetic hermeneutic when he comments on 2 Cor. 3:18- "As we maintain the Holy Spirit's continued indwelling and demonstrate obedience to His direction, we become so appealing to Jesus that we provoke His heart toward us. He draws near, and His love, righteousness, and power transform us."[62]

In reality the passage is actually speaking of our being transformed by beholding the Lord through the vehicle of His Word. Nowhere does the passage speak of our maintaining the Holy Spirit's indwelling. In fact, the idea that the believer must do anything to maintain the Spirit's indwelling is thoroughly unbiblical. Nowhere does the passage indicate that we make ourselves more appealing to Jesus and provoke His heart toward us. Bolz has simply inserted these unbiblical ideas out of his own fertile imagination into the text and completely altered the passages meaning.

Paul Keith Davis, another prophet with strong Kansas City connections and currently the leader of "White Dove Ministries" gives the following novel interpretation of Hebrews 4:12-13. He states that the word of God that is alive and powerful is not a reference to the Scriptures, but rather it is a person who can come and stand alongside the preacher during a meeting and reveal the hearts of those present to the one preaching. He draws this conclusion from verse 13 where he says that the phrase "nothing is hidden

74

from his sight" refers back to the Word. Unfortunately, for Davis, the "his" refers back to God grammatically. The author of Hebrews is definite that the word about which he is writing is the Bible and not a person because he uses the neuter pronoun "it". This word is never used to refer to a person.

Apostle Chuck Pierce takes the same passage to mean something completely different. In a chapter entitled, "Let Us Go that We May Worship Him!", Pierce discusses "ascending in worship" and coming to a place of abiding in our position in heaven with Christ, he writes,

> "As we seek the Lord and move into a posture of worship, our souls and spirits are divided. This is how we cut loose and ascend. Hebrews 4:12 declares: 'For the Word that God speaks is alive and full of power [making it active, operative, energizing, and effective]; it is sharper than any two-edged sword, penetrating to the dividing line of the breath of life (soul) and [the immortal] spirit, and of joints and marrow [of the deepest parts of our nature], exposing and sifting and analyzing and judging the very thoughts and purposes of the heart. (AMP)"[63]

Even with appealing to the Amplified Version, Pierce really is unable to find any support for his theory that our souls and spirits are divided in worship to allow our spirits to abide in our heavenly position in Christ. Once again, Pierce is reading into the passage what he wants it to say.

Comparing the interpretations offered by Pierce and Davis to the same passage illustrates the danger of the prophetic approach to the Bible. Each man can come to widely differing interpretations because there is simply no guide or grid for understanding the passage. The student is left with no way to actually determine what the verse means. Bible study becomes a case of each man determining what is right in his own eyes. The Scriptures cease to have any objective meaning whatsoever.

Pierce continues his sloppy handling of Scripture throughout the book. Later he writes,

> "The Word of God declares, 'But we all, with unveiled face beholding as in a mirror the glory of the Lord, are being transformed into the same image *from glory to glory*, just as by the Spirit of the Lord' (2 Cor. 3:18 emphasis added). Through our Lord Jesus' sacrificial death, He made a way for us to go into the Throne Room and experience His glory. We go from one place of glory to another place of glory."[64]

While it is true that the book of Hebrews says that we may boldly approach the throne, this was not the thought that Paul was sharing in 2 Corinthians 3:18. Context clearly shows that the beholding about which Paul was writing occurs as believers study the Word of God. In other words, we behold God through the Scriptures. Paul said that when the Jews read the books of Moses they do so with a veil over their face but in our case the veil has been removed. It is the Word of God that transforms us from glory to glory.

A post on the prophetic newsletter Elijah List by editor Steve Shultz, provides another classic example of the misuse of Scripture that is rampant within the prophetic community. In an article discussing the difference between modern prophets and psychics, Shultz turns the meaning of Deuteronomy 18:22 completely upside down when he writes the following:

> "However, even if a true prophet misses it once in awhile, the Bible tells you not to be afraid of that person. Just because a person makes a mistake doesn't mean he or she is a false prophet or a psychic. It only means they are still learning to hear accurately.
>
> *"If what a prophet proclaims in the name of the LORD does not take place or come true, that is a message the LORD has not spoken. That prophet has spoken presumptuously. Do not be afraid of him."*- Deut. 18:22"[65]

Notice Shultz's interpretation of this passage. He believes that God is saying that not only does an inaccurate prophetic word not negate the prophet's claim to be a prophet but that we do not need to be afraid to accept this person as a prophet. In other words, we don't need to be afraid that this person's message will hurt us. We can accept him as a prophetic person who is just learning to hear God correctly.

Although we have examined this passage in a previous chapter, let's again look at the passage he quotes in its fuller context.

Deuteronomy 18:18-22

> "I will raise up for them a prophet like you from among their brothers. And I will put my words in his mouth, and he shall speak to them all that I command him. And whoever will not listen to my words that he shall speak in my name, I myself will require it of him. But the prophet who presumes to speak a word in my name that I have not commanded

him to speak or who speaks in the name of other gods, that same prophet shall die. And if you say in your heart, 'How may we know the word that the LORD has not spoken"–when a prophet speaks in the name of the LORD, if the word does not come to pass or come true, that is a word that the LORD has not spoken; the prophet has spoken it presumptuously. You need not be afraid of him."

When viewed in its proper context, not only does Deut. 18:22 not teach what Shultz claims, it in fact teaches the EXACT OPPOSITE. The passage is actually saying the following: 1. If a true prophet speaks in the name of God and his words are not followed, God will hold the disobedient accountable. 2. False prophets are to be put to death. 3. The way to determine a false prophet is two-fold. Some will speak in the name of other gods. Some will speak a false word in the Name of the True God. 4. You can recognize a false prophet when his words fail to come to pass. (Then the prophet would die.) 5. You have no need to fear the false prophet (in context this would mean that you do not need to fear any retribution by disobeying him and you need not fear executing the judgment of God upon him.)

It would literally be possible to fill an encyclopedia with examples like the ones given previously and never move to another issue. It is hoped that the litany of examples given in this section are enough to demonstrate that this issue is systemic throughout the apostolic/prophetic community. This is not a problem with merely one or two of the prophets nor are these examples merely isolated instances. These "prophetic" teachers regularly run roughshod over the actual meaning of the text of Scripture in order to provide justification for their new doctrines. The approach to Scripture employed by the vast majority of these teachers is so consistently sloppy that many of their followers have no idea how the Bible should be properly interpreted. They have lost the ability to even recognize when the Bible is being misapplied. Their handling of the Scriptures is startlingly similar to the methodology employed by cultists as demonstrated in the example given in the beginning of this chapter.

Charismatic/Third Wave author Sam Storms, a former staff member under Mike Bickle, and former seminary professor, recognizes and expresses concern over this approach to the Bible. He writes, "All too often charismatics will find in a biblical passage a word or image or literary allusion that sounds analogous to their immediate circumstance and claim it as a promise, or use it to justify a novel practice, without regard for its original context or authorial intent."[66]   He continues by stating that he believes there is no intent to undermine the authority of Scripture. Storms states, "I suggest, however, that this is due more to a lack of hermeneutical sophistication than to any conscious diminishing of the texts inspiration and authority."[67]

I agree with Storms that in most cases it is not the intent of most those within the prophetic community to undermine the authority of Scripture. Many of these teachers have little or no training. Like Storms, I also prefer to give them the benefit of the doubt since I cannot know their hearts. Still the undermining of Scriptural authority is the **result** of many of their practices whether or not it is the actual intent. Additionally, as will be shown presently, not everyone within the prophetic community holds to a high view of Scripture.

The impact of this "prophetic hermeneutic" is serious indeed. In the first place, as has already been stated, this type of approach to Scripture causes the Bible to lose its ability to provide boundaries for doctrine and practice because the Bible simply has no objective meaning. The Scripture means whatever any particular prophetic teacher declares that the Spirit has told him it means today.

This style of teaching also serves to remove any definite understanding of Scripture from the common man who realizes that he simply cannot see all the things in Scripture that these teachers are seeing. This makes the average church person dependent on these inspired teachers in order to know what the Lord has said.

The words of the eminent theologian Charles Hodge seem particularly pertinent here. He wrote,

> "...what all the competent readers of a plain book take to be its meaning, must be its meaning. Secondly, because the Holy Spirit is promised to guide the people of God into the knowledge of the truth, and therefore that which they, under the teaching of the Spirit, agree in believing must be true."[68]

Allow me to restate the salient points of Hodge's comments. First the Holy Spirit has promised to lead God's people into truth. Therefore, if the church has never seen a particular doctrine or interpretation in all of its

2000 year history then either the Holy Spirit has not done His job or this new interpretation is false. Secondly, if the church has agreed for the last 2000 years about the meaning of certain passages in Scripture then either that meaning is the true meaning or the Bible is so obscure and unintelligible as to be completely meaningless. Charismatic theologian Wayne Grudem concurs, "...the Old Testament and New Testament frequently affirm that Scripture is written in such a way that its teachings are able to be understood by ordinary believers."[69] Grudem points to the *Shemah* of Deut. 6:4-9 which commands the Israelites to diligently teach the commandments of God to their children. Grudem rightly notes that the passage assumes that the commandments of God are understandable to both the Israelites and their children.

Additionally, due to the rampant misinterpretation of Scripture, many within the body of Christ are being led into false doctrines and practices. At a minimum these prove to be distractions from activities that are Biblical and spiritually edifying. At worst, they undermine the very foundations of the Christian faith. Contrary to what is normally believed in contemporary society, doctrine does matter. Attempting to document and discuss these aberrant doctrines and practices will be the purpose of much of the remainder of this book.

Another outcome of this approach to interpretation is that it directly undermines the ability to correct and witness to those involved in aberrant and cultic movements. For instance, how do we know that the Jehovah's Witnesses are incorrect in their doctrine that only 144,000 will actually inherit heaven? After all, they can point to a verse and they have revelation? What about the many revelations of Joseph Smith? How does one know what the truth is? How can one discern between the many prophetic declarations of today's prophets? How does an individual determine truth from error? One cannot respond that we need to look at the context of the passage for as we have amply demonstrated above, context is irrelevant according to most of these prophetic teachers, in interpreting the Bible. So are we merely left with a "my revelation trumps your revelation" response?

But lastly, and most seriously, the Bible simply deserves better treatment than this. One must ask if it is permissible to treat the modern prophet's words in the same manner that they treat the words of the Bible. In other words, can one take the statements made by Bickle, Joyner, Pierce et.al and rip them from their context, redefine the words, ignore any relevant historical detail, literalize metaphors and then claim that this is what the prophets are saying? One suspects not. In fact the first cry of these prophetic teachers when their doctrine is called into question is that they are being taken out of context. Their protests indicate that they expect that when one reads the works of these teachers, one is supposed to read them in context and use the standard definition of words, recognizing when they are using rhetorical devices such as metaphor, simile, hyperbole, etc. The question then becomes, "If it is improper to treat the word of men in this fashion, is it not even more improper to do those same things to the Word of God?" In other words, doesn't the Word of God deserve at least as much respect as the word of man?

The Word of God should demand greater honor than this.

The hermeneutical or interpretive issue is truly the root of many of the problems within the prophetic movement. This is the reason so much space is being given to documenting and discussing the abuses. Because these prophetic teachers do not approach God's Word properly, they reach false conclusions. These false conclusions then support aberrant doctrines and unbiblical practices. These unbiblical practices and false doctrines undermine the historic truths of the Church and distract Christians from the pure faith and the true work of the ministry.

Unfortunately however, the problems within the apostolic/prophetic movements with regard to the Word of God do not stop at improper methods of interpretation. Modern prophets are also undermining the inspiration, inerrancy, authority and the clarity of the Word of God.

Prophets on the Inspiration of Scripture

In his book, "The Final Quest", Rick Joyner lists 4 levels of inspiration, ranging from impressions to trances. The more advanced the level, the more certain it is that a word is coming from God in an uncorrupted form. What is immediately startling is that Joyner places the New Testament epistles at only the **second level of inspiration!** This is extremely concerning when one reads what he says about this level. Consider the following,

"The next level of inspiration is a conscious sense of the presence of the Lord, or the anointing of the Holy Spirit, which gives special illumination to our minds. This often comes when I am writing, or speaking, and it gives me much greater confidence in the importance or accuracy of what I am saying. **I believe that this was probably experienced by the apostles as they wrote the New Testament epistles.** This will give us great confidence, but it is still a level where we can still be influenced by our prejudices, doctrines, etc.[70] (emphasis added)

There are several things in this statement that are extremely alarming. Notice first that while Joyner says this second level gives us greater confidence than impressions (the lowest level of inspiration), this is still an area where we can be influenced by our own prejudices, doctrine, etc. In this single statement, whether intentionally or not, Joyner has completely undercut the authority of the epistles. (He will do this again later in the same book.) Apparently, we as believers now have the task of evaluating the epistles just as we would the words of modern prophets in order to see where Paul and the other apostles might have been influenced by their own flesh as they wrote. Theoretically at least, we would be free to ignore those passages where we believe that Paul is speaking out of his own prejudice and doctrinal bias.

Secondly, Joyner notes that he experiences this level of inspiration frequently when he speaks and writes. This would put his words on equal authority with Scripture since they come with the same level of inspiration. Therefore the canon is not closed. But even more shocking, Joyner lists two levels above this, open visions and trances, which he and all modern prophets claim to be receiving. This would obviously then place the words of these modern prophets as superior to some Scripture, especially the epistles. Therefore, we should judge Scripture by their words and not the reverse. Incidentally, it is at this extremely high level that Joyner claims to have received "The Final Quest", which would then make this book of a greater level of authority than any of the New Testament epistles. Joyner writes:

"The visions contained in this book all began with a dream. Some of it came under a very intense sense of the presence of the Lord, but the overwhelming majority was received in some level of a trance."[71]

If Joyner is accurate in his statements, then it would logically follow that "The Final Quest" deserves canonization within the New Testament itself for it carries a higher level of revelation than 2/3 of the books originally included. In fact one should be able to judge the words of the New Testament epistles based on their conformity with "The Final Quest" rather than the reverse because Joyner's book comes from a higher level of revelation. With these statements Joyner has undermined the doctrines of the authority of Scripture, the verbal plenary inspiration of Scripture, the inerrancy of Scripture, the infallibility of Scripture and the idea of a closed Canon.

How far removed are Joyner's comments from the claims of Scripture about itself.

> "All Scripture is given by inspiration of God and is profitable for doctrine, for reproof, for rebuke, for instruction in righteousness that the man of God may be perfect thoroughly equipped for every good work". (2 Tim. 3:16-17)

> "Every word of God is pure" (Ps. 30:5)

> "Knowing this, that no prophecy is of any private interpretation. For prophecy did not originate with man but holy men of God wrote as they were moved (literally born along) by the Holy Spirit" (2 Pet. 1:20)

The Bible knows nothing of these levels of revelation when it comes to the penning of God's word. The Bible claims equal revelation from cover to cover.

With these words, Joyner has placed himself well outside the camp of orthodox Protestant theology. Whether intentionally or unintentionally, he has rejected the historic doctrine of verbal plenary inspiration, the idea that the inspiration of the Holy Spirit extended to the very words the authors chose and that such inspiration occurred in the same measure to every writer in every instance so that every book is equally inspired and can equally be called the Word of God.

Wayne Grudem summarizes orthodox doctrine well when he writes, "The authority of Scripture means that all the words in Scripture are God's words in such a way that to disbelieve or disobey any word of Scripture is to disbelieve or disobey God."[72]

This is no minor issue. This is a foundational issue. Joyner's position is heresy, pure and simple, and we must call it such.

Prophets on the Value and Integrity of Scripture

Moldy Pages

Today's prophets repeatedly make statements that devalue the role of Scripture. Consider the following comment by Tommy Tenney from his bestselling book, "The God Chasers",

> "God chasers don't want to just study from the moldy pages of what God has done..."[73]

Notice that God's inerrant, infallible word is reduced to "moldy pages". According to Tenney, it is merely the record of what God has done in the past. It is the tracks of where God has been but it is not where God is at now. Obviously, the new words must be more important. The reader is led to look away from the sure foundation of God's Word, which has been established in heaven, to the shifting sands of the proclamations and manifestations of today's prophets.

Many errors in these old love letters

In similar vein, "prophet" Scott Hicks, whose words have regularly appeared on the Elijah List, posted the following in the discussion section of the "signofjonah" blog. His comments reveal a very weak appreciation for Scripture. The post is given here in its entirety so as to circumvent the claim that Hicks has been taken out of context. All emphases, grammar, spelling etc. are in the original.

> "The bible has many errors...Though I believe it does not in its ORIGINAL TEXT — However, How is it that you say the Bible is without error when one Scripture concerning Jesus visiting Gaderra — says that their was "one" demoniac that ran to Jesus and then other Scripture says that there were "two" domoniacs that ran to Jesus...
>
> The Bible we have "NOW" is tranlated text — while it is generally holy and inspiring, and full of old "love letters" there are still errors due to tranlational issues during translation – However, how can God's Rhema word be with error if it comes straight from the thone? – It can't! God

is without error – perhaps certain ones are with error when they claim God said something – but that doesn't pertain to every prophet of today….. While there are many false – did it occur to you that if translated Scripture is with error – then perhaps God does use men to speak through. So that all can have a clear message?..

You need to think about this real hard for a little bit…. Its funny that the first words out of the enemy's mouth - the first words ever recorded - He told Eve: "Surely God hath not said." … Surely God didn't say that…..That was his first words then and from the looks of this blog - it remains to be his words of deception…..Think about it…

-Scott"

Before getting into a point by point analysis of all that Hicks wrote in this comment, it would first be good to note the general attitude displayed toward the Bible. Hicks finds that the Bibles we have today, while "generally holy and inspiring" are basically unreliable. Despite Jesus' promise "heaven and earth will pass away but my words will never pass away", God has not reliably preserved His Word. In Hicks' mind modern prophets are today giving a clear message compared to the "old love letters" contained in those errant Bibles. Once again, one needs to compare the words of modern prophet Scott Hicks with the words given by the Holy Spirit concerning the Scriptures which have already been documented in this chapter.

Upon closer examination, a number of other problems are revealed in the way Scott Hicks relates to the Scriptures.

First, Scott misunderstands the doctrine of inerrancy which deals with Scriptures in the original manuscripts not in current translations. He apparently believes that Evangelicals are claiming that some modern translation is inerrant. That is not what the doctrine states.

That being said, we do have more than 24,600 ancient manuscripts of the New Testament plus the writings of the church fathers in which they quote Scripture. The New Testament we possess today is so pure that there is not even discussion about 98%+ of the text. The Dead Sea Scrolls added a wealth of support for the Old Testament as well. Every believer can have the utmost confidence that when they read any reputable translation, they are reading the Word of God. The Bibles we possess do not contain "many errors".

Second, Hicks seems to misunderstand the translation process. He appears to believe that errors have crept in as the Bible had to be translated over and over. One of two things is true. Either Scott believes that the Bible was translated from Greek/Hebrew/Aramaic into one language then another, then another until it is full of errors (much like playing the game "telephone".) or he really means to discuss transcription errors (i.e. errors in copying) instead of translation errors. Either way, his point is simply wrong. We do not need to go through a series of other languages to get back to the original. We can go directly to the original languages. Further, though errors were made in copying, since no one person or group ever had control of all the manuscripts, the same errors were not made in all the copies. Therefore scholars can compare manuscripts and reconstruct the original.

Next Hicks resorts to a failed tactic normally employed by liberal scholars and skeptics attempting to prove the Bible is unreliable in his mention of the Gadarene demoniacs. The different accounts within the gospels are not contradictions nor are they errors. They are eyewitnesses choosing to relate different details based on what they thought was important under the inspiration of the Holy Spirit. The fact that the Bible is difficult to reconcile in some places actually indicates that the authors of the Scriptures did not collaborate in fabricating stories about Jesus but were, as they claim, reporting eyewitness accounts. In the case of the Gadarene demoniac, this is not a contradiction. If one gospel writer had said there was only one demoniac and the other said there was more than one, we would have a contradiction. Such is not the case. One biblical author focuses on one of the men (possibly the main speaker) and another gospel writer adds the detail that another demoniac was also present. This is easy to reconcile and does not constitute an error.

Following this, Hicks actually makes a statement with which one can agree. He says that a word coming from the throne of God cannot be in error. To this statement a hearty "Amen" is in order. However, what neither Hicks nor any other member of the prophetic movement can produce is a modern prophet whose words actually are without error. In fact, nearly all of the modern prophets admit that they are not without error. As one pastor has said, "today's modern prophets are like a child playing an instrument and making numerous mistakes all the while claiming to be a prodigy. We are just supposed to ignore all the sour notes." Hicks fails to make the logical conclusion of his own reasoning. Since all of these prophets give prophecies that contain errors, these words must not be coming from the throne of God.

Lastly, Hicks sinks into a tired line of reasoning thrown at anyone who dares to question today's prophets, i.e. "You are doing the devil's work." Anyone who examines the prophets is immediately slandered as an "accuser of the brethren", having a Jezebel spirit, religious spirit, Judas spirit, Saul spirit etc. etc. ad nauseum. This ad hominem attack was dealt with in chapter four.

Apparently Hicks is unfamiliar with John's instruction. "Beloved do not believe every spirit but test the spirits whether they are of God for many false prophets have gone out into the world." (1 John 4:1) Or Paul's instructions to the Thessalonians given in the context of speaking about prophecy."Test all things. Hold fast to that which is good." (1 Thess. 5:21). Not to mention God's instructions in Deuteronomy chapters 13 & 18.

No, if one dares to attempt to be a Berean and examine the Scriptures to see if the things spoken by the prophets are so, one is dastardly. This is especially true should any attempt be made to warn the rest of the body of the falsehood. But Hicks is not alone among the modern prophets in his attitude toward the Scriptures.

Yesterday's Manna

In her enormously popular book, "Journal of the Unknown Prophet", Wendy Alec continues the prophetic attacks on the value of the Scriptures. In a section penned to today's prophetic teachers which was supposedly spoken by Jesus Christ Himself, Alec writes,

> "For the Word alone is **yesterday's manna** and even they [prophetic teachers] have seen deep in their hearts that **it is no longer enough to feed my people.**"[74] (emphasis added)

Alec's statement about "yesterday's manna" is significant. It's biblical/ historical antecedent comes from the pages of the book of Exodus when

God sent the manna to feed the nation of Israel. With the exception of the sixth day, the Israelites were to collect only enough manna for each day's needs. But some among them were disobedient and Moses writes, "Notwithstanding they did not heed Moses. But some of them left part of it until morning, and it bred worms and stank." (Exodus 16:20) So here Alec would have us believe, either intentionally or unintentionally, that Jesus Christ compares the teaching of the Word of God alone to stinking, worm infested bread.

Her statement, which is again supposedly directly from the mouth of the Lord Jesus, that the Word is no longer sufficient to feed the people of God is also remarkable. One cannot help but consider how different Alec's words are from those of the Word of God. For according to the Word of God, Scriptures are able to make us wise unto salvation, are able to perfect the man of God so that he is equipped for every good work, and are pure milk (not wormy bread) that we are to crave so that we may grow thereby. With these statements Alec demonstrates herself to be a false prophet and proves that whoever or whatever she may have encountered, it was not the Lord Jesus. For one thing is certain, God the Son will never contradict God the Holy Spirit, the author of Scripture. The Incarnate Word would never call His people to disdain the written Word.

Biblical Prophets Made False Prophecies Too

In order to attempt to explain why today's prophets continue to have so many failed prophecies--a real problem since the claim is that this generation of apostles and prophets will be the greatest in the history of the church--Rick Joyner writes the following,

> "No prophet is infallible, which is why new covenant prophecy must be judged. There are even cases where old covenant prophets missed a prediction or prophecy, but were still acknowledged as prophets by the Lord (Jonah, Isaiah, and Elijah all made statements that were not true or did not come to pass).[75]

This statement, if true would have serious ramifications for understanding the doctrine of inerrancy. It is interesting that Joyner offers no examples whatsoever to support his assertion. However, we can certainly guess what is in his mind with respect to Jonah. Jonah prophesied the overthrow of the city of Nineveh. It is true that Nineveh was not destroyed as Jonah predicted but the Bible tells us why. The city of Nineveh repented at the preaching of Jonah and God spared the city. This is perfectly consistent with what God has revealed in His Word. If God pronounces doom on a city or nation and that people repent, God has promised to turn from the calamity that He had declared He would send. Consider the Word of God through the prophet Jeremiah,

> "If at any time I announce that a nation or kingdom is to be uprooted, torn down and destroyed, and if that nation I warned repents of its evil, then I will relent and not inflict on it the disaster I had planned. And if at another time I announce that a nation or kingdom is to be built up and planted, and if it does evil in my sight and does not obey me, then I will reconsider the good I had intended to do for it." (Jeremiah 18:7-10)

Many scholars have recognized that historical contingencies affect how a declaration of God is carried out. Many times the prophecy itself was the means used by God to cause a humbling of the recipient(s) of the prophecy [as in the case of Nineveh] through which God was able to turn them from disaster.

As Richard Pratt notes,

> "Old Testament predictions did not necessarily seal the fates of those who received them. Instead, their recipients believed that it was possible for intervening historical contingencies—especially the contingency of humble prayer—to have significant effects on the fulfillment of prophecy."[76]

This is certainly a far cry from the prophets today like Joyner, Clement, Jones et. al who just plain regularly get it wrong. Despite Joyner's claim, Old Testament prophets did not have the luxury of simply missing. Joyner's comments however, are interesting because they, once again, illustrate just how far modern prophets will go in order to attempt to justify themselves.

Not All the Scripture is Equally Inspired

Not only does Joyner, in "The Final Quest", indicate that the epistles were written from only the second highest level of revelation, as we discussed previously, later on he indicates that the words of Paul in Scripture do not have as much authority as the words of Jesus in the gospels. The following dialogue was supposedly spoken by Paul to Joyner while Joyner was in heaven:

> "The foundation stones were laid by Jesus, alone. My life and ministry are not the example of what you are called to be. Jesus alone is that. If what I have written is used as a foundation, it will not be able to hold the weight of that which needs to be built upon it. What I have written must be built upon the only Foundation that can withstand what you are about to endure; it must not be used as the foundation. You must see my teachings through the Lord's teachings, not try to understand Him from my perspective. His words are the foundation. I have only built upon them by elaborating on His words. The greatest wisdom, and the most powerful truths, are His words, not mine."[77]

So according to Joyner, we have a multi-tiered Bible, a canon within the canon. There are the Words of Jesus, which provide the real foundation. These words are really, really inspired. Joyner would, I'm sure, add to this the Book of Revelation since it also contains the words of Jesus and was received in an open vision. Then you have the rest of the New Testament which is of a lesser level of revelation and inspiration. If we build our lives around these passages, the foundation will not be strong enough to hold the weight, especially for those of us in this last-days church.

This is sheer lunacy and is completely contradictory to the apostle's understanding of their own writings. For instance, Peter in commenting on the epistles of Paul, writes, "in which are some things hard to understand which unstable people twist to their own destruction, as THEY DO THE REST OF THE SCRIPTURES" (2 Pet 3:16 emphasis added) Notice that Peter here places Paul's words alongside the rest of the Scriptures in authority. He does not in any way indicate that Paul's words came with some lesser level of inspiration. Nowhere do the apostles in any way indicate that their words or writings will not supply a sufficient foundation upon which to build one's life.

Scripture is Impotent

Modern prophets, Choo Thomas, Mary K. Baxter, Bill Weiss, who have all become famous by virtue of their trips to heaven, hell or all of the above, all give the indication that their experiences and books are necessary because their testimonies will be able to convince people of the reality of these places whereas the Bible has been impotent to do so.

Choo Thomas's book, "Heaven is So Real" is absolutely filled with this kind of rhetoric. Consider the following words, supposedly to Thomas from Jesus:

> "My daughter, you are an End-Times prophetess,' the Lord told me, "and you are living proof of My Word and My prophecies......."He told me that many people don't believe His words and prophecies, and He said even some Christians do not believe them."[78]

She continues:

> "He wants me to serve as living proof of the Bible and His prophecies, because many people do not believe what they read in the Bible, nor do they believe He is coming soon for His people."[79]

And elsewhere she writes:

> "He had shown me how desperate many people are to know the truth about heaven, and I realized emphatically that my book would be the means whereby they could really know."[80]

Notice that Thomas realized emphatically that her book, not the Bible, would be the means used to satisfy the hunger of those desperate to know the truth about heaven. There is no way to understand these statements except that the Bible is deficient. Thankfully, the church now has Choo Thomas's personal experiences to verify the truth of God's promises. One wonders how generations of believers in bygone days were able to know the truth about heaven and the promises of God without the benefit of Choo's visions.

Mary K. Baxter makes very similar boasts. According to Baxter, Jesus said to her,

> "I am going to reveal unto you the reality of hell, that many may be saved, many will repent of their evil ways before it is too late."[81]

And later in the same book we read,

> "He said, 'I am Jesus Christ, your Lord, and I wish to give you a revelation to prepare the saints for My return and to turn many to

righteousness.... I want you to write a book and tell of the visions and of all the things I reveal to you. You and I will walk through hell together. Make a record of these things which were and are and are to come. My words are true, faithful and trustworthy. I Am That I AM, and there is none beside me.' "[82]

And again,

> "Behold, My child," Jesus said, "I am going to take you by My Spirit into hell so that you may be able to make a record of the reality of it, to tell the whole earth that hell is real, and to bring the lost out of darkness and into the light of the gospel of Jesus Christ."[83]

This last quote is particularly relevant. Once again we see that her book, not the Scriptures, will be the means of convincing people that hell is real and bringing the lost out of darkness and into the light of the gospel. The Bible is just not enough to do this.

In the light of the comments of Thomas and Baker, it is important to remember the teaching of the Lord Jesus in the story of the Rich Man and Lazarus. In response to the rich man's request that Lazarus be sent back from the grave to speak to his five brothers, Abraham replied, "They have Moses and the Prophets; let them hear them." The rich man seemingly followed a similar line of reasoning as that of Thomas and Baxter that the Scriptures alone are insufficient but someone coming back who had actually been to hell would do the trick. Abraham's response in Luke 16:31 is salient, "If they do not hear Moses and the Prophets, neither will they be convinced if someone should rise from the dead." If a person is unwilling to hear the clear teaching of Scripture on the subject of heaven and hell why would one assume that they would be convinced by the stories of those like Baxter and Thomas?

The New Testament Apostles Didn't Teach the Scriptures Either

Former Dallas Theological Seminary professor Jack Deere attempts to provide cover for all of the extra-Biblical teaching occurring in today's church by boldly asserting that Jesus and the apostles didn't teach the Bible either.

> "You know I'm gonna look up every reference to teaching in the Bible. So I just punched it in my computer concordance, looked up every single reference 'taught, teacher, teaching,' every single reference in the

New Testament and its astounding. Did you know not one time, not one time does it say that Jesus taught the Bible?.. Isn't that interesting? Not one time does it ever say that. It says He taught about the kingdom, taught about God, preached the Gospel of the kingdom, and the Good news. Not one time does it ever say He taught the Bible ... I looked up all the references with the apostles and did you know that with only one possible exception, it never says the Apostles taught the Bible?...Here's the last verse in the book of Acts, verse 31. Here's how it ends with what Paul's doing. v.31 'boldly and without hindrance he preached" not the Bible, the kingdom of God. And he taught, not the Bible, but taught about the Lord Jesus.' " [84]

Now in, the first place this statement is patently ridiculous since it would have been impossible for the apostles to be teaching from the "Bible" before it was finished and compiled. The apostles laid the foundation of the apostolic doctrine concerning Christ and the church. As with many of the new apostles and prophets, Deere fails to distinguish between the period when the Bible was still being written and the period after its completion.

Yet even having said that, the Scriptures do indicate that the apostles both taught and instructed others to teach the "Word of God" or "the Scriptures". Jack Deere is a former seminary professor and knows better. These words are at best misguided at worst they are intentionally misleading. The agenda seems to be to influence his listeners to be open to new doctrines and new revelations rather than holding steadfastly to the words of Scripture by holding up a skewed version of the ministry of Jesus and the apostles.

Consider for example Paul's admonition to Timothy,

> "I charge you in the presence of God and of Christ Jesus, who is to judge the living and the dead, and by His appearing and His kingdom: preach the word;" (2 Tim. 4:2)

Or look at Paul's admonition to Titus that adherence to the Word was an essential qualification for an elder,

> "He must hold firm to the trustworthy word as taught, so that he may be able to give instruction in sound doctrine and also to rebuke those who contradict it." (Titus 1:9)

Or consider this example from the ministry of Jesus as He instructs His disciples on the necessity of His death on the road to Emmaus,

> "And beginning with Moses and all the Prophets, he interpreted to them in all the Scriptures the things concerning Himself." (Luke 24:27)

Add to this the numerous times that Jesus and the apostles quoted Scripture in their teaching and Deere's point becomes patently ludicrous. The New Testament is absolutely loaded with teaching from the Scriptures.

Compare Deere's attitude with that of the great preacher Jonathan Edwards who wrote,

> "The devil has ever shown a mortal spite and hatred towards that holy book, the Bible: he has done all in his power to extinguish that light and to draw men off from it: He knows it to be that light by which the kingdom of darkness is to be overthrown.... He is enraged against the Bible and hates every word in it: And we may be sure that he never will attempt to raise persons' esteem of it or affection to it."[85]

Prophets and the Sufficiency of Scripture

The Word of God claims to be completely sufficient for life and godliness. 2 Timothy 3:16-17 boldly asserts, "All Scripture is given by inspiration of God and is profitable for doctrine, for reproof, for correction, for instruction in righteousness that the man of God may be perfect, thoroughly equipped for every good work." Now if this statement is true, then the Christian does not need anything that cannot be found and supported within the Word of God in order to live a life that is thoroughly equipped for every good work that God would have him or her to do. Peter expresses the same sentiment when he says that God's "divine power has given to us all things that pertain unto life and godliness, through the knowledge of him who called us to his own glory and excellence, by which he has granted to us his great and precious promises that through these we might be partakers of the divine nature..." (2 Pet. 1:3-4) Once again, we see that all the instructions we need in order to partake of the divine nature have been given to us in the Scriptures. Therefore there is no need to look to anything new. What we have been given is complete and sufficient for our needs. Instead of seeking a new revelation, we should pay closer attention to the revelation we have already been given.

The modern prophetic and apostolic movement consistently undermines this message. Anyone familiar with the movement can attest to the staggering number of new doctrines and practices being invented at a nearly daily rate that are supposedly needed by this end-times church in order to become the Bride of Christ and take her rightful place of dominion. Modern prophets are now teaching about spiritual portals, spiritual inheritances, spirit-ties, curses, vows, judicial intercession, philanthropic apostles, spiritual mapping, the Jezebel spirit and the list goes on and on.

It should be noted that the modern prophets continue to do this despite statements from within their own ranks that indicate that these new apostles and prophets should not use their prophecies to establish doctrine. For instance Rick Joyner says,

> "I must state emphatically that I do not believe that any kind of prophetic revelation is for the purpose of establishing doctrine. We have the Scriptures for that."[86]

In light of the statements we have previously quoted from Joyner, one is tempted to ask, "Which Scriptures? Do we mean the Old Testament Scriptures plus the words of Jesus or the words of Jesus only? Shouldn't we include books like 'The Final Quest' since they were given at a higher level of revelation?" But I digress.

Mike Bickle, in his book, Growing in the Prophetic, also gives a warning about the tendency of modern prophets to invent doctrine,

> "When prophetic people and evangelists become separate from the local church, they are often tempted to establish doctrine..."[87]

All of these statements would be fine if the prophets held to their own standard. But it is just not that simple. In the book The Final Quest, despite Joyner's own claim not to be establishing doctrine, he then emphatically declares a host of doctrines (such as civil war in the church and the demon possession of Christians) either by explicit statement or by implication. And these statements come with equal authority as Scripture because the revelations were received by Joyner, "in heaven where it is impossible for men to lie"[88] or via trance states as has already been documented. In fact, the entire book is a detailed description of eschatology and the end-time church.

Modern apostles and prophets are giving a host of extra-biblical instructions to direct the church. For example "apostle" Chuck Pierce issues monthly prayer initiatives and instructions based on the year and month of the current Hebrew calendar. Consider his discussion of the prophetic significance of the year 2008:

> "The Hebrew number system has always helped me as I focus each year on decreeing the 'best' the Lord has for me and my family and those connected with me. I do not think you have to understand the Hebrew year to know the will of God. However, in Hebrew, numbers have word meanings which have picture meanings, which have sounds. This brings a fuller perspective than just saying we have entered the year 2008. The Hebraic year 5768, which will encompass the Gregorian calendar's Year of the Lord 2008 A.D., is the 'Year of Smekh Chet!' That means we are coming into 'The Year of the Full Circle of Life—A New Beginning is Yours!"[89]

True to form, Pierce issued another prophecy concerning 2009. Entitled, "5769 A Year of Goodness in the Midst of Suffering."[90] Interestingly, just two weeks later in an apparent effort to influence the election, Pierce issued the following warning:

> "Also, the election for President in our nation will produce a major shift in the world. Do not forget to vote. Vote for righteousness to rule this nation! We need to stay focused in prayer. Stay focused, watch and pray! Remember that this year, 5769, 'A Year of Goodness in the Midst of Suffering,' can also mean that 'A Serpent Stands at Your Door to Constrict Your Future!'"[91]

If Pierce's words are to be taken seriously, and it is to be assumed that he believes we should do so, one must believe doctrinally that the numbers of the Hebrew calendar year are somehow prophetic. Pierce is establishing doctrine with these words whether he intends to do so or not. (In actuality this works out to be numerology, which is an occult practice, not a Biblical one.)

Bob Jones and Paul Keith Davis are among the many teachers to issue a yearly "Shepherd's Rod" with supposed insight into God's activities for the coming year and how Christians can get in line with God's purposes based on a doctrinal belief that all of God's sheep must pass under the rod every year for evaluation. (Incidentally, the belief in the Shepherd's Rod will be discussed in detail in the chapter on "Modern Prophets and the

Atonement" as it has serious ramifications for how one understands the sufficiency of the atonement of Christ.)

The church is being led in a host of extra-biblical practices built around extra-biblical doctrines. In spiritual mapping, participants attempt to discern by name the demons afflicting their geographic area so that they can bind them and close doors to them in the spirit world. Consider the account of spiritual mapping expert George in describing the work of a spiritual mapping team in Guatemala City:

> "To accomplish this, team members were divided into three working groups that investigated respective historical, physical and spiritual factors. The process began when God led the historical team to a Mayan archaeological site. As they reviewed the weathered remains it suddenly became clear that their spiritual challenges were part of an ancient continuum of idolatry and witchcraft. At this precise moment, the physical factors team (which had been operating independently) located a vacant house adjacent to the ruins where occult rituals were still being practiced. A third team, comprised of intercessors, received a revelation that the territorial spirit over that place was linked to a human coconspirator whose lifestyle included idolatrous and occult practices."[92]

As one reads this one is tempted to shout, "Stop!! When did Paul ever engage in this type of ministry? Certainly Paul encountered extremely idolatrous and wicked environments in cities like Corinth and Ephesus. Yet he felt no apparent need to engage in spiritual mapping and strategic level spiritual warfare. Why has no one in the history of the church ever seen this before? Why is there no instruction to do any of this in the New Testament?" At times one wonders why we even need Bibles any longer. Surely it must be obvious that the practice of spiritual mapping is based upon a number of doctrines, few if any of which can truly be established by Scripture such as territorial spirits, ancestral demons, the idea that man must achieve breakthrough in order for the gospel to penetrate, that such a breakthrough can be achieved by the application of certain practices and principles and many more.

Over and over again it becomes obvious that the modern apostles and prophets do not believe that the Scriptures give us the parameters for judging divine activity. For example, Mike Bickle in his book, "Growing in the Prophetic" writes the following:

"The Bible does not record all the possible divine or legitimate supernatural activities and/or experiences that have occurred or may yet occur among men and nations. Rather, it records examples of divine activity and legitimate supernatural experiences that fall into broader categories that are typical of how the Holy Spirit works. This concept is taught in John 21:25, in which John states that if all the wonderful works that Jesus did had been recorded, all the books in the world could not contain them."[93]

Once again Bickle shows his complete lack of concern for authentic interpretation. While John does indicate that not all of Jesus' works and words are recorded, the presumption of the passage is that those that are not recorded would be similar in nature to those that are. For example not every healing is recorded but we understand from the Scriptures that Jesus healed. In this sense Bickle is correct in stating that these examples fall into broader categories. However, there is no indication that we can expect *new* categories. We do not assume, for instance, that Jesus flew from place to place. And we cannot argue that Jesus did so based on John 21:25. But it is actually new categories of experience that Bickle is using this statement to endorse such as holy laughter, spiritual drunkenness and the other gross activities occurring in many of the "revivals" of the time. Nothing in this passage or any other passage in Scripture would lead us to expect or endorse the type of manifestations that were occurring in Toronto or Pensacola or the other "revivals" associated with them.

Bickle then makes his conclusion on the next page.

"To reject or call invalid a spiritual experience, the primary onus must be upon the skeptic to show biblically that something would be either contrary to the Scripture or somehow impossible for God to do. It does not first of all rest upon the one who has an experience to prove to others that it is valid."[94]

So the Scriptures do not give the believer the parameters for truly judging the work of the Spirit. Testing the spirits is now left purely to the subjective experience of the individual. Given all the bizarre manifestations that Bickle and others like him have endorsed throughout the course of their ministries, one wonders if a "skeptic", to use Bickle's term, could ever satisfy the burden of proof in Bickle's mind to indicate that something was not of God or impossible for God to do. Bickle has set up an impossible standard that leads to an "anything goes" approach to manifestations. This has truly opened up Pandora's Box to all sorts of paranormal experiences within the Body of Christ.

We will discuss many of these new revelations, new practices and new doctrines in more detail later. At this point, it is enough to demonstrate that these new teachings are in fact establishing new doctrines. For now we are simply seeking to illustrate the point that the logical and practical ramifications of much of the teaching of the modern apostles and the prophets is that the Bible is not a sufficient guide for faith and practice, at least not for this generation of believers. To reference Wendy Alec again, it is "no longer enough" to feed God's people. Instead, there are a whole host of doctrines that the "end-time" church needs to know that cannot be found within the pages of Scripture. And we must have these new apostles and prophets in order to bring them to us.

Prophets and the Closing of the Canon

The Church has long held that the sixty-six books of the Old Testament and New Testament contain all of the authoritative writings that God has given to guide His people. This belief is also being undermined by the words of the modern prophets.

One of the most direct, and brazen, comments to this effect comes from the lips of Kirk Bennett. Bennett was on the leadership team at IHOP for years and was in charge of training the prophets there. He is the founder of Seven Thunders Ministries. Bennett, in speaking to a class of potential prophets says,

> "There are going to be those in the end time generation who will have Daniel-types of revelatory experiences."[95]

Obviously, if these prophets are having "Daniel-types of revelatory experiences", then they would be speaking on an authority equal to the Word of God and therefore the Canon is not closed.

Mike Bickle makes the following comments concerning Wayne Grudem's book, "Prophecy in the New Testament and Today" which was discussed in chapter one. Bickle notes the following,

> "While affirming the value of the "mixed lot", Grudem argues from 1 Corinthians 14:36 that no prophets can ever speak "words of God".

Grudem has been very helpful in making a clear distinction between the authority of Scripture and prophetic utterances.

"However, I do not believe he convincingly eliminates the possibility of a person speaking a prophetic word or words that are 100 percent accurate in every detail and, as such, are God's words."[96]

Bickle continues,

"On occasion God speaks to His servants in an audible voice. Clearly these are His "very words" that may be reported with 100 percent accuracy. Additionally, open visions of the spiritual realm or of future events are familiar modes of communications to those who move in the prophetic realm with a remarkable degree of accuracy."[97]

Notice that Bickle is arguing that modern prophets can and do on occasion speak the very words of God. Since the "very word of God" cannot have less authority today than it ever has had in the past, this statement would mean that certain prophetic declarations given today carry as much authority as the written Word of God. If this is so, then the canon certainly is not closed. These words should be recorded, studied and preserved for future generations of Christians and should stand alongside Romans, Ephesians and the rest of the New Testament. Though Bickle would certainly say that this is not the case, it is the natural conclusion of his belief. Additionally, as we have pointed out numerous times in this book, if the prophet is claiming to be speaking from such a level of inspiration then that prophet is subject to the tests of Deuteronomy 13 and 18 and must be declared a false prophet if these words do not come to pass.

Bickle gives us an example of this kind of proclamation when he states, concerning his revelation that God is changing the understanding of Christianity, "...I heard the words themselves. There was no guess-work, this was not an impression, I heard the internal audible voice of the Lord."[98]

Once again, if true, then this word is absolutely binding and authoritative for all Christians.

This is a far cry from the type of prophecy advocated very modestly by Wayne Grudem, who on the contrary holds fast, to the idea of a closed canon. His words give a sober warning to the church in the midst of the outlandish claims of modern prophets.

> "*If* New Testament prophets today, for example, spoke words that we knew were the very words of God, then these words *would* be equal to Scripture in authority, and we *would be* obligated to write them down and add them to our Bibles whenever we heard them. But if we are convinced that God stopped causing Scripture to be written when the book of Revelation was completed, then we have to say that *this* kind of speech, uttering the very words of God, **cannot happen today**. And any claims to have new Scripture, new words from God, **must be rejected as false**."[99] Emphasis added. Italics in the original.)

Grudem's point is well taken. Once again we ask, how could the "very word of God" have less authority today than in the past? If therefore, these prophets are actually speaking "the very word of God", if they are truly visiting heaven and receiving revelation directly from the mouth of Jesus, then they are writing Scripture. Their words and pronouncements would have equal authority to the Bible.

Modern prophets simply can't have it both ways. Either they are speaking the very words of God and are the greatest apostles and prophets ever, in which case they would be subject to the tests of Deuteronomy 13 and 18 and must be infallible in their prophesying, or they are doing something much different with a completely different level of inspiration. They cannot continue to claim the level of revelation they are claiming while at the same time continuing to prophesy falsely.

Sadly, some of today's modern prophets have gone so far as to claim that their words are in fact of equal or greater authority than Scripture. We have already shown the comments of Rick Joyner, Tommy Tenney and Scott Hicks. Consider the following comments from Choo Thomas in her bestselling book, "Heaven is so Real".

> "Every word in this book is true. The words of Jesus have been transcribed exactly as He said them to me."[100]

And again:

> "Like John, I had been called to write, and my mission was the same as his-to let people know that the marriage supper of the Lamb has already been prepared, and blessed are those who are invited to be there on the last day."[101]

So Thomas's book cannot be evaluated by the Word of God because it is on the same level as the Word of God. If in fact, every word of it is exactly as Jesus gave it to her, then obedience and reverence must be the response of the Christian. After all, we do not make ourselves the judges of Scripture; we are instead to bow before its authority. If Thomas is correct in her claim, we must also do this before her book. Yet how are we to do this when the book clearly contradicts the words of Scripture?

The fact is that in all of these new doctrines and practices put forth by the modern apostles and prophets, well meaning Christians are being led away from Biblical truth and are participating in practices that do not have the blessing of God.

Prophets Ignoring Biblical Norms

Another troubling aspect of the prophetic movement as it relates to the Word of God is the tendency to ignore biblical norms. By a biblical norm I mean the regular way that God chooses to act. Our God is an amazing Being who does amazing things. But care must be exercised to differentiate between what God did once and what God is advocating as a regular part of the Christian life. An example should make this principle very clear.

The Old Testament book of Numbers tells of God getting a rebellious prophet's attention by speaking through the mouth of the prophet's donkey. Bible-believing Christians do not hesitate to affirm that Balaam's donkey talked. But suppose a teacher were to arise who founded "The Church of the Talking Donkeys". And suppose this teacher were to claim that his contribution to the body of Christ was to teach believers how to receive divine revelation through their household animals. Would this practice be Biblical? After all, the teacher has a verse. God did it once, He can certainly do it again. But is this Biblical?

The answer of course is "No". Such a practice would not be Biblical because, while God certainly did this activity once, there is no indication in the Bible that God has any intention whatsoever of repeating this event. Balaam's experience was not intended to be used to establish a norm. The Biblical truth is that God does not want us seeking revelation from our barnyard animals.

Now admittedly, this example is absurd. But consider the number of activities currently being advocated within the Body of Christ that are also based on one-time events that were never meant to establish norms for the Body of Christ.

For instance, anointed items. Acts 19 gives us the account of a dramatic move of God in the city of Ephesus where even cloths touched by the apostle Paul were laid on people and healings occurred. In today's church an entire cottage industry has sprung up producing "anointed" things. One can find anointed rubber bands, anointed wishbones, anointed prayer shawls, anointed prayer mats and even anointed anointing oil.

Visitations to heaven comprise another example of ignoring biblical norms. The Bible relates that Paul was taken to the third heaven. John certainly had some kind of similar experience. But nowhere in the Scripture is it ever suggested that Christians are to seek or expect such experiences. They are not meant to be the norm. But that is not what is taught today by the modern prophets. Heaven has a veritable open border policy and all who desire may enter, not upon death but right now. Indeed, a heavenly visitation seems to be one of the necessary experiences in order to garner a following as one of the modern prophets. In fact, it is being taught that heavenly visitation is one of the birth-rights of being born in this greatest-of-all, end-time generation.

For instance Shawn Bolz writes,

> "God is about to visit a generation with a manifestation of the Throne Room presence. More and more people are experiencing this reality than ever before. This is especially true because we are approaching a generation that truly lives with a manifestation of heaven on earth. The goal is to bring the greatest agreement and communion that has ever been seen in any generation between His desires in Heaven and our walk on earth. Are you ready to see heaven?" [102]

Bolz further states,

> "....it is the Father's goal to have a whole generation of heavenly minded believers who long for Jesus to return to Earth and claim His reward. Therefore, in our generation an access would be given to encounter Heaven experientially by the Spirit of Revelation."[103]

Mike Bickle states that his own experience of getting caught up to heaven can serve as a grid for those who will have this experience themselves.

> "The reason I'm going to describe it to you, I'm not going to describe it for curiosity's sake because I've very rarely told this in how many years since '84, uh, 18 years... so few times. People always ask me "Tell that story" and I go, "Nah," I don't want to get it on tape because I don't want to exalt mystical experiences, but the Lord is challenging me. He says, "The reason you struggle with this so much is because you had no grid for this and I'm gonna do this with so many people. Give them a grid so that they don't have to do that kind of real cool, dignified unbelief thing for five years. They can just enter in and begin to understand and they don't have to stay in kindergarten for the next thirty years in the Spirit." So we need to teach, we need to instruct. It needs to be not normal to where it's trite and over-familiar, but it needs to be not *so* bizarre that nobody can believe it or do it. Why should you waste three years, "I think I did, but I might not have but I could have," and "Oh aren't you sweet aren't you humble?" Oh *shut up!* Did you or *didn't* you!? Let's get *on* with it... That's why I'm going to give you some details, so we can just get rid of this distracting *other thing* and just get it out of its way. *Nothing* is more important than Scripture, *nothing* is more important than the exalting of Jesus and nothing is more important than the bringing in of the harvest. It's all about those kind of things."[104]

Notice Bickle's statement that God has said that He is going to "do this to so many people". Once again we see an isolated incident in Scripture is now being made a norm that many Christians should expect to experience. Perhaps even more alarming is the suggestion that Bickle's personal experience will be that which provides the grid for what other believers should expect. One might have thought that since Scripture did not provide a grid for these experiences that they were not meant to be normative in any age. But instead, despite tipping his hat to the importance of Scripture, Mike Bickle comes to the rescue and informs us that we can judge our mystical experiences by his to see if they are from God. In the immediate context, Bickle's statement that nothing is more important than Scripture seems particularly hollow.

Paul Keith Davis makes a very similar claim concerning heavenly visitations becoming the norm for the end-time church,

> "Many will also be taken into the third Heaven, and like Paul, experience God's realms that are impossible to communicate."[105]

Kirk Bennett goes even further in his audacity as he distorts the meaning of Hebrews 4:16, "let us come boldly before the throne of grace", to teach that **every believer has the right to a heavenly visitation.** He teaches that we are to cry out for it and say, "I am here to spend my admission ticket."[106] Seriously contemplate the brazenness of this teaching. Believers, according to Bennett, have the right to demand a Paul-like visitation to heaven because Hebrews 4:16 is their admission ticket and God must let them in. Bennett doesn't say whether or not this admission ticket is only good for one visit or if it can be reclaimed for multiple rides into the other world.

The apostle Paul was so humble about his own visitation to heaven that he didn't speak of it for fourteen years and even then did not use his own name in relating the story. How different from the idea that we can demand to "spend our admission ticket".

And finally, for the person who has difficulty getting caught up to heaven on their own and for whom the many teachings by the prophets on how to make this happen have proven insufficient, the Elijah List provides the following:

"Elijah List Dec. 26, 2005

"Third Heaven Vision Anointing Oil"
(** 1/2 oz - $10.00 Order **)
(** 1/4 oz - $8.00 Order **)

Third Heaven Vision Anointing oil is made with six ingredients from around the world: calamus, cassia, frankincense, myrrh, Rose of Sharon, and spikenard - in a base of virgin olive oil. Each fragrance was chosen from different nations and was individually prayed over and sanctified for the work of the Lord. May you have "third heaven" visions!"[107]

Tom Panich, the developer of the "Third Heaven Vision Anointing Oil" also has a teaching series to help would be heavenly tourists gain access to the abode of God.

Prophetic Teacher Michael Sullivant offers a corrective warning to this type of attitude (though sadly it seems few are listening) when he cautions that "overreliance on prophecy [or prophetic experience] for personal guidance" is one of the perils of the prophetic ministry. He writes,

> "People who have experienced or witnessed the dramatic guidance of the Holy Spirit in operation sometimes conclude that this is or should be considered the *normative way* for the Spirit to lead us through life's decisions. I have had many experiences with people who have imagined that they are hearing God's voice almost continually."[108]

He later says that people tend to look to the prophetic because they want to bypass the hard work of seeking to discern God's will through prayer, the study of Scripture and seeking godly counsel. These people are looking for a short cut.

Notice that Sullivant warns against seeing the dramatic guidance of the Holy Spirit and dramatic experiences as the norm for the Christian life. Sullivant's words are well-said but why should one do the hard work of studying the Bible when the words of the modern prophets are so accessible? Why spend time studying about heaven when Shawn Bolz, Choo Thomas, and Mary K. Baxter can describe it in detail? Or better yet, one can take Bennett's advice and cash in one's ticket demanding from the Almighty to be given access to see for yourself? The Bible simply ceases to be relevant in favor of the pursuit of experience.

Conclusion

So what can we conclude after this brief survey of the attitudes and words of the modern apostles and prophets concerning the Scripture? One would have to conclude that the Bible alone is an insufficient guide for the end-time church. New doctrines, not found in the Bible, are needed to perfect the Church. Scripture is generally inspiring but basically unreliable. It is insufficient to convince the world of God's truth, especially with regard to heaven and hell. It does not provide the parameters to faith and practice and does not give us the norms for the activity of the Holy Spirit. The Canon of Scripture is not closed and, in fact, many of the words of today's prophets carry a higher level of revelation, anointing and authority than some of the words of Scripture. And lastly, the Bible cannot be understood by any normal means. Grammar, history and context are completely irrelevant. The words of Scripture can be redefined, and ripped out of context to discover the "deeper" meaning for today's church. There is no objective interpretation or understanding of Scripture. The Bible means whatever one wants it to mean.

We should hasten to say, that none of today's prophets would agree with these assessments. They would immediately profess a belief in the authority and integrity of the Bible. Still, these assessments are the logical conclusions that must be reached based on the statements that the prophets make and the teachings they promote.

CHAPTER SIX

The Dumbing Down of the Church
Modern Prophets and the Decline of Doctrine

"We have filled the people with doctrines instead of Deity; we have given them manuals instead of Emmanuel."[109] - Francis Frangipane

On January 9th, 2007 in the city of Lee's Summit, Missouri, Misty Horner, a healthy 30 year old woman died of septic shock. Misty had given birth to a stillborn child a month earlier. Misty and her husband were part of a Christian group that does not believe in going to the doctor. On December 1st, after an entire week of labor, the baby began to emerge backwards. Caleb, Misty's husband, took a pair of household scissors and attempted to perform an episiotomy without anesthesia. The baby was stillborn. Misty finally succumbed to the resulting infection one month later.[110] This story is truly tragic. But unfortunately, many people miss the real lesson. Misty died as a direct result of false doctrine. The group's doctrine of never seeking medical attention cost Misty her life. Doctrine matters.

It may seem obvious, but everyone has doctrine. Doctrine is a statement of belief. A person may have sound doctrine or poor doctrine but everyone has doctrine.

The Scriptures place a high priority on sound doctrine. 1 Timothy 4:16 states, "Take heed unto yourselves and to the doctrine for in so doing you will save both yourselves and them that hear you." Jesus warned his disciples to beware of the teachings (doctrine) of the Pharisees and Sadducees (Matt. 11:16-17). Christians are commanded to test those who would teach them and the doctrine they bring (1 Jn. 4:1). They are commanded to cling to the truth and avoid false doctrine (1 Thess. 5:20-22). Church leaders are instructed to shepherd the flock of God because of false teachers attempting to draw away disciples after themselves (Acts 20:28-30). This emphasis upon doctrine is in perfect keeping with the nature of a God who declares Himself to be Truth (John 14:6).

It is important to understand that the Christian profession has content. That is to say that when we affirm that believing in Jesus saves, we are also understanding that there is a certain amount of content necessary for that profession to be real. In other words, it is the Jesus of the Scriptures, the second person of the Trinity, God incarnate, born of a virgin, tempted in all manner just as we are yet without sin, who suffered under Pontius Pilate, who was crucified and resurrected and who will one day come again to judge the living and the dead, who saves. Cults may refer to a "Jesus", but the content they pour into that name is very different. They teach a different Jesus.

All of this is to emphasize that doctrine matters. In fact, sound doctrine is vital to the spiritual life of the individual and the church.

Noted Christian apologist J.P. Moreland, who has shown some affinity for some members of the prophetic community, makes the following observation about the importance of doctrine:

> "*What* we believe matters—the actual content of what we believe about God, morality, politics, life after death, and so on will shape the contours of our life and actions. In fact, the contents of our beliefs are so important that according to Scripture, our eternal destiny is determined by what we believe about Jesus Christ."[111]

Moreland goes on to conclude:

> "Discipleship unto the Lord Jesus is a thoughtful life. The simple truth is that those who are not thoughtful about the real content of what they actually believe about God will not actually believe very much."[112]

Michael Sullivant, who served under Mike Bickle at Metro Vineyard/Metro Christian Fellowship, warns of the tendency of prophets to lapse into doctrinal eccentricity and the church's need to correct these false doctrines. He writes,

> "In some church circles prophetic people have been allowed to function unchecked, often because leaders have been intimidated by

their sometimes powerful gifting. This lack of accountability has allowed some to develop unbiblical ideas and ways and pass them off as normative and valid. In many cases they have become models of ministry for others to mimic."[113]

After listing a number of examples, Sullivant draws the following conclusion,

"The attitude behind these eccentricities is very far indeed from the spirit of the New Testament apostles and the plain ethical injunctions of their writings. Yet many have come to associate these kinds of things with prophetic ministry. This is why the prophetic has an uphill battle to reclaim credibility in the eyes of many sincere believers who are committed to the truths and values of Scripture."[114]

Sullivant's words ring with truth. His concern over the "doctrinal eccentricities", or more appropriately heresies, within the movement is justified.

But we hear a very different message from the majority of today's apostles and prophets. One of the most serious weaknesses within the movement is the tendency to downplay the importance of doctrine. In fact, doctrine is almost seen as a dirty word. Doctrine is seen as the inhibitor to growth.

Downplay Doctrine

In a passage extolling the virtues of Kenneth Hagin as a great teacher on the subject of supplication, despite some of his doctrinal imperfections, Mike Bickle states the following,

"I gave up on trying to make sure they're perfect before I buy into anything they say. That's a burden. If they have to be as perfect as you are doctrinally before you buy into anything, you're never, ever going to grow.....The profound error is to have all of our "i"s dotted and out "t"s crossed but to have no anointing to do anything.....I'm not afraid of the groups that are a little bit off because they're moving somewhere forward because I believe I have enough understanding and discernment and I've got enough people connected to me around the body of Christ and I'm connected to the word of God that I can handle some of the excesses and abuses of some of these camps."[115]

There are a number of problems with the previous statement. First, it may be true that a person's theology does not have to be perfect before we can learn from them, but certainly they should be correct on the central tenants of the Christian faith. Surely they must at least stand within the pale of orthodoxy before we place ourselves under their teaching. The New Testament repeatedly warns against false teachers and false doctrine and Christians are commanded to avoid them both. There have to be boundaries between orthodoxy and heresy.

Additionally, though Bickle is correct that the goal is not merely to have intellectual knowledge, he has set up a false dichotomy. We do not have to choose between sound doctrine and passion. It is possible to have both. It is possible to "move somewhere forward" while still maintaining the truths of Christ. Knowledge apart from practice has little value. But practice apart from knowledge is misguided and can end in disaster. We are not to be content with one or the other nor are we to play one against the other.

In counterpoint to Bickle's statement the words of Sam Storms, another former staff member under Bickle, are particularly poignant. He writes,

> "But good theology should never diminish zeal. God never meant it to. When truth is searched for, discovered, and defined it has the power to inflame the heart and empower the soul and energize the will to do what otherwise may seem burdensome and boring. **Theological truth is not the problem. Arrogance is.** Contrary to what some Charismatics have suggested, **the flesh is the enemy, not the "mind"**.[116] (emphasis added)

Zeal is an admirable quality. But zeal alone is also insufficient. Knowledge without zeal is dead but zeal without knowledge is dangerous. Those within the prophetic movement are in danger of producing followers not unlike the Jews of Paul's day about whom Paul wrote, "I bear them witness that they have a zeal for God but not according to knowledge." (Romans 10:2) Just as it is possible to find a number of churches that are dead in their orthodoxy, one can travel the country from one end to the other and find people doing incredibly foolish and harmful things based on zeal alone apart from the knowledge of the truth.

Bickle also seems unaware of Paul's admonition in Romans 16:17 to "mark those who cause divisions among you teaching contrary to the doctrine you have received and avoid them". It is imperative to note that the divisions of which Paul is speaking are doctrinal in nature for those who cause the division are "teaching contrary to the doctrine you have received". Notice also that Paul does not instruct his readers to pick through the teachings of false teachers in order to find the good. And frankly, in the light of Bickle's endorsement of spiritual drunkenness, spiritual mapping, contemplative prayer, and a host of other fads that have swept the church in the last two decades, it seems fair to begin to question how much discernment Bickle really does have despite his bravado on the subject.

Bickle elsewhere states that sound doctrine should not be a criterion for evaluating the validity of modern prophets. He writes,

> "My friend Richard is a dedicated and godly Nazarene pastor with an earned seminary degree. We pretty much are in agreement now, but at first he was absolutely shocked and offended at the idea that prophetic persons may be incorrect in some of their doctrines.

> "Richard used an easy but inaccurate equation to judge the spiritual gifts. He thought that a man with a history of accurate prophesies also must be uniquely godly and biblically sound on most areas of doctrine. I disagreed with him.

> "He had no experience with prophetic people, yet he had his theories clearly worked out. I had much experience with prophetic people and was receiving an ongoing education with regard to most of my old theories. Yes, prophetic people must be clear about major doctrines like the person and work of Christ and the place of the Scriptures. But on lesser points of doctrine, they might be misinformed."[117]

A couple of points are of interest. First we notice that for Mike Bickle personal experience trumps any other kind of learning. He is critical of his friend "Richard" because he had his theories worked out without personal experience (we can assume this came primarily from his study of Scripture and theological training since Bickle notes Richard's seminary degree). But there is no indication that Bickle might be wrong about his assumptions developed primarily from his encounters with people claiming to be prophetic. It never occurs to Bickle that he could be getting too close to some of these "prophetic people" to be truly objective. Nor does he indicate any Biblical reason for rejecting his friend's theories. In fact, he never appeals to Scripture at all. On the contrary, his personal experience with "prophetic people" has provided the real enlightenment on this issue.

But it is his statement that prophets must be correct on major doctrines and the Scriptures that is particularly telling. This is especially true if we consider it in the light of another statement that he makes later in the very same book. In discussing the heretical healer of the 1940's William Branham, Bickle states the following.

> "Branham ended up in some doctrinal heresy, although never to the extent of denying Jesus Christ as Lord and Savior or doubting the authority of the Scriptures. While affirming the deity of Christ, he denied the trinity. He allowed himself to be spoken of as the "angel" to the seventh church referred to in Revelation 3. This caused great confusion among his followers. They reasoned that if God could give him genuine prophetic information about people's lives, then why didn't God in the same way give him sound doctrine? But the gift of prophesy doesn't at all ensure that you will have the gift of teaching or vice versa."[118]

So apparently, according to Bickle, the doctrine of the Trinity is not a major doctrine and must not be included in the doctrines of the "person and work of Christ". A more thorough examination of the teachings of William Branham can be found later in this book. Suffice it for now to say that his theology was not at all sound. Regarding his view of Scriptures, he taught that God had given His Word in three forms, the Bible, the zodiac and the pyramids. But none of this is enough to disqualify him as a prophet in Bickle's eyes nor those of many others within the apostolic/prophetic community. In fact, fallen IHOP prophet and former Branham associate, Paul Cain, himself no stranger to false doctrine, calls Branham the greatest prophet who ever lived. It is also important to point out that there is a total lack of Biblical support for Bickle's assertion that a true prophet can have false theology and doctrine, despite Bickle's experiences to the contrary.

In direct contradiction to Bickle's apparent assessment that the doctrine of the Trinity is a secondary doctrine, consider the words of Bruce Ware. He writes,

> "The doctrine of the Trinity is both central and necessary for the Christian faith to be what it is. Remove the Trinity, and the whole Christian faith disintegrates."[119]

He continues by illustrating his point from the doctrine of salvation.

"In order for us sinners to be saved, one must see God at one and the same time as the one judging our sin (the Father), the one making the payment of infinite value for our sin (the divine Son), and the one empowering and directing the incarnate—human—Son so that he lives and obeys the Father, going to the cross as the substitute for us (the Holy Spirit)."[120]

The doctrine of the Trinity was considered a doctrine essential for salvation according to the author of the Athanasian Creed which states:

1. Whosoever will be saved, before all things it is necessary that he hold the Catholic [universal] Faith.

2. Which Faith except everyone do keep whole and undefiled, without doubt he shall perish everlastingly.

3. And the Catholic [universal] Faith is this:

That we worship one God in Trinity, and Trinity in Unity,

It might be good to note at this point, that when confronted with Branham's heresies, modern prophets will nearly uniformly condemn his doctrine just as Bickle did in the previous quotes. They will instead say that it is his power to which they are pointing. But, power is not the test. Jesus said "For false christs and false apostles will arise and show great signs and wonders in so much that they could deserve the very elect if that were possible." (Matt. 24:24) Or again consider this statement from the mouth of the Lord, "Many will say to me in that day, Lord, Lord in your name we cast out demons and performed miracles and did many mighty work and I will tell them, 'I never knew you. Depart from me you who work iniquity.'" (Matt. 7:22-23) It is for this reason we are commanded to test the spirits whether they are of God. (1 Jn. 4:1) It is important to state again that the test that John gives is a doctrinal test. "Every spirit that does not confess that Jesus Christ has come in the flesh is not of God." (1 Jn. 4:3)

Bickle continues with his efforts at de-emphasizing the importance of sound doctrine with the following statement.

"True Christianity is a dynamic relationship with a living God, and it cannot be reduced to formulas and dry orthodoxy. We are called to

113

embrace the mystery of God and not to lust after neatly tying up every doctrinal or philosophical loose end that we encounter."[121]

Once again, Bickle establishes a false dichotomy. Certainly we want more than a dry orthodoxy but we should still desire orthodoxy. The idea that a passionate heresy is somehow better is patently ridiculous. The implication that the pursuit of doctrinal soundness and the pursuit of spiritual passion are somehow incompatible is completely false. And while we may never be able to know all things or be able to tie up "every doctrinal or philosophical loose end", we can know some things certainly for God has revealed them. Furthermore, as we are attempting to show in this book, our argument with the modern apostles and prophets is not over areas that are ambiguous but over foundational doctrinal truths. Bickle's statement is just a smokescreen and nothing more.

Francis Frangipane takes a similar attitude toward doctrine. In his book, "The House of the Lord", he writes,

> "We have instructed the church in nearly everything but becoming disciples of Jesus Christ. We have filled the people with doctrines instead of Deity; we have given them manuals instead of Emmanuel."[122]

Frangipane seems oblivious to the fact that teaching people to become disciples of Jesus Christ would necessitate doctrinal instruction if for no other reason than because to teach them who Jesus is necessitates a doctrinal discussion. Additionally, how else is the church to follow the words of Christ given in the great commission and "teach them to observe all things whatsoever I have commanded you" without instruction in doctrine?

Once again, it is true that doctrine is not enough. Doctrinal instruction is not the stopping point but it is foundational. It is simply neither possible nor profitable to attempt to bypass doctrinal instruction. Discipleship may certainly involve more than merely doctrinal instruction but it cannot involve less. The prophetic/apostolic movement is attempting to develop an intimacy that is not based on truth.

Christians of nearly all stripes acknowledge that some doctrines are more critical than others. But we must understand that there are lines of no compromise. Doctrine is essential because we worship a God who declares that He is truth and who commands us to worship Him not only in Spirit but also in truth.

Later, Frangipane continues his undiscerning ways by saying this, "Let us not look for the apostasy anywhere else but in the areas of our own hearts."[123] This statement, while sounding very humble and holy, is actually completely contrary to the multiple warnings found in Scripture that we are to test the spirits whether they are of God because many false prophets have gone out into the world (1 Jn. 4:1).

Doctrine Divides

One of the mantras repeated frequently and in a variety of ways among the new prophets and apostles is that doctrine divides. Doctrine is seen as a negative force. Consider for instance the words of Rick Joyner when he writes,

> "We must first understand that our unity is not based on doctrines. Such unity is superficial at best. Our unity can only be found in Jesus. To focus our attention on Him and learn to love and cover one another is far more important than agreeing on all doctrines. Having like doctrines is not a basis for unity…it is a basis for division!"[124]

Joyner's quote sounds spiritual until one begins to examine it. He states that our unity can only be found in Jesus. Alright, which Jesus? The Jesus of Mormonism? The Jesus of Jehovah's Witnesses? The Jesus of the New Age? Once one begins to answer the question, "Which Jesus?", one is dealing in doctrine. And as we focus our attention on Him, aren't we learning of Him and from Him? This too would involve doctrine.

In one sense, it is true that doctrine divides. It must divide. Doctrinal statements are made in order to distinguish truth from error. Truth by definition is exclusive. If, for instance, our God is triune in nature then by definition all forms of Modalism (Oneness doctrines) and Arianism (like Jehovah's Witnesses) must be wrong.

However, it must be pointed out that according to Paul in Romans 16:17 it is those who are teaching contrary to the doctrine you have received who are responsible for the division, not those who point out their heresy. This is a critical distinction. Merely demonstrating that an individual has moved from a position of orthodoxy into heresy is not the cause of the division.

But are the divisions within various branches of orthodox Christianity as great as they are sometimes portrayed? The answer would appear to be "no". Christians of most denominations have believed for generations that we could fellowship together and cooperate together in a variety of activities, such as the pro-life movement, while not having to agree on every point of doctrine, so long as we held to the core doctrines essential to Christianity. This cooperation within the church does not seek to minimize the distinctives of the denominations or to view them as evil but rather subrogates these distinctives underneath the great truths, which all branches of true Christianity hold in common. These great truths may be found articulated in the historic Creeds of the church.

Other areas of doctrine are not deemed unimportant in the fact that one may still choose, for instance, to attend a church that practices baptism in the manner one finds most consistent with the Scripture or that holds to a form of church government in line with one's convictions. But within this there is recognition that other traditions also contain members of the Body of Christ with whom we can cooperate.

The failure of ecumenicism in all of its forms, including that advocated by the modern apostles and prophets, is that it seeks unity at the expense of truth by minimizing doctrine. Unity is achieved by downplaying all doctrine. In this way the church is left without doctrinal parameters. True unity can come through a recognition of which doctrines are essential and which are non-essential. The church unites around the essentials. In this way, the true church is still distinguishable from that which is aberrant.

Unfortunately, much of the apostolic and prophetic movement has slipped into a pure ecumenicism. As has been shown in the case of William Branham and as can be seen in the acceptance of Oneness teachers today within the prophetic movement, even the doctrine of the Trinity can be compromised without creating a stir. The only essentials seem to be a belief in the continuation of spiritual gifts and the offices of apostle and prophet. On these doctrines they allow no compromise.

Unity at all costs.

In the Latter Rain/Kingdom Now theology dominant within the apostolic and prophetic movement, the church must begin to move in unity under the direction of the modern apostles and prophets in order to achieve dominion over the earth. Therefore, there is a tendency to emphasize unity at the expense of truth. It is a peace-at-any-price approach to the Christian life.

As an example consider the words of Francis Frangipane, one of the few teachers who continues to proudly associate himself with Latter Rain doctrines. (Most of the modern apostles and prophets, while still holding to fundamental Latter Rain doctrines, do so under the guise of some other title due to the baggage associated with the Latter Rain movement of the mid twentieth century.)

> "The result of this new spiritual fullness will be a new level of unity. Fault-finding and gossip will disappear. In their place will be intercession and love. Wholeness will return to the Church. This also means that the ambition and division we see today between congregations will be identified as sins, which will be repented of before Jesus returns.
>
> The truth of this message must be made clear, for most Christians consider oneness within the body inconceivable before Jesus returns. They have not discerned nor warred against the enemy's lies, which have conditioned believers to accept strife and sectarianism in the Church. It is my passionate conviction that the Church which will ultimately be raptured will be free of strife and carnal divisions -- it will be a bride "without spot or wrinkle" made ready for her bridegroom.
>
> This scattering, dividing process among the Lord's sheep has gone on long enough. Jesus has set His heart to bring healing and unity to His body. In this regard, through the prophet Jeremiah, the Lord spoke a somber warning. He said, *"Woe to the shepherds who are destroying and scattering the sheep of My pasture!"* (Jeremiah 23:1). The Son of God is not pleased with the carnal divisions in His body! Indeed, the Lord promises to chasten those pastors who continue to build their kingdoms without laboring together to build His. To them He says, *"I am about to attend to you for the evil of your deeds"* (vs 2)."[125]

It is fascinating that Frangipane quotes a Scripture that, in context, actually is warning the leaders of Israel who caused the nation to be scattered in judgment because of idol worship and apostasy, in other words, false doctrine and false worship. It isn't that the people of Israel were scattered and fragmented from each other in some type of denominationalism but rather that they have been scattered as sheep from their true Shepherd through false prophecy. This passage is not dealing with distinctions within the Church over secondary doctrinal issues. It is also interesting because Jeremiah 23 also contains one of the gravest warnings on false prophets found in all of the Scriptures. Perhaps Frangipane should have read a little further and a little more carefully.

Mike Bickle in "Growing in the Prophetic" follows a similar approach as he indicates we shouldn't use doctrine as a boundary or guideline in determining true vs. false teachers. He writes,

> "Throughout church history there have been a lot of anointed people who have wound up with strange doctrines. Their constituency bought into the false assumption that a person whom God uses in a genuine prophetic or healing ministry *must* be 100 percent doctrinally correct. The most notable example in recent history is William Branham."[126]

Once again, a discussion of William Branham's doctrinal positions can be found in Appendix A, "Patron Saints of the Prophetic". Suffice it for now to say that Branham was a heretic in the truest sense of the word. However, no one is demanding that a teacher be 100% accurate in all of their doctrines. This is a straw man argument. But there are main and plain doctrines that provide lines of demarcation between Christianity and every other religion in the world. These lines cannot be allowed to become blurred.

In the same book, Bickle devotes an entire chapter to the tired cliché rampant within the prophetic community that "God offends the mind to reveal the heart". This false dichotomy, which has no basis whatsoever in the Word of God, is trotted out every time concerned Christians point to bizarre manifestations and question how they could possibly be caused by a God who claims to do all things decently and in order. The net result of this statement is to impress people that they are thinking too much so, "shut up and drink the kool-aid". This mantra has been repeated to the point that unfortunately few in the prophetic community seem to question its validity. But it is a blatant rejection of the command of God that we love Him with all of our heart, soul and mind. (Matt. 22:37). The call to follow Christ is not a call to shelve one's intellect.

As Christians we should seek unity. This can be done by recognizing which doctrines are essential and which are secondary. However it should never be done at the expense of doctrinal integrity over central issues of faith and practice. There are places where division is necessary in order to preserve the fundamental truths of the church.

No More Theologians

In another classic example of downplaying the importance of sound doctrine, founder and former leader of the International Coalition of Apostles, C. Peter Wagner wants to do away with the term and position within the body of Christ of "theologian". In an editorial in "Ministry Today", he writes,

> "Let's do away with the term "theologian." Why? The idea that certain members of the body of Christ are theologians while the rest are non-theologians is traditional thinking embedded in the old wineskins of the church.
>
> First, those called to lead the church and to equip the saints for the work of ministry are called apostles, prophets, evangelists, pastors and teachers (see Eph. 4:11). Theologians are not on the list. In fact, the word "theologian" isn't even in the concordance.[127]

One will immediately recognize the influence of the "five-fold ministry" concept to which we referred earlier in Wagner's remarks. At this point we will withhold evaluation of his "old wineskins of the church" comment, which relates to the supposed great change occurring in the Body of Christ in order to focus on his central premise.

It is particularly interesting that the man who gave to the church such novel titles as "philanthropic apostle" and "marketplace apostle", who has spread the myth of spiritual mapping and who supported every bizarre manifestation to infect the Body of Christ in recent memory, is suddenly concerned that a particular word is not in the concordance. One might be tempted to remind Dr. Wagner that the word "Trinity" is not in the concordance nor are the words, "Bible", "verbal-plenary inspiration" or "vicarious atonement".

But what is even more interesting is that one whose theology is so poor should call for the end of theologians. He continues, speaking of his time spent as a professor at Fuller Seminary.

> "If nothing else, we were forced to recognize the difference between theologians and non-theologians. The theologians saw themselves as the elite guardians of the truth. Their assignment was to make sure that the doctrines espoused by the seminary remained pure and uncontaminated. In their minds, we missionaries did not have the skills which the theologians had developed, and consequently we were regarded as mere practitioners, not serious thinkers."[128]

Judging by Wagner's own theology one might conclude that the theologians at Fuller Seminary were right about Wagner's theological abilities. For instance, his book, "Dominion" advocates both Kingdom Now or Dominion Theology and Open Theism.[129] However, this paragraph is particularly interesting because we might find some insight into Wagner's true motivation. He was snubbed by the theologians. His remarks concerning their assignment to keep the doctrines of the seminary pure and uncontaminated (as though that's a bad thing) seem to be dripping with sarcasm. Later he states that these same theologians brought him up on heresy charges. (Obviously they weren't impressed with how important he was as the head of the International Coalition of Apostles. He was ultimately cleared, not because his theology was deemed acceptable, but because he had tenure and the seminary feared violating his academic freedom.[130]) It would seem that at least part of Wagner's issue is personal.

But would not Wagner himself have felt that he had particular abilities in his own field of study? Does not a doctor rightly conclude that he has more knowledge in the field of medicine than someone who may also work in the field but who did not pursue the same level of degree like perhaps a lab technician or nurse? Wouldn't an attorney who specialized in wills believe that he has more knowledge in that particular subject than an attorney specializing in a different area? Is it so remarkable and inappropriate that professors who have given serious study to the subject of theology might feel that they have a level of expertise not found among professors whose expertise was in other disciplines?

Wagner now comes to his idea of how theological disputes should be resolved.

> "Such is not true, however, among the churches moving in the stream of the New Apostolic Reformation. We do not have an ecclesiastical office of theologian nor do we have recognized functional equivalents. We do not agree that an elite group of individuals who happen to have advanced academic degrees in theology should be recognized as our doctrinal police force. Take the typical vertical apostolic network for an example. In an apostolic network the person in charge of maintaining the DNA of the network is the lead apostle, who consults with those he or she chooses, and no one else."[131]

Well there you have it. We don't need these godly men who have given their lives to meticulously studying God's Word in order to bring clarity to the Body of Christ. We do not need a "doctrinal police force". No we just need to go to the "lead apostle" of whatever vertical apostolic network (good luck finding that concept in your concordance) we are associated with and allow him to sort it all out as he consults with "those he or she chooses and no one else". This John Wayne approach to theology will insure an even greater fragmentation within the church than what we are seeing today as each lead apostle does what is right in his own eyes. It will also lead to a further deterioration of doctrine within the Church of Christ because, as has already been shown, many of these lead apostles have no stomach for doctrine altogether or even for serious systematic study of the Scriptures. Wagner's disdain for theologians and those who have a concern for doctrinal purity and integrity shows through bright and clear.

But this was not the attitude of the apostle Paul. This same apostle who prayed that the church might walk in unity, recognized the importance of sound doctrine and the necessity of divisions on the basis of truth. He wrote to the Corinthian church, "In the first place, I hear that when you come together as a church, there are divisions among you, and to some extent I believe it. No doubt there have to be differences among you to show which of you have God's approval." (1 Cor. 11:18-19) It is this same apostle who commanded the church at Rome to mark those who teach a contrary doctrine and avoid them. (Rom. 16:17)

The real issue is not whether or not the church will continue to refer to some men as theologians but whether or not the church will prize truth and doctrine as valuable and necessary.

The Absence of Essential Doctrines from prophetic teaching

Though this book will attempt to deal with the teachings of the prophets in many specific doctrinal issues, it should be noted that this is not an easy task. The fact is that it is difficult to find statements from the various prophets on many key doctrinal issues. They simply do not come up. This is, in and of itself, a very disturbing trend within the prophetic community.

Conspicuous by their absence in the vast majority of teachings by the notable prophetic figures is any in-depth discussion of the Trinity, Fall of Man, Sovereignty of God, the Gospel or any other substantive issue that one might find in any systematic theology. I do not mean by this to suggest that most of the prophetic teachers do not believe in these things (although many are extremely weak in their understanding of essential Christian doctrines and especially of the sovereignty of God leaning almost or even completely as in the case of Wagner to an Open Theist position), but rather to say that these issues simply are rarely discussed and addressed by the prophetic teachers.

Instead we find such teachings as the breaker anointing, judicial intercession, cleansing your land, spiritual mapping, prophetic art, the Josiah generation, the Zadok priesthood, restoring David's tabernacle, open heavens and the list goes on and on.

For all the talk about raising up a generation of apostles and of apostolic power and apostolic lifestyle, very little attention is given to apostolic doctrine. The central doctrines of the Christian faith do not occupy center stage in the teaching ministries of today's apostles and prophets.

Wagner, in discussing the courses given at the Wagner Leadership Institute, states the following:

> "One of the realities of this new tailored approach that quickly came to our attention was that if we offered traditional courses in systematic theology, epistemology or the history of dogma, practically no one would sign up for them."[132]

It should be noted that Wagner does not view this occurrence as a cause for alarm but rather celebrates it. This approach of offering and requiring only those classes students wish to take is ridiculous. Imagine the educational output of a high school that only offered classes that were popular with the students. In writing of these new apostolic churches Wagner states,

> "These leaders do not seem to carry the excessive amount of doctrinal baggage many of their predecessors carried."[133]

Translation: They are more poorly educated and therefore more malleable for false teachers like Wagner. These leaders then in turn, poorly educate their followers and pass on a host of unbiblical ideas.

How different from the early church in Acts 2 who continued daily in the "apostle's doctrine." How sad to see doctrine spoken of as "baggage" as though it were something that needed to be discarded.

It is not surprising to hear that students would not want to enroll in classes like Systematic Theology. These classes are difficult and require rigorous thought and study. What is surprising is that an institution devoted to training Christian leaders would not require such an education. While leaders within the apostolic movement consistently downplay the importance of heavy doctrinal subjects like Systematic Theology, this type of training is actually essential. Douglas Wilson explains why when he writes,

> "Unless I read the whole Bible cover to cover every time I preach, or every time I share the gospel, or every time I answer a question, my speech necessarily has to be a summary of the contents of the Bible. It must be a systematic abstraction....Now I may either summarize poorly or well. But I cannot talk about the Word without summarizing. *That* is inescapable."[134] (Italics in the original)

To be uneducated in the great themes of the Bible (which is fundamentally what Systematic Theology does), means that one's teaching will at best be superficial, at worst, heretical.

There is clear Scriptural support for teaching systematic theology. Jesus Himself engaged in this type of instruction. In His encounter with His disciples on the road to Emmaus, after rebuking them for being slow to believe all that the prophets had spoken, the Bible states, "And beginning with Moses and all the Prophets, he interpreted to them in all the Scriptures the things concerning himself." (Luke 24:27) This is nothing less than systematic theology. Jesus walked His disciples through the entire Old Testament teaching them what the Scriptures revealed about the Messiah and the necessity of His suffering. Additionally, the entire book of Romans is a systematic treatise on the glory, of God, the fall of man, and the nature of redemption. It is one of the greatest theological expressions ever penned and once again demonstrates what a far cry the attitude of today's so-called apostles is from the apostles of Christ.

Further, instruction like Systematic Theology is important because of what has been referred to as the organic nature of doctrine. That is to say that doctrines are related. Changes in one doctrine necessarily produce changes down the line in other doctrines. In fact, one of the central premises of this book is that some of the seemingly secondary doctrines being taught by the prophets and apostles actually undermine the Christian faith in essential areas. This will be demonstrated clearly in the succeeding chapters.

Rick Joyner goes even further in his writings, seemingly even saying that knowledge in and of itself is bad. In a horribly befuddling book replete with mystical interpretations of Scripture entitled, "There Were Two Trees in the Garden", Joyner writes the following.

> "The Tree of Knowledge and the Tree of Life are symbolic of two spiritual lineages, or 'family trees.' The Bible, from Genesis to Revelation is a history of two lineages. Understanding the lineages can help us to understand the most common errors besetting the human race, including the church.
>
> "Satan did not tempt Eve with the fruit of the Tree of Knowledge just because the Lord had made it taboo. He tempted her with it because the source of his power was rooted in that tree. Furthermore, the Lord did not make it taboo just to test His children; He prohibited the eating of its fruit because He knew it was poison."[135]

Joyner concludes by saying, "It was not just man's disobedience that brought death to earth; it was also the fruit from this tree."[136]

There are so many things wrong with the previous quotes that it is hard to know where to begin to address them. It should be remembered that God planted the garden. The Tree of Knowledge was God's tree not Satan's. God never planted a poisoned tree nor did He plant a tree that was the source of Satan's power. Never does the Bible state that the source of Satan's power is the Tree of Knowledge. And contrary to Joyner's revelatory information, the Bible clearly declares that it was disobedience that caused the fall and death. Paul writes, "Therefore just as sin came into the world through one man, and death through sin, and so death spread to all men because all sinned….For as by the one man's disobedience the many were made sinners, so by the one man's obedience the many will be made righteous." (Romans 5:12, 19)

The result of the entire book by Joyner from which the previous quotes were drawn seems to be to cause Christians to fear and eschew doctrine and even knowledge. Doctrine is repeatedly attacked within the pages of this book.

This lack of emphasis on foundational truth produces a Christianity that is void of any substantive doctrinal content. It produces a people who are hardly in a position to discern truth from error, are easy prey for false teachers and are easily carried about by every wind of doctrine that blows through the church. It produces a wishy-washy, touchy feely, gullible people who will chase every fad that claims to be from God. Recent history in the church proves that this is so. But then, it is completely understandable that teachers whose own theology is so poor and whose teachings are so false would want a generation of people incapable of telling the difference.

It is truly interesting that while leaders in the apostolic and prophetic movement claim that this move away from propositional truth is an act of the Holy Spirit, they are in fact merely mimicking the spirit of the times. This disregard for propositional truth within the prophetic is really no different than the postmodernism of our day that views all truth as personal and subjective. Nor is it really any different than the actions of extreme segments of the Emergent Church movement. All of these are merely different manifestations of the same disease. They are the result of following the spirit of the age not the Spirit of Christ.

Support of False Teachers

Another evidence for the movement's disdain for doctrine and a disturbing trend among many within the prophetic movement is their persistent support of and references to other false teachers both in the past and in the church presently. As was noted earlier, the only issue where there seems to be no room for compromise is a belief in the continuation of miraculous gifts and the offices of apostle and prophet. Beyond that, anything goes. One can deny the Trinity, the sufficiency of the atonement, the authority of

Scripture or introduce a number of extreme doctrines into the church and still be revered. This is especially true if there are stories of power associated with one's name.

We have already demonstrated the admiration that Mike Bickle and Paul Cain have for William Branham. But they are not alone. A recent visit to the Elijah List revealed no less than 35 prophecies referencing Branham as a spiritual icon and example to follow. The words of Paul Keith Davis of White Dove Ministries are indicative of the type of praise Branham regularly receives.

> "During the 1930's an extraordinarily gifted prophet began to emerge as a spiritual leader of a new ministry model.....God wonderfully graced this humble man with a revelatory gift and supernatural power not seen since the early Church......In this experience God gave William Branham a forerunner message for his life and ministry. **I believe he was a token or prototype of an entire body of people who will emerge as Jesus' bridal company.**"[137] (emphasis in the original)

Another key character from the past that is getting a great amount of attention from today's prophets is John G. Lake. Lake was a healer whose ministry in America was based primarily in the Northwest. Lake was steeped in early dominion theology. He believed that communication with the dead was acceptable. He was also arrested for fraud. A more detailed and documented treatment of John Lake can be found in the Appendix. Lake is another questionable teacher who receives high praise in prophetic circles.

Mike Bickle states that John G. Lake has influenced him "more than any man other than Jesus".[138] Later in the same message he states that for an entire month he didn't read anything but John G. Lake and Madame Guyon (a Roman Catholic mystic).

Cal Pierce, a member of the International Coalition of Apostles and who has operated "healing rooms" in the tradition of John G. Lake for the last 10 years, states the following in his biographical information, "Inspired by John G. Lake's healing ministry, Cal Pierce visited Lake's gravesite once each month for over one year to pray."[139]

Paul Keith Davis lists Lake among those who operated in a higher level of authority. He writes, "When I first began to study the lives of several 20th-century leaders, I discovered there were a few that seemingly were set apart and functioned in this higher realm of power and authority. These included Maria Woodworth-Etter, John G. Lake, William Branham and others." Branham has already been discussed. For those unfamiliar with her, Etter is sometimes known as the trance evangelist because she would fall into trance states in the middle of her preaching.

Kenneth Hagin, the father of the Word Faith Movement, also receives due benevolence from prophetic leaders. Mike Bickle, while disagreeing with Hagin's crasser prosperity doctrines, refers to Hagin as the greatest teacher on petition in prayer of this generation.[140]

Perhaps one of the most troubling examples of this proclivity for teachers whose theology is errant is the affection that many of the modern prophets have for Roman Catholic mystics. A visit to the IHOP bookstore will reveal an entire section of the works of Madame Guyon, Julian of Norwich, Henri Nouwen, Thomas Keating, the desert fathers and many, many more. A professor friend who accompanied me remarked, "It's as though the Reformation never happened." These mystics are read primarily for their teachings on contemplative life and prayer.

The point is this: These prophetic leaders give evidence of their lack of regard for biblical truth and sound doctrine by their blatant endorsement of false teachers. They not only endorse these teachers but they are training their disciples in their ways.

The reality: Everyone has doctrine

As stated earlier, it is impossible to avoid doctrine. The statement, "Jesus is Lord" is a doctrinal confession. The belief that apostles and prophets still exist today, a non-negotiable axiom to those in the apostolic/prophetic movement, is a doctrine.

And it is not a choice between doctrine and intimacy. Doctrine is a statement of truth. To know someone intimately demands that one know them truly. Truth and intimacy are inseparable. Someone who claimed to be intimate with the Keith Gibson who is writing this, while at the same time stating that he likes country music, is single, has blonde hair and works as a circus clown would be giving evidence that they don't know Keith Gibson well at all. None of those things are true. In the same way, many today have great emotional attachment to Jesus, but when they consistently make statements about Him that are patently untrue, one must begin to question the level of their intimacy.

God grant us that we may love Him and know Him as He is in truth.

CHAPTER SEVEN

Poor God and Other Heresies
Modern Apostles and the Nature of God

"The Church has surrendered her once lofty concept of God and has substituted for it one so low, so ignoble, as to be utterly unworthy of thinking, worshipping men. This she has done not deliberately, but little by little and without her knowledge; and her very unawareness only makes her situation more tragic."[41]

"What comes into our minds when we think about God is the most important thing about us."[42] A. W. Tozer

There is no more important objective in teaching than to impart to the hearers a true knowledge of God. It is imperative that a minister attempt, despite his human frailty, to present God to the congregation in all of His biblical majesty taking into account the full counsel of God. This is not an area for theological sloppiness. There is no greater subject.

Because the doctrine of God is so central to the Christian faith, one might assume that at least in this area we would find agreement with those in the apostolic and prophetic movement. At least here, we would find these leaders standing solidly within the pale of biblical orthodoxy. At least on this topic we should find no compromise. Such assumptions would unfortunately be sadly mistaken.

Instead we find that the modern prophetic movement is undermining the church's understanding of the nature of God. This is most obvious when we consider the statements of the prophets that seem to misunderstand God's Triune nature, either by teaching outright modalism or what would amount to tri-theism. While many within the prophetic community have been leaning toward Open Theism for years, at least one leader has now

129

openly declared it to be the most biblical paradigm for understanding the nature of God. Still others, regularly speak of a God who is far less exalted and far less sovereign than the God of Scripture. This is what I will refer to as "weak God" or "poor God" theology. The God of the new prophets appears to need man's help frequently to accomplish His purposes.

This digression from the biblical picture of God appears in many cases not to have come purposefully or intentionally. Rather it appears to be the result of poor hermeneutical principles and exegetical skills, lack of exposure to solid systematic theological teaching, and the attention given to historical figures, like William Branham, reported to have accomplished great miracles but whose teachings were gravely flawed.

Modalism and Tritheism

While these two heresies are significantly different, they both stem from a fundamental lack of understanding and application of the doctrine of the Trinity. By understanding, it is not meant that any finite human can truly understand *how* the doctrine can be so but rather *that* the Bible states it to be so. It is also possible to give a proper definition of the doctrine itself based on the revelation of God's Word. In other words, one may not be able to comprehend how it is possible for God to be triune in nature but one may understand that the Bible teaches that there is one and only one God who eternally exists in three Persons, Father, Son and Holy Spirit. One can apprehend that Scriptures teach that the members of the Godhead are one in essence and different in Person while not fully comprehending the mystery of how this can be.

Wayne Grudem provides a good definition of the Trinity. He states it this way,

> "God eternally exists as three persons, Father, Son and Holy Spirit, and each person is fully God, and there is one God."[143]

Modalism or Oneness Theology

Modalism is essentially the belief that there is only one God who manifests Himself or reveals Himself as Father, Son and Holy Spirit. In modalism, God takes on different roles or characters, much like an actor in a play, but He does not eternally exist in three distinct Persons at the same time. God reveals Himself as Father in creation, Son in Redemption, and Spirit in the Church but there is truly only one Person.

Modalism's great weakness is that it cannot appreciate and account for the relationships between the members of the Trinity. Further it confuses the true teaching of redemption that the Son came to do His Father's will and on the cross endured the Father's wrath against sin. The example of the Son's submission is lost as is the full concept of God at one and the same time judging sin (the Father) and atoning for sin (the Son).

It seems pertinent to consider the words of Bruce Ware once again,

> "In order for us sinners to be saved, one must see God at one and the same time as the one judging our sin (the Father), the one making the payment of infinite value for our sin (the divine Son), and the one empowering and directing the incarnate—human—Son so that he lives and obeys the Father, going to the cross as the substitute for us (the Holy Spirit)."[144]

We have already noted in previous chapters that William Marion Branham who is regularly lauded by members of the prophetic community held to a form of Oneness doctrine. In fact, Branham went so far as to refer to the Trinity as a doctrine of demons. But Branham is not alone in his rejection of this central tenant of the faith.

For instance the doctrinal statement for T.D. Jakes ministry states, "God--There is one God, Creator of all things, infinitely perfect, and eternally existing in three Manifestations: Father, Son, and Holy Spirit." This is modalism pure and simple. The Biblical doctrine is that there is one God, eternally existing in three Persons. The persons within the Godhead are eternal and distinct. It is not merely that God manifests himself in three different roles.

Tommy Tenney, like Jakes, has a background in the United Pentecostal Church. In fact his father was a leader in that denomination. Tenney is best known for his book, "The God Chasers". Tenney left the UPCI after ministering within the denomination for more than 10 years because of some of its legalistic stands. He did not leave it because of its errant view of the Godhead. Tenney attempts to avoid doctrinal statements whenever possible however, the doctrinal statement concerning God on his website is word for word the same as that of Jakes.

Modalism is an ancient heresy. It has always had a certain appeal because of its simplicity. What is new is not that there are teachers proclaiming modalistic heresies but rather that they are now accepted into the mainstream of the church as leaders in Christianity.

At the complete opposite end of the theological spectrum is Tritheism. This belief separates the three Persons of the Godhead so completely that one is left with three Gods.

During the heyday of the Toronto Blessing, Carol Arnott slipped into Tritheism in relating a supposed conversation that she had with the Holy Spirit. She said the Holy Spirit told her, ""You know, the Father, and Jesus, and I have been together for all of eternity. But when Jesus went back to heaven to be with God the Father, I came to earth.' And He said, 'I am so lonely for Jesus.' He said, "So that when people really, really love Jesus, and really honor Him, and really worship Him,' He said, I love to be around those kinds of people.'...He misses Jesus and He misses the Father."[145]

So we see that the Father, Son and Spirit are so distinct that they are actually separate from one another completely. While Arnott probably did not intend to espouse Tritheism, that is the net result of her teaching. Further, if this conversation with the Holy Spirit actually took place then Tritheism is absolutely true for it is impossible that the Holy Spirit could be wrong about His own nature. Of course, the more plausible explanation is that the supposed conversation with the Holy Spirit is actually the product of Arnott's fertile imagination or the result of a conversation with a spirit of a different nature altogether but, as we learned in our last chapter, one is not supposed to consider such options.

Lack of Omnipresence

Additionally, if Arnott's conversation with the Holy Spirit is true, then God obviously is not omnipresent. The Father and Son are now localized in heaven and the Spirit is localized to some degree on the earth.

Arnott is not alone in bringing messages that would have this impact. Commenting on Genesis 18:16-22, Denny Steyne makes the following startling statements,

> "When God has to visit a place in order to see it, Apostolic Love has covered it. Often I have heard people say that Lot had no business

living in Sodom and that he was a compromiser! I believe Lot was a righteous man (2 Peter 2:7) distressed by the world around him. Lot was nevertheless touched by the hand of God to love those around him to the degree that his love for them 'covered' their sins to such a degree, that God couldn't see them from Heaven, but had to take a road trip to find out the truth!"[146]

Moving past the revelation that Lot was an apostle—interesting considering he is an Old Testament saint--one must consider what this word teaches about the nature of God. First we see that God is not omnipresent. He is apparently located in heaven and must "take a road trip" in order to find out the facts about Sodom. This idea that God is somehow spatially located necessarily leads back to either a tritheistic or modalistic view of God logically. We also find that God is not omniscient because He must visit Sodom in order to get the facts because Lot's extravagant love has hidden the city from God (a belief that must be read into the text because it is certainly not found in a plain reading of the passage). It should be noted that if God is not omniscient, He cannot in perfect justice judge world because there could be facts of which He is not aware. Further it must entail that God is not sovereign since obviously if there are events happening in Sodom of which He is not aware this must also entail that these activities have occurred outside of His control.

The point is not to state that Denny Steyne actually believes these things. Rather, it is to point out that this sloppy handling of the Scripture has implications. If this word from Denny Steyne is true, then a number of biblical doctrines must be seriously revised if not rejected completely. While attempting to elevate the impact of a believer's love, Steyne has unwittingly (It is to be hoped) sacrificed the greatness and majesty of God.

Much of the errant expressions of the nature of God within the prophetic movement can indeed be attributed merely to a sloppy handling of the Word of God. This is not said to excuse such an abuse of Scripture but rather to point out that most of today's prophets do not bother to examine their revelations in the light of Biblical revelation so their errors are not the result of conscious thought. This is not true of all of them however.

Open Theism

As has already been noted, C. Peter Wagner is no minor or fringe figure in the apostolic and prophetic community. He is the founder and first president of the International Coalition of Apostles which at the time of this writing boasts nearly 500 members all claiming apostolic status of some kind. Since these individuals are all exercising some governing authority over prophets, teachers and other leaders within the church, Wagner's potential impact is great indeed. Not to mention his impact via those who read his books who are not a part of his apostolic network. It is therefore alarming when a leader like Wagner casts his lot with an openly heretical teaching like Open Theism.

It is beyond the parameters of this book to give an exhaustive treatment of the subject of Open Theism, and many others more eminently qualified have already done so[147]. But a brief description and rebuttal are in order.

Gregory Boyd is perhaps the most notable figure advancing the theory of Open Theism today. We will allow him to speak for the movement. Boyd writes,

> "In the Christian view God knows all of reality—everything there is to know. But to assume He knows ahead of time how every person is going to freely act assumes that each person's free activity is already there to know—even before he freely does it! But it's not. If we have been given freedom, we create the reality of our decisions by making them. And until we make them, they don't exist. Thus, is my view at least, there simply isn't anything to know. *So God can't foreknow the good or bad decisions of the people He creates until He creates these people and they, in turn, create their decisions.*"[148]

Open Theism is nothing short of a radical departure from the historic Christian faith. It is an all-out attack on the fundamental nature of God. It is a rejection of how the church has traditionally understood the nature of God, especially with regard to his exhaustive foreknowledge and immutability. It is a reinterpretation of the Bible's teaching on God, as one Open Theist said to me, "in the area of the *omni's* and the *imm's*" (for instance omniscience and immutability). God does not possess exhaustive foreknowledge of the actions of his creatures because these actions have not been performed therefore there is nothing for God to know. Therefore God is not omniscient in the sense that the church has historically defined omniscience. God is not immutable because He grows in His knowledge of His creatures as they act out their free choice and as He adapts to these choices. God is more omnicompetent than omnipotent. God is not completely beyond time. He learns by watching the actions of His creation.

Space will not permit a full discussion, but following the hermeneutic of Open Theism to its logical conclusion will lead one to reject God's omnipresence as well.

This teaching has incredible implications for the Christian life. Predictive prophecy looks more like God playing the odds. God is the infinitely good guesser. God is constantly responding to the actions of creation, playing catch up if you will. The Divine Counsel could be incorrect in certain circumstances as issues arise that God did not foresee. One Open Theist says that God might have to apologize for the counsel that He has given. Although God is pictured as the infinitely wise chess player, it is still possible that He could direct moves that turn out to be disastrous. Evil that happens in the world may be random and pointless. Your suffering may not have a place in the divine plan, though we are to be comforted that God hurts along with us and will work really hard to bring good out of it. Still, since the future is uncertain, we have no definite assurance that God will be able to do so. These are just a few of the many issues that are at stake.

But Open Theism is not the biblical picture of God. Consider the following Scriptures as just a sampling of the biblical material.

> "O Lord, you have searched me and known me! You know when I sit down and when I rise up; you discern my thoughts from afar. You search out my path and my lying down and are acquainted with all my ways. Even before a word is on my tongue, behold, O Lord, you know it altogether....Your eyes saw my unformed substance; in your book were written, every one of them, the days that were formed for me, when as yet there were none of them." Psalm 139:1-4, 16

Notice that God knows our thoughts before we think them, our words before we speak them and has written all the days appointed for us before even one of them exists.

Some of the most majestic passages in the Bible on the foreknowledge of God can be found in the book of Isaiah.

> "Thus says the LORD, the King of Israel and his Redeemer, the LORD of Hosts: 'I am the first and I am the last; besides me there is no god. Who is like me? Let him proclaim it. Let him declare and set it before me, since I appointed an ancient people. Let them declare what is to

come, and what will happen. Fear not, nor be afraid; have I not told you from of old and declared it?" Isaiah 44:6-8a

"Assemble yourselves and come; draw near together, you survivors of the nations! They have no knowledge who carry about their wooden idols, and keep on praying to a god that cannot save. Declare and present your case; let them take counsel together! Who told this long ago? Who declared it of old? Was it not I the LORD?" Isaiah 45:20-21a

Notice that in these two passages God declares that one of the characteristics that sets Him apart from the idols of the nations is the ability to declare what is to come. He challenges the idols to do the same. In other words, foreknowledge is an essential attribute of deity. Foreknowledge is one of the attributes that makes God, God.

The Lord declares his foreknowledge directly in Isaiah 46, speaking of the calling of Cyrus before he had even been born.

"remember the former things of old; for I am God, and there is no other; I am God, and there is none like me, declaring the end from the beginning and from ancient times things not yet done, saying, 'My counsel shall stand, and I will accomplish all my purpose, calling a bird of prey from the east, the man of my counsel from a far country." Isaiah 46:9-11a

With this basic understanding we now return to C. Peter Wagner. While admitting that the subject of Open Theism is controversial, Wagner nevertheless states that he has reached a conclusion on the subject.

"I believe what is known as 'open theism' provides us with the most biblical and the most helpful theological framework for doing our part in seeing 'Your kingdom come, Your will be done on earth as it is in heaven.'"[149]

Wagner attempts to comfort his readers that he is not drifting into heresy when he writes,

"The issues at stake are not those that threaten the validity of Christianity, or those that could be labeled 'heresy' or those that question the authority of Scripture. They are simply respectable theological differences of opinion."[150]

Wagner could not be further from the truth. As we have already discussed, the issues at stake in this discussion go right to the heart of one's fundamental understanding of the nature of God and His work in the world. This is more than just a minor academic discussion. And these positions are being labeled heresy by responsible theologians across the denominational spectrum of Christianity.

Wagner outlines what he believes was the problem as he was educated in a Reformed seminary.

> "Now that I look back, I see that our underlying problem was that no theological alternatives were presented to us. We were taught that God is sovereign, infinite, eternal, omniscient, omnipotent, and omnipresent, that He was unchangeable and that He was just."[151]

Remember that Wagner is claiming that being taught these fundamental beliefs about God was the underlying *problem* in his theological education. As the paragraph continues, Wagner then lists some of the particular distinctives of Reformed Theology into which he was educated in seminary and which he also finds problematic, however it should be stressed and understood that the attributes listed thus far have, until recently, been believed by Christians of all times and all places regardless of their denominational perspective and are thoroughly biblical. If Wagner is looking for theological alternatives to these core beliefs about God, as he states that he is, then he is abandoning the God of Scripture.

Weakness in God

One of the great sources of confidence for believers throughout history has been the understanding that the Most High God rules over all. Nothing escapes His notice. Nothing is outside of His foreknowledge and nothing can occur apart from His will either directly or permissively. Despite outward appearances, the world is not out of control for God is supremely in control. All things have a purpose in the providential plan of God even when we cannot fathom what that purpose might be. Nothing is random. And though God, out of His benevolence and goodness, allows man to participate in what He is doing, He is in no way dependent on man for anything. He does not need anything, or anyone, including us, though He chooses to give our lives meaning and purpose by working through us.

Notice how the Scriptures describe the all-sufficient, sovereign God we worship.

> "Who has measured the waters in the hollow of His hand, or with the breadth of his hand marked of the heavens? Who has held the dust of the earth in a basket, or weighed the mountains on the scales and the hills in a balance? Who has understood the mind of the Lord, or instructed him as his counselor? Whom did the Lord consult to enlighten Him, and who taught Him the right way? Who was it that taught Him knowledge or showed Him the path of understanding? Surely the nations are like a drop in a bucket; they are regarded as the dust on the scales; He weighs the islands as though they were fine dust. Lebanon is not sufficient for altar fires, nor its animals enough for burnt offerings. Before Him all the nations are as nothing; they are regarded by Him as worthless and less than nothing. To whom then will you compare God? What image will compare to Him?" (Isa 40:12-18)

Or again in Psalm 50:7-15:

> "Hear, O my people, and I will speak, O Israel, and I will testify against you; I am God, your God. I do not rebuke you for your sacrifices or your burnt offerings, which are ever before Me. I have no need of a bull from your stall or of goats from your pens, for every animal of the forest is Mine, and the cattle on a thousand hills. I know every bird in the mountains, and the creatures of the field are mine. If I were hungry I would not tell you, for the world is mine and all that is in it. Do I eat the flesh of bulls or drink the blood of goats? Sacrifice thank offerings to God, fulfill your vows to the Most High and call upon Me in the day of trouble; I will deliver you, and you will honor Me."

Notice that God's sovereignty and foreknowledge extend even to those who are unbelievers.

> "This is what the Lord says to his anointed, to Cyrus, whose right hand I take hold of to subdue nations before him and to strip kings of their armor, to open doors before him so that gates will not be shut: I will go before you and will level the mountains, I will break down gates of bronze an cut through bars of iron, I will give you the treasures of darkness, riches stored in secret places, so that you may know that I am the Lord, the God of Israel, who summons you by name. For the sake of Jacob my servant, of Israel my chosen, I summon you by name and bestow on you a title of honor, though you do not acknowledge Me. I am the Lord, and there is no other; apart from Me there is no God. I

will strengthen you, though you have not acknowledged Me, so that from the rising of the sun to the place of its setting men may know there is none besides me. I am the Lord and there is no other. I form the light and create darkness, I bring prosperity and create disaster; I, the Lord, do all these things." (Isa. 45:1-7)

In fact, this was the great lesson that had to be learned by Nebuchadnezzar in the book of Daniel. He lost his mind and lived as an animal until he came to acknowledge, "that the Most High is sovereign over the kingdoms of men and gives them to anyone He wishes." (Dan. 4:25) In the conclusion of Nebuchadnezzar's letter in Daniel chapter 4, the king acknowledges,

> "I honored and glorified Him who lives forever. His dominion is an eternal dominion; his kingdom endures from generation to generation. All the peoples of the earth are regarded as nothing. He does as He pleases with the powers of heaven and the peoples of the earth. No one can hold back his hand or say to him: 'What have you done?'" (Dan. 4:34-35)

But this is not the picture of God portrayed in the writings of far too many of the modern apostles.

God is Weak on Earth

Disturbingly, in the writings of many of the modern prophets, one finds strains of thought that reach back to E.W. Kenyon and have been popularized through Word Faith teachers such as Kenneth Hagin and Kenneth Copeland. One of these strains is the idea that God lost his rule over the earth in Adam's fall. The line of reasoning, which is thoroughly unbiblical, runs like this. Adam was created as a god-class type of being. Adam was given dominion over the earth. When Adam fell, he forfeited his dominion over the earth to Satan. God was removed from the earth realm. God needed (and still needs) man to cooperate with Him in order to accomplish His purposes on the earth.

The absolute fallacy of this type of reasoning may be seen in several things. First, the Bible never says that Adam was made in the god-class. This is not what is meant by being in the image of God. Second, any dominion that Adam was given was always subordinate to the absolute dominion and sovereignty of God. The situation with Adam might be illustrated by a company owner who hires a manager for his warehouse.

The manager may have a degree of dominion over the warehouse. He may be able to hire the employees and terminate employees that do not meet his satisfaction. He may determine how he warehouse operates on a day-to-day basis. But his dominion is always subordinate to the owner. The owner may, at any time he chooses, step into the warehouse and dictate what is done because he is the ultimate ruler of the company. The Bible teaches that God is the absolute sovereign over the earth. He has never for one second forfeited His absolute reign. Any authority given to man is only subordinate authority. When Adam fell, God did not bemoan being kicked out of the earth realm but instead promptly kicked Adam out of the garden. The entire Bible is a record of God exercising his sovereignty. The book of Daniel is particularly poignant when it declares emphatically that "the Most High rules over the nations of men and gives them to whomever He chooses."

Kenyon's view of God leaves God on the outside looking in until He can find a man to cooperate. Echoes of Kenyon's weak God may be seen in many of the modern prophetic writers.

In their 2007 edition of "The Shepherd's Rod", Paul Keith Davis and Bob Jones make the following comments:

> "The Bible declares that the heaven of Heavens belongs to God, but the earth has been delegated into the hands of man. Dominion of the earth was first entrusted to Adam. Unfortunately, that heritage was lost in the Garden of Eden. The spirit of this world has usurped the true spiritual authority originally given to mankind."[152]

One can easily hear the voice of Kenyon behind the words of Davis and Jones. The spirit of the world has usurped the dominion given to man. God has to some degree lost control of the earth. This teaching has serious implications because it seems to place the burden on man for making things right. In Word of Faith circles, God had to find a man to speak His faith-filled words into the earth. Similarly Jesus, as a man, had to speak God's faith-filled words into the bowels of the earth in order to conquer Satan and be resurrected. In the prophetic community, man has to clear the heavens for God to be able to move. We have to seek a breaker anointing to "allow the work of God to go forward in new dimensions"[153] (Bickle). Or we have to roar to "release God's judgments" (Todd Bentley). We must engage in strategic level spiritual warfare by spiritually mapping our city (Otis, Joyner, Frangipane et. al.) etc. etc.

Davis and Jones indicate something similar as they continue in discussing the "spirit to overcome" that we should seek from God. It is essential that the church receive this spirit to overcome for once we do;

> "When this transpires, we will learn how to release God's dominion in the Earth."[154]

Notice that we must "learn to RELEASE God's dominion on the earth". God's dominion is somehow bound. God must wait for us. Once again this is completely contrary to the clear teaching of Scripture that God is right now exercising complete dominion over the earth even as He allows evil to continue to exist for His own glory and His own purposes.

Bill Yount also demonstrates this same misconception when he writes,

> "As I read this Scripture in Romans [8:22], the word "now" jumped off of the page! I sensed the Lord saying, "Now, means now!" I sensed the earth itself is groaning to come under it's original ownership of the Lord of all the earth! It is crying out for a deep cleansing to be redeemed into God's Kingdom. **I saw as the Heavens and the earth were being shaken violently, many regions of the earth were shaken into the Kingdom of Heaven."**[155] (emphasis in the original)

Though Yount earlier in this same prophecy quotes Psalm 24:1 which states, "the earth is the Lord's and the fullness thereof", his later comments completely contradict this verse. After all, how can the earth be groaning to be under its original ownership? The earth has never belonged to anyone other than the Lord. Listen again to the words of God as recorded in Psalm 50:10 "For every beast of the forest is Mine, and the cattle on a thousand hills." Does this sound like God has ever lost ownership of the created realm? Romans 8:22 teaches that the creation longs (metaphorically) to be released from the curse that it received through the Fall of Adam not that it desires to return to divine ownership.

Todd Bentley, in explaining how to make decrees to activate the heavenly court (we will discuss apostolic decrees more later as one of the many new doctrine prophets are currently inventing) seems to draw from the same polluted well when he writes,

"In the last teaching, we explained the concept of prophetic decrees. Remember, God created Adam and Eve in the beginning to have dominion over the earthly realm, to have authority to make decrees on earth. But because they disobeyed God's instructions, the Devil succeeded in stealing their dominion from them. (Gen. 3) To make matters worse, their disobedience caused all of humanity, all of us, to suffer under the curse of sin and to lose our dominion over the earth. We all lost the power to make kingly decrees."[156]

This is a classic case of reading back into the Scriptures what one wishes to find. Nowhere does the Bible indicate that Adam and Eve, as a part of their dominion over the earth, had the right to make kingly decrees in the sense that Bentley is using this term. Bentley heaps error upon error as he falsely reasons; 1. Adam and Eve had the right to make kingly decrees on behalf of God 2. This sovereignty was lost in the Fall and God lost some ability to have His purposes carried out on the earth 3. This ability is restored in Christ and finally 4. Believers must activate the heavenly court through decrees in order for God's purposes to be done on the earth.

He continues, "Angels freely execute the judgments of God echoed in heaven after we decree what God has spoken to use on the earth."[157] And again later he writes, "Failing to accept our responsibility to make the decrees God has spoken, hinders angels from intervening in our lives."[158]

Notice again how man-centered, man-exalting the theology of the modern prophets is. Man had dominion. Man lost dominion. Man has the capacity to thwart the purposes of God. Man has the ability to activate and release the judgment of God. Heaven is waiting on Man to get it right before heaven can act. Man is responsible for initiating the change.

Never one to be outdone where teaching a new heresy is concerned, Wagner jumps on board the human dominion bandwagon stating,

"Then when God delegated authority for dominion over creation to Adam, along with free moral choice, Satan saw an opportunity to take back the authority that he had lost [in his fall from heaven]. God would not have given it back to him, but Adam now could. This may sound strange at first, but think about it. God gave Adam the authority to give his authority over to Satan!"[159]

After Wagner discusses the need for Jesus to regain this lost authority, he comes to the inevitable conclusion drawn from this teaching. Quoting Steve Thompson he writes,

> "Jesus, having won back authority on earth, could now mediate and rule in the affairs of earth. However, Jesus did not stay on the earth to rule it. He ascended to the Father and is seated at His right hand. So who now is responsible to rule and reign in the earth? Believe it or not, the church, which is the body of Christ."[160]

There are so many problems with this last statement it is difficult to know where to begin. First we notice that Jesus had to win back authority on the earth in order to mediate and rule in the affairs of earth. This is utter foolishness as Jesus is God and the passages discussed previously demonstrate God's sovereignty in the earth. But we also notice that since Jesus did not stay on the earth in His physical human nature, He is no longer ruling at the present time. Apparently Thompson assumes that He must not be omnipresent in His divine nature and therefore is not available to rule. Finally, it would appear that neither the Father nor the Spirit are in a position to rule because the only candidate Thompson can land on is the church. We now must exercise God's dominion.

Of course, the entire scheme leads to another issue. If Adam had God's delegated authority and turned it over to Satan through disobedience, is it possible that the church could turn the authority that Christ won over to Satan through disobedience again? If the church does this will God have to send another Redeemer? Fortunately, we don't have to worry since this entire doctrinal superstructure is false to begin with.

Bickle also echoes this similar sentiment that God's will and power must be released by believers. In a document entitled, "Authority of the Believer: Prophetic Decrees", Roman numeral II "How God's Power is Released in the earthly Realm", we read,

> "A. The spriitual principle is that the Spirit moves at God's word (Gen. 1 principle). In Genesis 1, the darkness and the Spirit were there. But nothing happened until words were spoken.
>
> B. God created humans in His image and then gave us His Word to release His will on earth. God taught Adam to have dominion over the earth in the same way God did by speaking words.

C. When our heart and words agree with God's will then they release His power. If our words agree with Satan then we release his power. Jesus resisted Satan by speaking God's word (Matt. 4:4-10.)

D. Faith does not come by asking but by hearing the Word. Many have "faith" in the devil's word.

So then faith comes by hearing, and hearing by the word of God. (Rom. 10:17).[161]

Look again at what Bickle is teaching, "when our hearts and words agree with God's will then they RELEASE HIS POWER. If our words agree with Satan we "RELEASE HIS POWER". So the determining factor here is man and not God. Man determines whose power is released. Beginning with the dubious teaching that God exercises His authority only through the words He speaks, Bickle determines that man is able to exercise dominion in the same way through the spoken word. While this may make many feel incredibly important, it simply cannot be squared with the Biblical data. In fact Bickle is wandering perilously close to the teaching of Word Faith theology that our words create our reality.

This document on prophetic decrees then goes on to give a list of dubious examples all in an attempt to show the biblical nature and authority of this practice. However it ends with this interesting caveat.

"We make decrees to the elements of nature and to inanimate objects (wind, fig tree, mountains, etc.). We make decrees over geographic regions. We should not give decrees over individuals that are sick to rise up (without it happening because it disheartens them)."[162]

So in other words prophetic decrees that could not in any way have any verifiable results are all okay. But don't decree healing because if it doesn't happen it will be disheartening. If all of this decreeing works, why is there a need for this admonition?

Shawn Bolz takes a similar approach. In discussing blueprints for buildings God wants to have built on earth which Bolz claims he was shown while being given a guided tour of heaven, he writes, "God's plans are *this* complete, needing only our agreement in order to manifest in our generation." [163] He continues by making this remarkable statement, "I couldn't believe how many things God desires to own that currently exist now on the earth."[164]

There are two issues with these statements by Bolz. First, according to the Scriptures, God already owns all things. Bolz's assertion that he couldn't believe how many things God "desires" to own is patently ridiculous in the light of Biblical revelation. But secondly, notice that Bolz indicates that God's plans are complete but they need "our agreement in order to manifest in our generation". Once again, the Bible gives a completely different picture of God. According to Ephesians 1, God is working all things according to the counsel of His own will. Nowhere does the Bible indicate that the sovereign God of the universe needs the agreement of His creation in order to accomplish His plans. The picture that Bolz paints of God is that of a weak deity wringing His hands hoping that men get it right and come into agreement with Him so that His plans can be actualized.

God is Weak in Heaven

Not only has God lost His sovereignty over the earth. But apparently God is unable to maintain control even over heaven.

As Bolz continues his tour of heaven, we continue to see a picture of God that is far less than that given to us in Scripture. In the "creative inventions room", Bolz discovers the following,

> "Angels guarded certain inventions. I tried to discern why guards existed in this area, then I noticed some people trying to gain illegal access through witchcraft to steal these inventions. I was incredulous that the enemy was so bold, yet as I watched one invention, I began to understand why" [Shawn then tells of a man who was to steward one of God's inventions but he ran into financial trouble and didn't turn to God. A wealthy man was sent by a demonic force to meet this Christian and fund his invention. He then stole the technology] "So the enemy stole and won the use of a precious, divinely inspired communication system, which Satan has used to defile humanity all over the globe with every form of perversion. After this, I understood why guardians watched over this and other areas of the heavenly storehouse."[165]

The idea that men are able to somehow penetrate heaven through witchcraft to steal ideas for inventions from God is laughable. The idea that somehow the enemy was able to accomplish this in the past is ludicrous. One begins to wonder how impotent the God that Bolz worships truly is. This is certainly not the picture of the omnipotent God given in Scripture.

But Bolz is not done. He next visits the "music room". In this room the Spirit is inspiring new song that angels take and impart to human for use in worship. Once again Bolz sees trouble in paradise as demons are infiltrating this room and plagiarizing God's music in order to pervert the sound and impart it to rock bands. But not to fear, for Bolz sees that,

> "Heavenly guard angels, however, armed with something like giant fly swatters, would search for demonic intruders. They would squelch the enemies who were trying to steal a peek or listen in on the music arts section."[166]

So here apparently we have angels involved in some sort of heavenly whack-a-mole in order to keep the demons at bay and protect the music that God wants to bring forth on the earth. The fact that Bolz maintains any form of credibility in the Christian community only testifies to the sad state of the modern Church. The entire scenario would be laughable if it weren't for the tens of thousands of young people who believe Shawn Bolz is a prophet.

Before moving on to other prophets, I want to give one more example from Bolz. He writes,

> "a friend named James had a vision at age 18....People were chained against walls and writhing in pain. Precious gold, which he knew belonged to the Lord, was locked up in boxes. Demons were holding on to prophetic promises that clearly belonged to Jesus. James wondered where he was, and he was shown that this deeply oppressed place was a treasury of God that had been captured and laid up in the second heaven.....James began to intercede—praying that the enemy would return what was rightfully the Lords—and he began to exhibit an unusual spiritual authority that was beyond his eighteen years. He clinched an agreement with the God of Heaven, and God began to answer his prayers........The enemy is the master of exploitation and deception. He wants to use the very vehicles of ministry against the beautiful, precious treasure God is birthing. The enemy uses nine parts truth mixed with one part lie and spreads his dominion by having those who would compromise agree with these deceptions."[167]

Surely this is nonsense. The promises of God do not go unfulfilled and none of them have been or ever will be captured by demons. One wonders how, interceding to God for the enemy to release and return these possessions would be of any value at all if God wasn't strong enough to keep these promises and treasures from being stolen by the enemy in the first place. The only possible reason is that when man comes into agreement with God in intercession the balance of power is finally tipped in God's favor. Once again, the picture is of a God who is in need of the assistance of His creation in order to accomplish His divine purposes. It is the "unusual spiritual authority" of James that finally turns the tide and wins the day. This is not the picture of God given to us in Scripture. Bolz's book indicates that it is he who has been deceived by the "master of exploitation and deception" as well as an overly fertile imagination.

Scott Hicks seems to take a page out of Bolz's book when he writes the following,

> "I was thinking of something the other day that many would say is crazy, but I was thinking by inspiration from above, **"Everything that the secular world has should have been a Kingdom thing first!"** Every building; every business; every idea; every corporation; banking system; and all the way down to children's playgrounds!....I'm convinced that not all of, but many of the secular things of today should have been invented or birthed by the body of Christ. Many secular business owners and inventors are of Christ, while some are not. But those that are not, somehow got the revelation, the understanding, and the drive to accomplish the tasks of success. I wonder at times how this could be? Is it that the body of Christ has neglected such things, or is it that the ungodly has entered in another way and discovered a divine secret that was meant for the body of Christ? Both may be the case, however, by the latter suggestion, the ungodly have climbed into the sheep fold some other way, rather than through Jesus Christ!"[168]

Hicks' first idea that everything in the secular world should have been in the kingdom first, which he claims came from inspiration, is found nowhere in the Bible. Lost people still bear the image of God, and God, in His divine sovereignty can still use them (as He did with Cyrus) to accomplish His purposes and permit them to invent and create beautiful things. The idea that because something didn't come from a Christian that God was not involved is blatantly, Biblically false.

However, the belief that the ungodly have somehow climbed into the sheepfold by another way other than Jesus and stolen secrets that belonged to the body of Christ is just absurd. Once again we must ask, "how weak is the God of the modern prophets?"

God is Weak in Answering Prayer

A classic example of the weak God of the modern apostles and prophets can be found in the writings of International Coalition of Apostles' member Dutch Sheets. Sheets writes,

> "Recently, I believe the Lord showed me what sometimes happens when we come to Him with a need, asking Him to accomplish what He says in His Word. In answer to our requests, He sends His angels to get our bowls of prayer to mix with the fire of the altar. But *there isn't enough in our bowls to meet the need!* We might blame God or think it's not His will or that His Word must not really mean what it says. The reality of it is that sometimes He cannot do what we've asked because we have not given Him enough power in our prayer times to get it done. He has poured out all there was to pour and it wasn't enough! It's not just a faith issue, but also a power issue."[169]

Pay close attention. Sheets claims to have received this teaching through divine revelation. According to Sheets, here is what sometimes happens when believers bring a need to the Lord in prayer. Notice that Sheets indicates that our prayers can line up with what God has already promised in His Word, may be according to His will, and that God may actually attempt to answer our prayer. But the Lord may be unable to do so because we have not given Him enough power through our prayers in order for Him to accomplish His will. So apparently God is not able to keep His own promises without our help. We have to give God the power to act. Here again we come face to face with the Almighty Man of prophetic teaching. God is reduced as man is enthroned as the one who is truly determining the course of the universe. Once again, the source for this word simply cannot be God despite Sheets' claim that it came from the Lord.

God is Weak in Salvation

Despite the fact that the Bible teaches that the Gospel is the power of God unto salvation and is sufficient to turn men from darkness to light, Austin, Otis, Bickle, Frangipane and nearly every other apostolic and prophetic teacher have invented another doctrine, spiritual mapping, whereby man must help God out. In spiritual mapping, a city is researched historically, through seeking divine revelation, and physically in order to discern the demonic activity in the city. One must determine how the demons gained and maintain legal control over the city and who the ruling principalities over the city are. These demons are then catalogued by name so that intercessors may clear the heavens by binding and loosing, repenting for the past sins of the city and a number of other practices that have more in common with the occult than historic Christianity, in order that the gospel and the Spirit of God might be released over the city. Spiritual mapping was discussed previously in chapter 5 so the point will not be belabored here. This teaching makes salvation primarily a work of men by the use of principles and techniques. It is Pelagian to the core. Consider the following quote by George Otis Jr.,

> "Transformed communities do not materialize spontaneously. If they did we might legitimately wonder why an omnipotent and ostensibly loving God did not turn the trick more often. We would also be left to ponder our own value as intercessors. Fortunately, such thoughts can be banished immediately. This is because community transformation is not an arbitrary event but rather the product of a cause and effect process."[170]

Otis is concerned to take God off the hook for the resistance of some communities to the gospel. He also is concerned to make certain that our place as intercessors is preserved. But his answer comes with a heavy price tag. Salvation and awakening are no longer the works of God sovereignly moving but rather the programmed response to the proper application of principles. In counterpoint to this consider the words of William Willimon:

> "...revivals are miraculous, that the gospel is so odd, so against the grain of our natural inclinations and the infatuations of our culture, that nothing less than a miracle is required in order for there to be true hearing."[171]

It should be noted that when forced to justify their positions biblically, practitioners of strategic level spiritual warfare (spiritual mapping) must admit that the Bible states very little, if anything at all, about territorial demons and certainly contains nothing concerning how to deal with them. These theories are based on a pragmatic approach, looking at what appears to be working elsewhere, rather than on the Word of God. This alone should be a cause for concern.

In addition to these issues, in spiritual mapping the cross is no longer central. Individual salvation is replaced with community transformation, individual sin is replaced by corporate sin and spiritual warfare replaces the proclamation of the gospel.

God is Weak in Eschatology

In another example, Bill Hamon seems to indicate that the Father needs our help in order to accomplish the return of the Son. Hamon asserts,

> "The full restoration of apostles and prophets back into the Church will then bring divine order, unity, purity and maturity to the corporate Body of Christ......That will in turn bring about the end of this world system of humanity and Satan's rule. The fulfillment of all these things will release Christ, who has been seated at the right hand of the Father in heaven, to return literally and set up His everlasting kingdom over all the earth."[172]

We will deal with Hamon's declarations about the absolute necessity of modern apostles and prophets later. For now, notice that the Lord cannot accomplish order, purity and maturity in the church without them. Notice also that it is up to the church to end the world system of humanity and Satan's rule. But most importantly, notice that all this is necessary in order to "RELEASE" Christ. Jesus is bound apparently with His hands tied until the church does what is necessary to enable Christ to return.

In contrast to the modern apostolic/prophetic movements assessment of a God who is needy and waiting for men to act, consider the words of Bruce Ware,

> "Does God need us to do his work? Does God need us to help others grow in Christ? Does God need us to proclaim the gospel so that others hear the good news and are saved? The answer is an emphatic no. He doesn't need any of us to do any of this. Being the omnipotent and sovereign Ruler over all, he would merely have to speak, and whatever He willed would be done. Recall the words of Paul in Acts 17:25, that God is not 'served by human hands, as though he needed anything.' No, the humbling fact is that God doesn't need any of those whom he calls into his service. So why does he do it this way? Why does he call us into service, and even command us to 'serve the Lord'

(Ps. 100:2)? The startling answer is this: He calls us into a service that he doesn't need because he wants so very much to share with us. He's generous. He loves and delights in giving a portion of his glorious work to others and empowering them to do it. Recall that it is his work. He could just do it, but it is as if he says, 'No, I want you to participate in the privilege and pleasure of my work;'[173]

The true biblical picture is that God is completely all-sufficient in Himself. He is not dependent on nor in need of anything from His creation. He is the sustainer and supplier of His creation. The church is given the privilege of joining God in His work but God is not dependent upon us. In fact, God could do the work alone and chooses to use people out of His great benevolence. This teaching is crucifying to the flesh and exalting to the God of all. It is the exact opposite of the man-centered, prideful teaching of the modern apostles and prophets.

Prophets Can Force God to Act Prematurely

The God presented in Scripture is the ultimate Sovereign. He works all things according to the counsel of His own will (Eph. 1:11). He operates on His own timetable.

The God of the prophets is a remarkably different character.

For instance, in a prophecy purportedly coming directly from the mouth of God, Theresa Phillips states the following:

> **"It's not the Armageddon time.**
>
> "Be careful what you prophesy," says the Lord. "For you can bring Me to do something ahead of My time. For I hear the voices of My prophets even now writing out the dispatches as if it were now.
>
> *But America, I'm giving you another golden chance.*
> *America, I'm giving you the Kingdom of advance."*[174]

The prophecy itself, which is much longer, is quite confusing but at least one thing seems to be certain. The prophets must be careful about what they prophesy or they might force God to act before He is ready. It would appear that they might interfere with the second chance that the Almighty declares that He is giving to America.

Of course, nowhere in Scripture does God indicate that He is under any compulsion to act simply because a prophet spoke a word. One might expect that the prophet would be judged for speaking presumptuously. The God of the modern prophets however, is forced to jump when His messengers speak even if to do so means that He must act prematurely. Behold the power of the modern prophet.

One must look at the God Phillips is proclaiming and ask who is really in charge? Is it God or the prophet? It almost seems as though God must take orders from those claiming a prophetic gifting.

God Was Lonely

Allen Hood states that God brought all the animals before Adam for Adam to name to cause Adam to long for a companion. In this way Adam could understand how God longed for a companion, which is why He created man in the first place.[175] The implication of this kind of teaching is that God is not sufficient within Himself relationally.

In contrast, the Bible indicates that God created man for His own glory, not from any sense of need or longing. Among the relationships within the Trinity, God was perfectly satisfied relationally. Again, while our flesh loves to believe that we have in some way fulfilled or completed God, such is simply not the case. Once again the comments of Bruce Ware are helpful.

> "He is by nature a unity of Being while also existing eternally as a society of Persons. God's tri-Personal reality is intrinsic to his existence as the one God who alone is God. He is a socially related being within himself. In this tri-personal relationship the three Persons love one another, support one another, communicate with one another, and in everything respect and enjoy one another. They are in need of nothing but each other throughout all eternity. Such is the richness and the fullness and the completion of the social relationship that exists in the Trinity."[176]

God the Gossip

Today's modern prophets give the impression that they walk through life receiving direct communication from the Almighty on an almost moment by moment basis. If Moses was the friend of God, they are God's personal confidants or bff's. The stories that are told in this vein would be charming if it weren't for the impression that they give of God.

For instance, Kirk Bennett relates the anecdotal story of Mike Bickle and Paul Cain meeting for the first time. Cain asks Bickle if it would be alright to move to a table in an unoccupied section of the room. When Bickle questions him as to the need of this, Cain replies that he is having difficulty eating because God has told him information about all the people around them; the waitress has kidney problems, another man is in a homosexual relationship and so on. Bickle wonders if they should minister to the people but Cain says no. God didn't disclose this information in order for Cain to become involved in ministry at this time. Bickle questions why God would share such things unless it was to have them minister. Cain remarks, "Because I am His friend and friends share things together."[177]

Undoubtedly, this story has a certain appeal to it. How impressive that Paul Cain could become so intimate with God that the Lord would just share with him even the secrets of other people's lives. However, normally when one shares another's secret with a third party who is neither a part of the problem nor part of the solution, it is called gossip. Here, albeit inadvertently, God is portrayed as the Heavenly gossip who shares the secrets of others for no apparent reason whatsoever. Apparently God just needs to get it off His chest. He needed to unload. In fact, the sharing of all of this personal information about the others in the restaurant doesn't even produce greater intimacy between God and Cain because the information is such a burden that he can't eat until they move.

The story does serve the critical purpose of making Paul Cain look very important however.

Nowhere in the Bible do we see God act in such a manner.

The Risky God who has Faith in You

Allen Hood alarmingly teaches that God is full of faith toward you. Hood boldly declares to an audience of young people, "The same heart who climbed up on the cross and said, "I bet my life, he'll say yes." Is the same heart who has faith in what we will be."[178]

This is another example of the radical beliefs of the modern prophets tending toward Open Theism. It is difficult to understand how the God who knows every word on our tongue before we even speak it, who has all of our days written in a book before even one of them is lived, who knows us from before we were born (Psalm 139) can be full of faith toward us. God operates on perfect knowledge, not faith. In addition, even classic Arminians believe that God has known from before the foundation of the world who would be saved. Jesus did not "bet [His] life [we'd] say yes." It is absolutely foolish to think of the Son of God in these terms. Hood's teaching represents a radical departure from Biblical truth regardless of one's position on election. Jesus was not gambling at the cross.

Though it is popular in the modern culture to talk of a God who takes risks (ala Wild at Heart), risk is a ridiculous attribute to assign to God in the light of His absolute foreknowledge, omnipotence and sovereignty. It just doesn't follow. A God who already knows the outcome cannot be taking a risk in anything that He does. Risk by definition involves a level of uncertainty concerning the outcome. God is not uncertain. Such poetic license is inappropriate when dealing with a subject as awesome as the character of God.

God is no Longer our Master

Kirk Bennett states God is no longer operating in the "master role". He calls us friends.[179] Jesus said I do not call you servants but friends, "for a servant does not know what His master is doing." Bennett also quotes from Hosea 2:16 where God speaks to Israel and says that they will call Him, "husband". No longer will they call Him, "Lord". Bennett's students are taught that God relates to us as husband today not Lord.

It is one of the joyous truths of the Christian faith that we become the children of God and the friends of God. In addition to the passage that Bennett quotes, we could site 1 John where John is almost rapturous as he says, "Behold what manner of love the Father has given unto us that we should be called the sons of God." It is truly amazing.

But we must not emphasize this truth to the exclusion of other, equally biblical truths. We are the sons of God, but we still call Him Lord which means He is our master. Paul, perhaps the greatest saint who ever lived called himself a bondservant of Jesus Christ. We may glory in our sonship but we must also bow in reverence before the God of all. Jesus also said to His disciples, "You call me Lord and Master and you say well for this is what I am." We must never forget this. Though God condescends in His love for us, God is infinitely greater than we are and demands our reverence, worship and obedience. God has never ceased to operate in the Master role. We do not have the right to choose one aspect of our relationship with God and emphasize it to the exclusion of all others.

And Finally it Gets Absolutely Ridiculous

Today's prophetic teachers appear to have no boundaries on their vain imaginations and the encounters that they claim to have with God. We will close with one more extended quote from the prophet Shawn Bolz,

> "One day while grocery-shopping, I began to hear a low rumble. Having grown up in California, I had lived through many earthquakes. I expected an earthquake was coming, and so I braced myself for the ground shaking, but nothing happened. Again the sound came, yet no one around me appeared distressed. At that point, I wondered if I was having a spiritual experience! As I got to my car, the sound in my ears grew louder. Finally I asked, "God, what is happening?"
>
> "I am hungry," was His strange reply."
>
> "Suddenly I realized those noises were from God's stomach rumblings! He was letting me hear His hunger pangs."
>
> "As I began to pray about this, I was led to Mark 11:12-14: "The next day as they were leaving Bethany, Jesus was hungry. Seeing in the distance a fig tree in leaf, he went to find out if it had any fruit. When he reached it, he found nothing but leaves, because it was not the season for figs. Then he said to the tree, "May no one ever eat fruit from you again." And his disciples heard him say it."
>
> "In this Scripture, Jesus shares a parable that illustrates a divine hunger. Jesus is hungry for the fruit of our lives—the offerings of those who desire to feed the heart of God. Jesus longs for the fullness of what was promised to Him by the Father in heaven."[180]

Surely the above story doesn't even need a response.

Conclusion

A.W. Tozer wrote,

> "The heaviest obligation lying upon the Christian Church today is to purify and elevate her concept of God until it is once more worthy of

Him. We do the greatest service to the next generation by passing on to them undimmed and undiminished that noble concept of God which we received from our Hebrew and Christian Fathers of generations past."[181]

The doctrine of the new apostolic and prophetic movement diminishes God rather than exalting Him. The theology of this movement is utterly man-centered. The portrait of God being painted by the modern apostles and prophets simply does not fit with the revelation of God given in the Bible. The God of the modern prophets is weak and limited. The prophet's view of sovereignty is totally lacking biblical substance. The God the modern prophets proclaim is waiting for man to act. It is man who is the true determiner. It is man who seems to have the final say. This God supplies the power but it is man who determines when and where the power is delivered. God can't even protect what He has in heaven sufficiently to keep both demons and unbelieving men from stealing it away. He can't protect His promises sufficiently to keep them from being hijacked by the Devil. He is unable to answer prayer unless men have given Him the power to do so. He can't save unless men clear the heavens of demonic beings so the gospel can bear fruit.

Such a God is hardly worthy of worship.

CHAPTER EIGHT

Jesus: Your Personal Boyfriend?
Modern Prophets and Jesus

*"There is a tendency to continue relating to Him as 'the **MAN** from **Galilee.'** Jesus is not a man. He was and is Spirit. He took the **form** of a servant and became a man for a brief time."* – Rick Joyner

In our last chapter we saw that modern prophets present a distorted picture of the Godhead from the one given to us in Scripture. The modern prophet's problems do not stop there. They appear to be reinventing Jesus.

The person and work of Christ is central to Christianity. It has been said that you can take the founders of other religions away and still have their religion. But if you remove Christ from Christianity you have nothing left. This is because Christianity is not first and foremost a religious system and ritual, it is a relationship with a person. If we are going to move into deeper intimacy with the person of Christ, the place where the modern prophets claim to be taking the church, it is essential that we are growing in the truth about Christ. One of the fundamental premises upon which this book stands is that true intimacy requires truth.

In this chapter, we will examine where the modern prophets are taking the church in relation to their understanding of Jesus, the second member of the Trinity. Once again, we see that these are not secondary issues. And once again we will demonstrate that the modern apostles and prophets have wandered far away from an orthodox understanding.

The Incarnation of Jesus

Rick Joyner denies the two natures of Christ when he writes the following:

"There is a tendency to continue relating to Him as 'the MAN from Galilee.' Jesus is not a man. He was and is Spirit. He took the form of a servant and became a man for a brief time."[182](emphasis in the original)

This is a direct denial of the hypostatic union. Joyner states that Jesus was only a man for a brief time. Orthodox Christianity has understood for centuries that once the second person of the Trinity voluntarily took to Himself a human nature, this was a permanent joining. Jesus did not take on some sort of a rent-a-body which was discarded some time after the resurrection. He has not divested Himself of the human nature that He added in the incarnation. Either Joyner is unaware of this, he does not understand it, or he is intentionally denying it.

Wayne Grudem again states the orthodox position when he writes,

"All of these texts indicate that Jesus did not temporarily become man, but that his divine nature was permanently united to his human nature, and he lives forever not just as the eternal Son of God, the second person of the Trinity, but also as Jesus, the man who was born of Mary, and as Christ, the Messiah and Savior of his people. Jesus will remain fully God and fully man, yet one person, forever,"[183]

This mistake by Joyner is critical because the New Testament links the ongoing intercessory and mediatorial work of Christ to his humanity. The apostle Paul stated,

"For there is one God, and there is one mediator between God and men, the man Christ Jesus" 1 Tim 2:5

Likewise the author of Hebrews writes,

"Now there have been many of those priests, since death prevented them from continuing in office; but because Jesus lives forever, he has a permanent priesthood. Therefore he is able to save completely those who come to God through him, because he always lives to intercede for them." Hebrews 7:23-25

Apparently, the writers of the New Testament shared this tendency to think of Jesus as a man. Joyner's understanding is contrary to that of the apostles.

One also wonders from this quote how Joyner views the bodily resurrection of Jesus if Jesus was only a man for a brief time. Was His body raised? If so, did He discard it when He divested Himself of His humanity? When did this divestiture take place? Joyner's statement calls his understanding of multiple central Christian truths into question.

Shawn Bolz demonstrates that he also completely misunderstands the incarnation of Christ when he writes

> "Jesus always used language that pointed to eternity. He longed to be there so much—even while He was on the Earth—that Jesus could not separate eternity from His very being."[184]

For Bolz's statement that Jesus longed to be back in eternity while He was on the earth to be true, Jesus must have laid aside certain aspects of His deity (in this case omnipresence) in order for Him to take on humanity. This is outside the orthodox position. In the incarnation, Jesus did not become God minus certain attributes. Instead, He retained all the attributes of deity while at the same time adding an additional human nature. No recognized teacher for the first 1,800 years of the church taught that the emptying of Christ included laying aside or forfeiting any of His divine attributes. This teaching, like the teachings on dominion covered in chapter 7, may stem from the influence of E.W. Kenyon, in this case, his false theories about the kenosis.

Unfortunately, the doctrine of the incarnation is so poorly taught in most church circles today that few believers have a solid understanding of the doctrine. Therefore some detailed explanation is in order. In the text in Phil. 2:7, the key passage in Scripture for understanding the humbling of Christ, Paul clearly associates the emptying and humbling of Christ with the taking on of a human nature. In coming as a man, He took a status lower than that which He deserved. He forever united Himself with a being whose nature is infinitely lower than His own. In other words, the humbling act of Christ came through what He added to Himself not in giving any attributes up. What He relinquished was His right to glory, majesty and honor. Though the church often uses language that states that Jesus left heaven (especially in music), this is really a metaphor and probably one that should be discontinued because it is so easily misunderstood. Jesus, as God, is omnipresent. In the orthodox understanding of the kenosis, or emptying, Jesus humbled Himself by veiling His glory and taking to Himself a human nature. He did not, however, forfeit His divine nature in any way. He could now, as the God-man, choose to act out of either nature. Therefore as a man, Jesus could rightly state that He did not know the day nor the hour of His return while, since He is also fully God, the Scriptures could state that He knew what was in every man. The essential point is this, while the Son of God, took to Himself permanently an additional nature, that of a man, He NEVER RELINQUISHED ANY OF THE ATTRIBUTES THAT MAKE HIM GOD, not even temporarily. One of the attributes of God is omnipresence. Grudem again is helpful when he states,

> "In fact, if the kenosis theory were true (and this is a foundational objection against it), then we could no longer affirm that Jesus was fully God while He was here on earth. The kenosis theory ultimately denies the full deity of Jesus Christ and makes him something less than fully God."[185]

Therefore, there is no way that Jesus could be lonely for heaven for in His omnipresent divine nature, He was still there.

Undeniably, the hypostatic union and the incarnation present us with some of the greatest mysteries of the Christian faith. Much like the doctrine of the Trinity, the human mind is simply too weak to fully grasp the glory of the truth. Because of the greatness of this majesty, it is difficult to put into words and certainly today's modern prophetic leaders are not the first to stumble at this point. But it is precisely for this reason that many of today's apostles and prophets would be well-served to get some theological training or at least read a good systematic theology book *before* they begin writing books themselves that will influence the spiritual development of tens of thousands of people. A Jesus who is lonely for heaven may tug at our heart strings and gain our sympathy. But a Jesus who is less than fully God cannot make an atonement for sin that is of infinite worth. We feel that we are able to relate to this lonely Jesus as a man but we are less drawn to worship Him as the majestic God that He is.

Weak Jesus

In the previous chapter, we saw that the modern apostles and prophets present a view of the Father that is far less than what is given to us in Scripture. We showed that in many of their teachings the Father is weak and needing the help of His creation to accomplish His purposes. The same can be said of the prophet's view of the second person of the Trinity, Jesus Christ.

Shawn Bolz, in relating his encounter with the Angelic Minister of Finance (an extra-biblical character if there ever was one), shares an incident in which the angel presents him with a large ring of keys. Shawn then states the following,

> "These keys were for tangible resources that humanity would have stewardship over, bringing Jesus ownership of the souls impacted by the resources....This vision made the reality of what Jesus was called to inherit extraordinary in my perspective! There were so many natural things that came under His dominion. Quite honestly, I had never understood that He would be so influential on the earth" [186]

Once again, we see that Jesus is very limited. There are things that are currently not under His dominion. Jesus does not yet have ownership of the souls impacted by some of these resources. The church must use these keys and take stewardship over these resources before Jesus can gain ownership. This is a far cry from the biblical picture of Jesus to Whom belongs "all authority in heaven and earth" (Matt. 28:18) and who "is before all things and in Him all things hold together" (Col. 1:17).

Then Bolz makes the incredible statement that he did not realize that Jesus "would be so influential on the earth". So Bolz did not understand that the sovereign Lord of creation was to be so influential? Bolz did not understand that the Jesus who is presently reigning until all of His enemies have been made His footstool would be so influential? The clear teaching of Scripture that at the Name of Jesus, "every knee will bow, of things in heaven and things on earth and things under the earth" (Phil. 2:10) didn't cause Shawn to see that Jesus was going to be "so influential"? This statement makes no sense when evaluated in the light of biblical revelation. Bolz never stops long enough to evaluate his own revelations and experiences in the light of biblical teaching to see the extreme disconnect. If he had, he might have wondered if the angel he was dealing with was actually from heaven or possibly an angel of light.

Later Bolz describes Jesus in the following terms:

"You see, Jesus is a desperate man. He's not impatient or unknowing...just desperate. His Father promised Him a world as His inheritance (Psalm 2:8, John 3:16), and therefore, His desire will remain unsatisfied until that inheritance is fully released....All heaven shares Jesus' desperation."[187]

We might think that these were simply misstatements if Bolz hadn't described Jesus in exactly the same way in his previous book,

"If we can understand the desperation Jesus feels to inherit His reward, we will never be the same! In fact Jesus is our reward, and I believe a whole generation will be His inheritance."[188]

The word desperate means "without hope and despairing". No description of Jesus could be further from the truth. As sovereign God, Jesus could never be without hope nor would He ever despair. But a desperate Jesus is perfectly in line with Bolz and other modern prophet's man-centered, man-deifying theology. In this book Bolz constantly refers to resources that Jesus "needs" in order to secure his reward. He says that in order for Jesus to receive His reward people have to be sent into every arena of culture and society. Notice the emphasis carefully. Christ's reward is ultimately dependent on the efforts and the activities of man. If this were true, Jesus would certainly have every reason to be desperate. But thankfully, God's promises will be fulfilled. Though, out of His abundant love and generosity, God invites men to participate in His work, the outcome is never in doubt.

Jesus Neglecter of the Family

Bolz continues with his misunderstanding of the person and work of Christ as he describes Jesus in almost stoic terms as abandoning His family. Bolz writes,

"Jesus disengaged Himself from the temporal relationships of Earth, demonstrating a new value system. This value system favored relationships that were eternal. In addition, it would not honor relationships that were not eternal.

"His rebuke to His mother and brothers was a rejection of the temporary, earthly family unit. It shook up people's thinking about Jesus. How would He claim to be the Son of Love and then reject the ones He was supposed to love the most? He did so by setting a new standard for love!

"Jesus cleansed Himself from life's common goals, such as the support of a natural family community that didn't revolve around God's love as much as the love of another. Jesus was modeling to us how to pursue higher goals."[189]

The real impact of this teaching becomes clear when Bolz makes the following statement just two paragraphs later,

"We cannot walk in Heaven's nobility unless we cleanse ourselves from all other common identities."[190]

It is true that Jesus placed the will of His Father in heaven above any earthly attachment and that He calls His disciples to do the same. It is not true that Jesus disengaged Himself from temporal relationships on earth. Jesus had deep, committed friendships both with His disciples and with other followers such as Lazarus, Mary and Martha. And Jesus cared for His mother. One of the most beautiful statements of Jesus on the cross was His charge to His disciple John to care for His mother. In His hour of greatest distress, Jesus saw to the need of His mother. Jesus cared enough for His brother James that He appeared to Him after His resurrection (1 Cor. 15:7) Jesus did not reject the natural family unit. He honored it, blessed it and sanctified it. His first miracle was performed at a wedding in Cana. The implications of Bolz's statements run completely contrary to the teachings of Scripture on the subject of the family. The family unit was established by God, Himself. It is the basic unit for human society, including Christian society. It is so much more than just a "common identity". It is the God-ordained means of raising godly offspring (Malachi 2:15). The family unit is the crucible for learning some of life's most important lessons. Marriage is to be a picture of the relationship of Christ and the church. Again, Jesus placed His divine stamp of approval on the family unit by performing His first miracle at a wedding in Cana. And though, the first commandment is to love God with all of our heart, the second commandment is the love of others, which would include our family.

In a day when we see the family crumbling all around us and see the resulting destruction within society, the last thing we need are irresponsible statements by supposed prophets indicating that the family doesn't rate very highly on God's agenda. It is frightening to hold up this misconception of Jesus as the example for us to follow.

One sincerely hopes that Bolz rethinks his positions on this issue before considering marriage.

Jesus Your Personal Boyfriend

One of the most disturbing portrayals of Jesus that is consistently arising with the modern apostolic and prophetic movement is what we will call the "Romantic Lover" or the "boyfriend" Jesus. Jesus is frequently described in terms more fitting for a smitten teenager than the Lord.

It is important to understand that Jesus loves us deeply with a love that surpasses all human understanding. But He is not romantically in love with us as we would normally use that phrase in modern culture. Jesus does not pine over us. He doesn't get butterflies in his stomach or sweaty palms. However, modern prophetic teachers constantly refer to Jesus in terms that indicate a romantic involvement between the Lord and His people. One constantly reads terms like "lovesick", "ravished heart", "the lover God" and many more within prophetic literature. The metaphor of the bride as given in Scripture is overly literalized to the point that it loses all balance and biblical meaning. Further the bridal metaphor is frequently emphasized to the exclusion of all other word pictures of the relationship between Christ and the church giving a very distorted picture of the relationship.

We have already noted the "lovesick Jesus" of Allen Hood in the chapter on modern prophets and the Scriptures. Previously, we also noted that Kirk Bennett frequently teaches that the church is no longer in a servant relationship with Jesus and that God should not be called Master. This is in stark contrast to the attitude of the apostle Paul who frequently referred to himself as the "bondservant" of Jesus Christ. I mention them again only to remind the reader. We will now move on to other examples of this same error.

Choo Thomas illustrates the "boyfriend" Jesus as well, albeit in its milder form. In a story about an encounter with Christ that she supposedly had on December 25th, she writes that Jesus appeared to her in His Christmas gown and crown and said to her,

"Sweetheart, I am happy to be celebrating my birthday with you."[191]

Forgetting for a moment the ludicrous idea that Jesus was actually born on December 25th, nowhere in Scripture does Jesus call any of His followers, "sweetheart". But, as with so much of the mythology of the modern prophetic movement, the story does leave one with a clear impression of the importance of Ms. Thomas.

In addition to an extreme allegorical approach to Song of Solomon which will be discussed momentarily, one of the primary attempts to justify this kind of language biblically is supposedly found in the apostle John. In his gospel, John relates the events at the Passover Meal many translations give the following rendering,

> "Now there was leaning on Jesus' bosom one of His disciples, whom Jesus loved. Simon Peter therefore motioned to him to ask who it was of whom He spoke. Then, leaning back on Jesus' breast, he said to Him, 'Lord, who is it?'" John 13:23-25 (NKJV)

This rendering of the text, coupled with an inadequate understanding of the historical context, lends itself to a false mental impression. Commenting on John, Bickle writes,

> "To be a man who lays his head on the Lord's breast and receives His embrace will set your heart ablaze."[192]

Here Bickle commits an error based on an improper understanding of history. When men ate they reclined at the table, leaning on pillows. To be leaning on Jesus' breast meant to be the one directly in front of the Lord, who had to lean back to speak to him. Jesus and John were certainly in close proximity but they were not cuddling. They were not embracing. Consider the same text in a different translation.

> "One of the disciples, whom Jesus loved, was reclining at table close to Jesus, so Simon Peter motioned to him to ask Jesus of whom he was speaking. So that disciple, leaning back against Jesus, said to him, 'Lord, who is it?'" John 13:23-25 (ESV)

Read in this way, the passage gives a much different picture, one that is more biblically and historically accurate but which of course would not allow Bickle to make his point.

The extent to which this concept can be distorted was demonstrated by a man in one of the prayer ministries who, when interviewed by the author, said that he spent about 30 minutes of his quiet time holding Jesus against his chest and about 30 minutes being held by Jesus with his head against the Lord's chest. He was not joking and did not believe he was speaking metaphorically.

The Bridal Paradigm

The package used to present this teaching of the lovesick, romantic Jesus is termed "the Bridal Paradigm". I have been troubled for several years over the teaching of the "Bridal Paradigm" but had difficulty putting my concerns into words. While researching for this book, I read an exceptional article by the good folks at Spiritual Counterfeits Project that contained a section on the "Leaven of Bridal Mysticism". Jonathon Rice is the primary author of this section. This article was tremendously beneficial in helping to clarify many of the problems arising from this distortion of this biblical metaphor. While I won't be quoting the article directly, I want to give credit to Mr. Rice for helping to provide structure to my own thinking.

For those who might be unaware of this teaching, the bridal paradigm is the doctrinal position that the image of the Bride is the primary identity for the church, especially the church of this unique end-time generation. This generation will be the first to fully understand its identity as the Bride. This teaching has strong dominion theology undertones as there is a strong emphasis on the Bride co-reigning with Christ. Esther is seen as a type of the end-time Church.

The bridal paradigm becomes the grid, in a sense its own hermeneutic, through which all Scripture is interpreted and through which all spiritual activity is engaged. Thus we have teachings like Bridal intercession, the Global Bridegroom fast, the cross in the bridal paradigm etc. All of the Scripture is seen as the relentless pursuit of the heavenly lovesick groom for the bride of His heart's desire or the search of the Father for a bride for His Son who will be equally yoked to Him in love.

This message truly stands the gospel on its ear. No longer is the emphasis on a God who is working for His own glory and displaying His majesty in redeeming a lost and unworthy humanity. Now the story of redemption is on God seeking a suitable mate for His Son. No longer is the cross seen primarily as the place where Jesus makes propitiation for our sin and satisfies the justice, holiness and wrath of God, or the place of redemption where the price is paid for our ransom, which are the pictures the Bible uses. Now the cross is the dowry that is paid for the bride[193], a statement that the Bible never makes. Dowries (or more accurately bride prices) are paid because of the worth of the bride. But according to the Scriptures we had no worth. We had nothing to commend us to God. It was all grace. But this message will never do in the man-centered theology of the new prophets. So it must be reinterpreted through a new paradigm.

Jesus is described as "in-love", lovesick, the passionate Bridegroom, or as having a ravished heart. He is the Lover with fire in His eyes for His bride. He goes to the cross to woo His bride and win her heart with love by fighting unto death for her.

The church is to respond in similar manner as we pray for our love to be awakened, to be ravished by the love of the Bridegroom etc. etc. Images and language from Song of Solomon abound. Sometimes this language is used of the Father as well.

This teaching, while drawing upon a legitimate metaphor and the language of Scripture, pushes the metaphor beyond the boundaries of its proper understanding leading to an improper and unbiblical picture of Christ and His relationship to the Church.

The first problem is the emphasis on the metaphor of the Bride to the exclusion of all other images used to describe the Church. Yes, the church is the Bride of Christ, but that is not all that is said of the Church. The Church is also called the Body (1 Cor. 12), the children of God (Eph 3:14, 1 Jn. 3 and others), an olive tree (Rom. 11), a field (1 Cor. 3:6-9), a temple (1 Pet. 2:5), a royal priesthood (1 Pet. 2:9), a holy nation (1 Pet. 2:9), God's house (Heb. 3:6), the flock of God (1 Pet. 5:2), and an inheritance (Eph. 1:18). And this is just for starters! Consulting any good systematic theology book will yield a veritable host of metaphors, titles and images of the church. Therefore right from the beginning we should understand that any teaching that focuses almost exclusively upon one metaphor is necessarily out of balance. Each of these titles is meant to teach us some important truth concerning the people of God. One simply does not have the right to fixate upon one metaphor to the neglect of the others. One does not have the right to elevate one expression to the place of primary position and evaluate all of Scripture through this lens. In like manner, Jesus is the Bridegroom but that is not all that is said about Jesus. This teaching is seriously out of balance.

The second issue is that, while it is true that the metaphor of the Bride is used for the church as a whole, this same metaphor is never used for the individual believer. This may seem minor at first but it is actually very significant. It is the entire church that is the Bride of Christ. Each believer is a part but is not the Bride. It would appear that many of the prophetic teachers either misunderstand this or choose to ignore it. Due to this confusion, many of the statements of the prophetic teachers cause Jesus to sound like our personal boyfriend instead of our Lord. Consider again the man who claimed that he held Jesus for the first 30 minutes of his quiet time and then had Jesus hold him for the last 30 minutes. Jesus is not your boyfriend or lover. It is inappropriate to consider Him in this way.

The roots of this error in Protestant Christianity (there are other roots in Roman Catholicism) seem to stretch back to Sister Aimee Semple McPherson. It seems that Sister Aimee was among the first, if not the first, to personalize the concept of the Bride to the individual. Historian Matthew Avery Sutton writes,

> "McPherson's emphasis on 'Bride of Christ' imagery provoked the most explicit criticisms. In one representative sermon she insisted that the marriage of Old Testament figures Isaac and Rebecca, 'a remarkable type of Christ and His Bride', signified God's work with his people. Isaac represented Jesus, while Rebecca represented 'the Bridal Body.' Quoting the biblical account, the evangelist preached, 'the damsel was very fair to look upon, a virgin, neither had any man known her.' She turned to the audience, observing, 'As I look over your faces it seems I can almost pick out the Rebecca's who have come here tonight."[194]

According to Sutton, it was McPherson, in her sermon "The Bride in her Veil of Types and Shadows", that introduced the concept that the Bride was the central metaphor of the church and her theology. It was McPherson that began to interpret the story as a divine romance. It was for this reason that she began to preach dressed completely in white.

According to Sutton, this imagery was not missed by other ministers of the day.

> "Messages like these, in the context of McPherson's own proclivity for wearing white, did not escape the attention of her rivals. Shuler sarcastically pointed out, 'She does not wear white for nothing. She wears white so that she will have on the wedding garments when the Lord returns for His bride.' He further declared that she had presented herself as 'almost, if not, His bride.'"[195]

So we see that Sister Aimee was guilty of two of the fundamental errors found in the Bridal Paradigm today. She taught that the image of the Bride was the church's primary identity. Secondly, she personalized and literalized the Bride metaphor to the individual. However, today's teachers take the notion well beyond anything that Sister Aimee could have imagined.

A third issue with the Bridal Paradigm is that the statement is a metaphor. It is not a literal statement. The metaphor is meant to teach us the truth about God's love and commitment to us and our need for holiness and submission and yes, love for Him and a number of other things. But it is not meant to be literalized and physicalized (If that's not a word, it should be.) Today's prophetic teachers, as many before them, see in the Song of Solomon an allegory of Christ and the church. This has been a common approach to this book throughout much of church history and though it is not the correct approach to the book in my opinion, it is certainly orthodox. However, prophetic teachers then go a step further, moving beyond the boundaries of orthodoxy, by literalizing the allegory and interpreting the divine love in terms more fitting for human romantic love.

This third issue brings a host of problems into play. It should be noted that, as with teachings on Contemplative Prayer, the source of much of this teaching is Roman Catholic mysticism. Teresa of Avila, St. John of the Cross and Madam Guyon, along with many others, have provided the foundation for this thought. This, in and of itself, should be a problem. Why would we go to those whose overall understanding of God is so poor expecting to find truth? Why would we draw from the polluted well of Roman Catholic mysticism hoping to find pure water? I have been told that it is because of their passion and certainly these authors can write passionately about God, but they can and did write just as passionately about the Virgin Mary! This indicates to me, that the emphasis of the leaders of this movement is not at all grounded in a desire for truth but merely a desire to feel. And many of the "passionate" statements written by these mystics are squarely unbiblical. Consider the words of Catherine of Sienna who used to pray:

"O divine madman, you are crazed with love and drunk with love for me."

Surely a less Biblical picture of God could not be painted than that of a crazed madman drunk with love.

This literalizing of the metaphor can be seen in the abundance of overly romantic phrases used to describe God's love for us and ours for God. We read that God is "lovesick" or ravished for us. These phrases portray a God who simply cannot find true joy apart from us, who will never be satisfied without us. These statements are more appropriate for an adolescent than Almighty God. Jesus is finally sent to earth "When He couldn't take it any longer." This is a far cry from the God of the Bible who is completely sufficient within Himself and needs nothing. (Ps. 50, Isa 40) But the Scriptures indicate that the triune God is complete within Himself, lacking nothing including relationship. Once again the words of Bruce Ware are helpful.

"He is a socially related being within himself. In this tri-Personal relationship the three love one another, honor one another, communicate with one another, and in everything respect and enjoy one another. They are in need of nothing but each other throughout all eternity."[196]

Certainly Christ does love us. He loves us with a love that is beyond comprehension in its height, depth, width and breadth (Eph 3:18-19). But He is not romantic about us. He is not attracted to us. He is not "in-love" with us as we commonly mean that term today. There is a difference.

Because God is complete within Himself, His love is completely free and gracious. It comes with no strings attached because God does not need anything out of us. His love is given to us without the neediness that characterizes even the best illustrations of human love. His love can be completely sacrificial.

This overly romantic language can be seen in much of the modern worship music and unfortunately is almost sexual in its connotation. Consider the words to the song, "True Love".

Jesus I need to know true love
Deeper than the love found on earth
Take me into the King's Chambers
Cause my love to mature
Let me know the kisses of Your mouth
Let me feel Your embrace
Let me smell the fragrance of Your touch
Let me see Your lovely face.

In the East, the King's Chamber was the place where he was sexually intimate with His wives and concubines.

Or consider the disturbing vision of Bobby Connor in his 2007 Shepherd's Rod proclamation where he leans in longingly to Jesus desiring that his lips meet with the lips of his Lord.

"I extend my face and lips, preparing to kiss the sword–which is placed flat against Christ's lips. As I lean forward to kiss the sword, He turns the sword so that the extremely sharp blades face His lips and mine.........as the sword begins to penetrate, making its way into my lips, I felt only pleasure not pain. So I press even harder as my deepest longing is for my lips to meet the lips of the Master. My heart is filled with the plea of Song of Songs: "Let Him kiss me with the kisses of His mouth, because His mouth is altogether lovely.""[197]

As one reads the vision by Connor, one must remember that Bobby Connor is male. The incarnate Christ who lips he longs to kiss is also male. Couple this with the imagery of a sword cutting into Connor's lips and this vision is utterly grotesque and disturbing.

This literalizing of the metaphor can further be seen in the ridiculous practice currently in vogue of having "marriage" or "remarriage" services to Jesus. At several of "The Call" gatherings, led by Lou Engle, multitudes of young people stood to be married to Jesus. At a local ministry here in Kansas City, a woman dressed in white was carried in on a palanquin couch and a formal marriage ceremony was performed to marry her to Jesus. This "wedding" was attended by friends and family.

The woman changed her name (to Rose) and went on a honeymoon. This makes as much sense as having some type of spiritual surgery service in order to re-attach us as individuals to the Body of Christ. Maybe we could have re-adoption ceremonies to place us back in the family of God or re-citizenship ceremonies to re-establish our citizenship in heaven. This is the height of foolishness! A person is a part of the Bride through new birth, not ceremony.

But the insanity wouldn't be complete without also having divorce ceremonies. These decrees of divorce are written to divorce the church, individual, state or the entire country from Baal. One only has to google "divorce decree from Baal" to bring up several versions. Supposedly using these decrees properly will free the one(s) using it from the consequences of false religion. Here is the version used at "The Call" Nashville which took place July 7, 2007.

> "Divorce Decree for The Call Nashville
>
> We decree that:
>
> ...America's marriage to Baal is terminated, and the fruit of that marriage will come to an end.
>
> We decree that:
>
> ...the stronghold of sexual sin in America is being broken, including sex outside of marriage, homosexuality, incest, adultery, and pornography. We decree that in its place will come a revival of purity and holiness.
>
> We decree that:
>
> ...the sin of covenant breaking, manifesting through divorce, generational breaches, disloyalty, racial strife, lying, disrespect of authority, and broken relationships in general is now being broken in America. We decree that in its place covenant faithfulness will once again prevail.
>
> We decree that:

...witchcraft, idolatry and the power of false religions are broken off of our land.

We decree that:

...the sins of violence and anger—murder, abortion, rape, incest, self-mutilation, cutting and other forms of violence are being broken off of America.

We decree that:

...in this divorce settlement we receive custody of the children. We decree that Baal and Molech will not continue to steal, kill, and destroy our children, but rather that a great awakening is coming to America that will save a generation.

We decree that:

...America is turning back to God and His Son, Jesus Christ, and that we are renewing covenant with Him through Jesus Christ. We declare that love is stronger than death, that the fire of love for God is stronger than the fire of lust. We decree that America will once again burn with holy passion for God."[198]

For the readers of this book who are not familiar with the language and theology of this movement, one should remember that those participating in this activity fundamentally believe that their decree alone created a reality in the supernatural realm. In other words, they really believed that the speaking of this decree would bring about change in the supernatural realm that would be manifested in the natural realm. In this regard, the worldview of the prophetic is not significantly different from that of the Word Faith Movement. I'm sure the authors of this decree meant well. Having spent a brief amount of time in the past being involved in some of the activities of Strategic Level Spiritual Warfare, I have no doubt that the tens of thousands of people, primarily young people who made this decree and others like it at various meetings around the country were very sincere. I have no doubt that they felt very powerful and important. But this is pure nonsense. Space does not permit a full discussion of the errant approach to Scripture that under girds this type of activity except to say that it is based on a false understanding of Old Testament covenant principles relating to Israel. But while I'm sure this was a highly emotional moment for those

173

who participated, it is pure mysticism and a complete waste of time. At the time of this writing it has been over four years since this event. Have any of these decrees come to pass? It is no wonder that people in this movement ultimately burn out. The answer for our nation is the preaching of the gospel not the making of decrees. It is the gospel that is the power of God unto salvation. It is the message of Jesus Christ and Him crucified that can turn men and women from darkness to light. It is the transforming power of grace that will set them free from bondage to sin. The church is being diverted from its true mission into activities that feel powerful but produce little.

Literalizing the metaphor of the Bride can also create a good deal of gender tension among males. Andrew Strom is correct when he writes that this practice is effeminate at best. Normal males in regular life are forced in prayer and worship to conceive of themselves in a feminine role. This is beyond the bounds of what the Scripture is teaching. Jonathon Rice ponders whether or not this might have some bearing on the rash of homosexual scandals within the Charismatic wing of the church. Only God knows for certain.

But in addition to all of that, this emphasis of the Bridal paradigm seems to make subjective emotional feelings the height of spirituality. Yes, the first commandment is to love the Lord our God with all of our heart, soul, mind and strength. But this means far more than just some blush of emotion that we get while in prayer or worship. It is not difficult to work up an emotional state while attending a conference of any kind. Feelings alone are never the ultimate goal, especially when they are based on teachings that lack foundational truth. This love for God will ultimately be manifested in obedience, holiness and growth or it has no lasting value. Jesus said, "He that has My commandments and keeps them is the one that loves Me..." (John 14:21) Agape love is much deeper than an emotional high that comes during a meeting filled with manipulative activity and moving music.
The Bridal paradigm is just one more example of the prophetic community re-interpreting Christianity. It alters our view of God, the atonement, and the church. It sounds Biblical but it is not Biblical.

Jesus didn't build the church

And finally, we find that, despite His promise to the contrary, Jesus didn't build the church. In her incredibly self-aggrandizing book, Choo Thomas relates the following encounter with Jesus,

"My precious daughter, I came to tell you and show you some things. You have many things to do for Me before I come for My people. You must be patient with Me. Many of My people are not ready for me to come for them. My kingdom is completely ready for anyone who wants to enter.

Every believer must stand before Me at the end, and many of those who don't live by My words will be very disappointed.

I want all of My children to come to My kingdom. Whoever reads this book, I want them to believe and realize how they have to live in the world in order to enter the kingdom.

Daughter, I will bless you until you can't contain it. I will bless you more than you ever expected or asked for."

"Lord, the only thing I want to be blessed with is being able to serve You and make You happy."

"Daughter, you have already made Me so happy. That is why I chose you for this work. You and your husband will serve Me greatly until the last day. Tell your husband I am pleased with the work he is doing on this book.

After everything is done, I want you to build My church."[199]

A careful reading of the previous dialogue will reveal a number of serious problems. First we see that Jesus can't come and establish His kingdom until His people, in this case specifically Choo Thomas, do something. Secondly we notice that entering the kingdom is the result of what one does not grace and that not all of Christ's children will get to enter His kingdom. Fortunately, the church will have Choo's book to tell them how they should live. The reader is constantly impressed with how very important Choo Thomas is. The reader sees that she was chosen for this work because she is so pleasing to the Lord. But moving past all of these issues, one notices that Christ has given Choo Thomas a very special commission. She will build His church.

Even elementary Bible students might remember the words of Jesus at this point.

"...and on this rock I will build my church and the gates of hell shall not prevail against it." Matt 16:18b

Jesus Christ Himself has claimed the task of building the church. He has not delegated it to another. He is the author and finisher of the faith. He is the foundation, the Cornerstone. The building of the church is His work. It is the Lord who "added to the church those who should be saved." This is not to deny that Christ works through His children. But it is His work. It is difficult to believe that this message came from the Lord Jesus.

So once again when the words of the prophets are weighed in the balance they come up wanting. The Jesus being proclaimed in much of the modern apostolic and prophetic movement is very different from the Jesus of Scripture. For all of their talk of Jesus and all of the love songs being written to Him, the theology of the movement remains largely man-centered.

CHAPTER NINE

What Did the Cross Accomplish?
Modern Prophets and the Atonement

"I used to think that whoever was 'saved' and went to church would go to heaven and wear a beautiful wedding gown. I was wrong." – Choo Thomas

What did the work of Christ on the cross accomplish? Is this work once and for all? Is this work alone sufficient? What happens to a person in salvation?

The Bible teaches that the sacrifice of Christ was completely sufficient to satisfy the wrath of God, that it was once for all (Heb. 10) and that this atonement is complete in order to bring us all the way to glorification. (Rom. 8) In fact Jesus emphatically declared that He would not lose one of the children that God brings to Him.

> "All that the Father gives me will come to me, and whoever comes to me I will never cast out. For I have come down from heaven, not to do my own will but the will of him who sent me. And this is the will of him who sent me, that I should lose nothing of all that he has given me, but should raise it up on the last day. For this is the will of my Father, that everyone who looks on the Son and believes in him should have eternal life, and I will raise him up on the last day." John 6:37-40

Once again, these are critical issues and here again we see the modern prophets contradicting and denying essential Christian doctrine. The words of the prophets express confusion with regard to this fundamental issue.

The Sufficiency of the Atonement- Not all Christians go to heaven

We touched on Choo Thomas's view of salvation briefly in a previous chapter, but the "gospel" presented in her enormously popular book deserves closer scrutiny. In this book we find that salvation is really not all of grace but rather is dependent upon what we do. Thomas writes,

> "Innocence, trust, purity of heart, fascination, a sense of wonder, belief, joy, happiness, present-moment living-all these are some of the magical qualities of childhood that God wants us to exhibit to get to heaven."[200]

Notice again that according to Choo Thomas's description salvation is not all of grace. There are character qualities that we must exhibit in order to "get to heaven". In her theology, character is the prerequisite for salvation not the result of having received salvation. It is important to remember the claims made by Thomas which were discussed in chapter 2. According to Thomas every word of her book is true and is given to us exactly as Jesus gave them to her. If Thomas is correct then the atonement of Christ is not sufficient.

This is exactly the position that Thomas articulates in her book. Consider the following revelation she claims to have received:

> "When we got to the top, I looked over a brown and lifeless valley. Everywhere there was brown. The whole region seemed to be filled with dead grass.

> "I noticed multitudes of people who were wearing sand-colored robes roaming aimlessly in the vicinity of the pit's yawning mouth. Their heads were hanging low, and they looked very dejected and hopeless.

> "Who are these people, Lord?" I asked.

> *"They are disobedient 'Christians"*

> "How long will they have to stay in this barren, lifeless place?

> *"Forever, My daughter. The only ones who will enter My kingdom are the pure of heart-My obedient children."* [201]

So once again we see that the atonement of Christ is not enough. This is not a slip of the pen but is central to Thomas's theology. She writes later,

"My hope is that every Christian will be raptured and be able to enter the kingdom of God, instead of being left behind or have to go [sic] into the valleys of heaven. The Lord told me so often that whoever is raptured will have to stand before the judgment seat before the wedding takes place. The worst thing that can happen to any Christian is not being raptured or not seeing Jesus' face. This is the reason the Lord showed me the two valleys for disobedient and sinful Christians. I used to think that whoever was 'saved' and went to church would go to heaven and wear a beautiful wedding gown. I was wrong. The only ones who will see Jesus' face and wear the wedding gown are those whose hearts are pure as water. God is so holy that defiled things cannot enter His kingdom. That is why the Lord prepared the valleys for those who are not holy enough to enter His kingdom."[202]

Thomas is correct in her view that unholy things cannot enter the kingdom of God but in Thomas's view the answer to this dilemma is not the cross but one's own efforts to perfect oneself. Thomas, whether realizing it or not, has fallen into pure Pelagianism. Her understanding of the atonement is completely defective. On the cross Christ did more than just pay our sin debt, thus bringing us back to zero. He also granted to us His righteousness. We are able to enter the kingdom because we have been clothed in the righteousness of Christ. We have been made acceptable in the Beloved. We can boldly come before the throne of grace because of the new and living way made for us by the blood of the Lamb. As the Scriptures declare,

"For our sake he made him to be sin who knew no sin, so that in him we might become the righteousness of God." 2 Cor. 5:21

This is truly good news. This is a salvation that exalts the grace of God and meets the need of sinful man. The gospel proclaimed by Thomas is hopeless for sinners are unable to reform themselves and could never attain to the righteousness required to enter the presence of God. In Thomas's gospel, much like that of cults, the cross is merely the starting point. The cross gives man the opportunity to save himself by good works and righteous effort. The warning of Michael Horton seems particularly relevant here. He writes,

"I have identified Pelagianism as the default setting of the human heart: the religion of self-salvation. Much of Christianity in America, as elsewhere, stops short of being fully Pelagian. If asked directly whether we can save ourselves by moral effort apart from grace, I suspect most evangelicals would answer in the negative. However, grace is primarily seen by evangelicals as much as by the medieval church as divine assistance for the process of moral transformation rather than a one-sided divine rescue."[203]

Horton's comments are well said and apply directly to the teachings espoused by Thomas. For Thomas, grace is the divine assistance so that man can transform himself into someone fit for heaven. Biblical grace is a divine rescue done by God alone.

Further, the Bible only tells of two final destinations for the soul but Thomas reveals a third and fourth. Here those who are not quite fit for heaven but who have apparently been delivered from hell, wander in a desert for all of eternity. Thomas's teaching has more in line with the Roman Catholic idea of purgatory than it does with Biblical Christianity. Here is another example of prophets establishing new doctrines prophetically despite all of their claims that this prerogative belongs to Scripture alone.

The Sufficiency of the Atonement- Jesus must offer His blood yearly

According to Bob Jones in an interview with Steve Shultz of Elijah List for Prophetic.TV, Jesus comes every year on the Day of Atonement to offer His blood again in the Holy of Holies in order to buy us another year of life.[204] He expands this teaching to state that all Christians should look to God for revelation on the Day of Atonement because that is the day that we must all pass under the "Shepherd's Rod" for God to evaluate our lives and ministries. It is a yearly judgment. Jones attempts to ground this teaching in Scripture by referring to Leviticus 27:32. Multiple prophets give "Shepherd's Rod" prophecies yearly around the Day of Atonement. This is another doctrine and practice that has become so entrenched within the prophetic movement that it is rarely, if ever, questioned.

When asked by Shultz how this teaching can be reconciled with the book of Hebrews which states that Christ was offered once for all, Jones states that Jesus was offered once for all for salvation but this offering is for our promotion or demotion. Here again we see the notion that the cross was enough to get one started, but after that, there is more to be done. As one progresses through the interview, one finds that though Jones attempts to tip his hat to grace by saying that the blood of Jesus offered yearly buys us another year, the real work is done by the individual. Jones states that any place in us that God sees maturity, He opens up destiny. We need to be constantly reminded of Paul's admonition to the Galatians,

> "Let me ask you only this: Did you receive the Spirit by the works of the law or by hearing with faith? Are you so foolish? Having begun by the Spirit are you now being perfected by the flesh?" Gal. 3:2-3

In the book of Hebrews, we find that the sacrifice of Christ is greater than the offering of bulls and goats because these offerings had to be repeated. Christ's sacrifice on the other hand was indeed once for all and it was perfect and complete. The author of Hebrews states,

> "And every priest stands daily at his service, offering repeatedly the same sacrifices, which can never take away sins. But when Christ had offered for all time a single sacrifice for sins, he sat down at the right hand of God, waiting from that time until his enemies should be made a footstool for his feet. For by a single offering he has perfected for all time those who are being sanctified." Heb. 10:11-14

The author of Hebrews does not make any distinction in the offering of Christ, nor does any other author in the New Testament. In requiring Jesus to present His blood yearly, Jones has reduced the sacrifice of Christ to being little better than the blood of animals. One wonders if this will have to continue for all of eternity.

The Cross as a Dowry

Another interesting twist on the atonement that is presented by the modern prophets is that the cross was the dowry that Jesus had to pay to receive His bride. This teaching is directly related to the Bridal Paradigm which, as discussed elsewhere, becomes its own hermeneutic through which all of Scripture is evaluated.

Allen Hood in a teaching on "The Cross in Bridal Perspective" states, "Why do you think there's a dowry on the earth? You think that just popped up in somebody's mind one day? Ok. A dowry. The man's gotta pay something to get her. You think that just popped up? No! That was born in the heart of God. He's going to pay a high price."[205]

For the sake of clarity, what Hood calls a dowry is most normally called a bride price. The bride price was paid by the groom for the right of marrying the bride and was to compensate the family for the loss of her labor and as a statement of her value. A dowry is normally that which is paid to the bride by the Father and was to insure her future security in the event that the husband failed to provide for her. Hood uses this word to refer to the bride price so we will do so as well in order to be consistent.

Several things about this should be noted. The most striking is that there is not one place in the Scripture that refers to the cross as a dowry. And the illustration really doesn't fit because there is no family of the bride to whom the dowry would be paid. Additionally, a dowry is paid because of the value of the bride but according to the Scripture, we did not have anything inherent in us that deserved any price at all. What we deserved was judgment. As emotionally satisfying as this concept is, it must be admitted that it is truly a complete reinterpretation of the gospel. Once again, there is no place where Scripture refers to the cross in this way.

The atonement is not a minor issue. It is the heart of the Christian message. Teachers of God's word simply do not have the right to interpret the atonement any way they wish, any way that they find emotionally satisfying. The Scriptures primarily, though admittedly not exclusively, speak of the cross in terms of substitutionary atonement, propitiation of wrath, and legal acquittal. It is the language of the courtroom not the language of the romance novel that fills Scripture.

One is on dangerous ground when one begins to reinterpret doctrine like the atonement by using metaphors and symbols that God Himself has not used.

Fused into God

While some of the modern prophets undermine the sufficiency of the atonement, leaving much of the work to man, others see the atonement as bringing man almost into complete Deity.

In a foundational teaching entitled, "Fellowshipping with the Holy Spirit", IHOP founder, Mike Bickle teaches that the spirit of the redeemed person and the Holy Spirit become synonymous. A number of quotations will be given lest it be assumed that this is merely a slip of the tongue that does not reflect Bickle's true intention. Please consider the following quotations.

"As you learn to contact your spirit, you're going to find number one, there will be a spontaneous flow of wisdom coming into your awareness. See, God dwells in your spirit, right? So your spirit and God's spirit become one. So it is accurate to say that wisdom flows from God's spirit, or I can say that wisdom flows from your spirit. I can call it God's spirit or your spirit. The terminology makes no difference because they're one and the Scripture uses them interchangably.[206]

Of course, Bickle offers no examples of where the Scripture uses "our spirit" and "God's Spirit" interchangeably. We are just supposed to accept this because he says so. Bickle continues:

"That power is in your spirit the day you were born again. That power, that wisdom and those desires rise up into the realm of your soul and then you experience them. So it's vital to understand that... **because until you learn to fellowship with your spirit, or to fellowship with God's Spirit, it's all the same thing,** you can from the day that you were born again and your spirit is made one with God's, from that day forward, **you can say, "My spirit said to me..." or you can say, "God's Spirit said to you..." it makes no difference the terminology you use because your spirit and God's Spirit are one** from that day forward."[207]

Notice that Bickle repeatedly indicates that the spirit of the believer and the Spirit of God are one in such a way that there is no distinction between them. The subject/object distinction between us and God is completely removed. He then gives believers the following advice:

"always go inward to meet the Spirit of God and to develop a life in him. And then, as the Word of the Lord rises, as the burden of the Lord rises, as the wisdom of the Lord rises, I go right to the Father in worship and in prayer and it's effective and it's powerful."[208]

Never, not one time, does the Scripture indicate that believers are to go inward to meet the Spirit of God. The practice of going within oneself to find God has more in common with the mystical practices of Eastern religions generally and with Yoga or Transcendental Meditation in particular than it does with Biblical teaching.

"Beholding the spirit of God is when you set your mind on your spirit or on God's spirit, it's interchangeable, or on the glory of God, it makes no difference. And with an attitude of faith and with an attitude of obedience, **I release the activity of God's spirit in the realm of my soul."**[209]

Once again, there are so many issues with the above quotations that it is difficult to know where to begin. The Bible does not use the spirit of the man and the Holy Spirit interchangeably. Though God does graciously condescend to indwell those who are born again, there always remains a distinction between the spirit of the man and the Holy Spirit. The Spirit abides with us and in us, according to the Scriptures, but He does not replace us. Nor does He fuse with us in such a way that we become some sort of god-man in our spirit. Secondly, as previously stated, we are never told in the Scripture to "go inward" to meet with God as Bickle instructs. The Bible does not conceptualize our relationship in this way for once again it blurs the distinction between the believer and God Himself. Bickle expands on this erroneous concept in his series on contemplative prayer, a practice that will be considered in detail later.

Michael Tyrell echoes a similar teaching when he states,

> "Suddenly, the Lord gently spoke, "Part of you knows the truth and sees what I see, because he's sitting with me, let him speak." Then I saw it! In our triune nature, 1/3 of us is perfect because our spirit is seated in Heavenly places, and our spirit sees and knows. Our body is earth bound, but our spirit is in close proximity to our Father in Heaven. Thus, we can say, "On earth as it is in Heaven."
>
> It's tragic that this is a stretch for us to understand, but we're certainly not the first to experience it. Turn to 2 Corinthians 12:1-5, "It is not expedient for me doubtless to glory. I will come to visions and revelations of the Lord. I knew a man in Christ above 14 years ago (whether in the body I cannot tell, or whether out of the body I cannot tell, God knoweth). Such a one caught up to the third heaven.
>
> And I know such a man (whether in the body or out of the body, I cannot tell, God knoweth). How that he was "caught up" into paradise (3rd heaven) and heard unspeakable words, which it is not lawful for a man to utter."
>
> There is no doubt Paul was in Heaven, the problem is he couldn't tell if he was all there or partially there. We know he was there in the Spirit, for our mortal bodies cannot glory in His presence. This is huge!"[210]

Tyrell takes a common though disputed view of human nature, the tripartite view, and then declares that 1/3 of us is already perfect because of the atonement of Christ, something Scripture never declares. He then takes another great leap beyond the truth of Scripture to say that our spirits are already seated (actually) in heaven, therefore our spirit already "sees and knows". So the problem then becomes that we must get in touch with our spirit in order to get this revelation knowledge. Tyrell does not explain how it is possible for our spirit to actually be in heaven and yet still with us nor does he explain what it means for our spirit to see what God sees. He simply asserts it to be so.

But this is not Biblical. When Paul talks about us being raised with Christ and seated with Him in the heavenly places, he was speaking positionally. We do have access to the Father through Jesus. We do have the delegated authority that Christ has given to the believer. But there is not a part of us that is already in heaven and has perfect knowledge. We still "know in part and prophesy in part".

Contemplative Prayer Digression. Transcendental Meditation for Christians.

One of the truly alarming trends within Christianity today across many spectrums is the growth of contemplative prayer, sometimes referred to as "centering prayer". This form of prayer, which has been practiced primarily by Catholic mystics until the present time, bears little resemblance to Biblical prayer which is mentally active. In contemplative prayer, the Christian becomes mentally passive and merely experiences and encounters something of the divine. The Scriptures never teach anything remotely close to this kind of activity. I want to deal with this subject here because of the relationship that it has with Bickle's idea of Fellowshipping with the Holy Spirit. In fact, in many ways the two teachings are synonymous.

The prophetic community is certainly not alone in its endorsement of contemplative Christianity but it is definitely a problem that is rampant within the prophetic. It may go under many titles including soaking prayer or even "marinating in the Holy Spirit".

The fact is that contemplative prayer has much more in common with Buddhism and other Eastern religious practices than it does to anything Christian. In order to evaluate this teaching we must first understand it.

To that end we will allow one of the leaders within the movement to define the practice for us. Consider the words of Father Thomas Keating, one of the leading proponents of Contemplative or Centering Prayer, whose books are found in large number at Bickle's International House of Prayer along with the works of other Roman Catholic Mystics. I have chosen to include a very lengthy quote to avoid the charge that I am taking the author out of context. Keating writes,

The Method of Centering Prayer

Centering Prayer is a method designed to facilitate the development of contemplative prayer by preparing our faculties to cooperate with this gift. It is an attempt to present the teaching of earlier time (e.g. The Cloud of Unknowing) in an updated form and to put a certain order and regularity into it. It is not meant to replace other kinds of prayer; it simply puts other kinds of prayer into a new and fuller perspective. During the time of prayer we consent to God's presence and action within. At other times our attention moves outward to discover God's presence everywhere.

The Guidelines

Choose a sacred word as the symbol of your intention to consent to God's presence and action within.

Sitting comfortably and with eyes closed, settle briefly and silently introduce the sacred word as the symbol of your consent to God's presence and action within.

When you become aware of thoughts, return ever-so-gently to the sacred word.

At the end of the prayer period, remain in silence with eyes closed for a couple of minutes.

Explanation of the Guidelines

"Choose a sacred word as the symbol of your intention to consent to God's presence and action within." (cf. *Open Mind, Open Heart*, chap. 5) The sacred word expresses our intention to be in God's presence and to yield to the divine action.

The sacred word should be chosen during a brief period of prayer asking the Holy Spirit to inspire us with one that is especially suitable for us.

Examples: Lord, Jesus, Abba, Father, Mother

Other possibilities: Love, Peace, Shalom

Having chosen a sacred word, we do not change it during the prayer period, for that would be to start thinking again.

A simple inward gaze upon God may be more suitable for some persons than the sacred word. In this case, one consents to God's presence and action by turning inwardly toward God as if gazing upon him. The same guidelines apply to the sacred gaze as to the sacred word.

"Sitting comfortably and with eyes closed, settle briefly and silently introduce the sacred word as the symbol of your consent to God's presence and action within."

By "sitting comfortably" is meant relatively comfortably; not so comfortably that we encourage sleep, but sitting comfortably enough to avoid thinking about the discomfort of our bodies during this time of prayer.

Whatever sitting position we choose, we keep the back straight. If we fall asleep, we continue the prayer for a few minutes upon awakening if we can spare the time.

Praying in this way after a main meal encourages drowsiness. Better to wait an hour at least before Centering Prayer. Praying in this way just before retiring may disturb one's sleep pattern.

We close our eyes to let go of what is going on around and within us. We introduce the sacred word inwardly and as gently as laying a feather on a piece of absorbent cotton.

"When you become aware of thoughts, return ever-so-gently to the sacred word."

"Thoughts" is an umbrella term for every perception including sense perceptions, feelings, images, memories, reflections, and commentaries. Thoughts are a normal part of Centering Prayer.

By "returning ever-so-gently to the sacred word", a minimum of effort is indicated. This is the only activity we initiate during the time of Centering Prayer.

During the course of our prayer, the sacred word may become vague or even disappear.

"At the end of the prayer period, remain in silence with eyes closed for a couple of minutes."

If this prayer is done in a group, the leader may slowly recite the Our Father during the additional 2 or 3 minutes, while the others listen.

The additional 2 or 3 minutes give the psyche time to readjust to the external senses and enable us to bring the atmosphere of silence into daily life."[211]

Mike Bickle has done more than perhaps any other teacher to introduce this mystical practice into the prophetic community. The bookstore at IHOP literally abounds with the writings of Keating, Nouwen, Pennington and other mystics. In his own series on Contemplative Prayer, after telling his listeners that they are going to have to cross the aisle and study the Catholics in order to really learn about this type of prayer because there are virtually no Protestants that write about it other than Richard Foster, Bickle attempts to justify this practice Biblically. To do so, he resorts to his standard methods of Scripture twisting. The passage he selects is 2 Cor. 3:18.

"And we all with unveiled face, beholding the glory of the Lord, are being transformed into the same image from one degree of glory to another. For this comes from the Lord who is the Spirit."

Bickle refers to the practice of Contemplative Prayer as beholding the glory of the Lord within oneself.[212]

Taken in context, this passage has nothing to do with sitting mindlessly and passively consenting to the activity of God within oneself, whatever that means. The passage actually clearly refers to beholding the glory of God through His word. Consider the broader passage,

> "Since we have such a hope, we are very bold, not like Moses, who would put a veil over his face so that the Israelites might not gaze at the outcome of what was being brought to an end. But their minds were hardened. **For to this day, when they read the old covenant, that same veil remains unlifted,** because only through Christ is it taken away. Yes, to this day, **whenever Moses is read** a veil lies over their hearts. But when one turns to the Lord, the veil is removed. Now the Lord is the Spirit and where the Spirit of the Lord is, there is freedom. And we all **with unveiled face beholding the glory of the Lord,** are being transformed into the same image from one degree of glory to another. For this comes from the Lord who is the Spirit." (2 Cor. 3: 12-18)

Paul is not speaking about Contemplative Prayer at all in this passage. Notice that he says that the unbelieving Jews have a veil over them when the read Moses and the old covenant because of their hardness of heart. But in Christ this veil is taken away. The unbelieving Jews do not see the glory of God in the old covenant but believers can. Therefore Paul is talking about the ability to behold the glory of God, not in some inward, mystical experience, but rather through the study of His Word. We behold the glory of the Lord in the study of the Scriptures because in Christ they are no longer veiled to us.

In the same message Bickle claims that contemplative prayer is the most effective and dynamic way to fullness of God in Ephesians 3:19, "to know the love of Christ that surpasses knowledge, that you may be filled with all the fullness of God." But despite the boldness of his claim, Bickle is unable to provide one clear passage that even remotely looks like the teachings of Keating and others like him. Nor can he provide one clear example of any saint, either Old Testament or New Testament that ever engaged in the practice. The Bible does not teach Contemplative Prayer either by precept or example.

After nearly four complete sessions spent demagoguing on the need for the church today to practice contemplative prayer, Bickle finally gets around to an explanation of how to do it. Many IHOP defenders claim that what is meant by contemplative prayer at IHOP is significantly different than the mindless, wordless, trance-like meditation advocated by the Catholic mystics in spite of the fact that Bickle himself holds the mystics up as examples. Therefore it is important to see what Bickle actually states. Here is a lengthy transcription from his message.

"This is my name for Him and I call Him this, and I call Him Consuming Fire. Consuming Fire seal me with love. I put together Song of Solomon and Deuteronomy 4. Consuming Fire, Consuming Fire seal me with love. And one thing I've understood...well I'll just do all three of them. The second name I give the Holy Spirit when I call Him. I call Him Majestic Brightness. Majestic Brightness fascinate me with beauty. Fascinate me with God's beauty, with the beauty of redemption that you've imparted to us, how beautiful I am within You in the grace of God, show me beauty, many dimensions of beauty. And the third one, I call Him "River of Life immerse me in Your presence. Immerse me!" Now these three prayers, I use them a lot. I was taught by the contemplative books some years ago, that this.. that you don't want a lot of words. You don't want...You're not machine gunning your prayers. (speaking very fast) Holy Spirit immerse me. Please immerse me. Please, please (becomes unintelligible) It's not like that. As a matter of fact I start for a few moments and I start gazing on this bright, radiant Person. He is life. He is God the Holy Spirit. He is very God Himself. He is not just representative. He is as much God as the Father and the Son and I go, and I gaze "Consuming Fire." And I start with the phrases, "Consuming Fire seal me with love. And I'm using Song of Solomon 8:6, seal me with love. And I do the phrases a little bit. And I do it and I pause for a minute or two. And after a few moments I throw away all the phrases and I just say, "Consuming". I reduce the title, (whispering) "Fire" . Wait....one... two...three. It's not like I'm counting. But I'm giving you the idea. It's not rushed. Now I've got the whole sentence in my being deeply. "Fire". I'm talking to Him. He's a person. "Fire". I'll pray in the Spirit. And I use my prayer language. In 1 Corinthians 14:18 Paul says, "I pray in tongues more than all of you." And I use my prayer language and I gaze into that radiant, majestic brightness, that consuming fire. I just praise You. Now I don't mean pray in the spirit hard and fast, just every now and then. And it becomes in a real short amount of time wordless. There's no words. I'm just...(very long silence)...Gazing at the Fire. Pray in the spirit, quiet. And when I get distracted I use the English words. When my mind gets distracted and I get easily distracted I'll go back to words because when I say the words even gently out loud it makes my mind be obedient. So I really use the words because of the weakness of my mind to bring it back into order. And then when I'm focused, and there's a lock-in factor, there really is. I don't know how to say it theologically but there's a lock in point. And I don't say the words. And then a minute, two, three, five, ten. It's normally one or two minutes later and I get distracted and I use the words again and I bring it into the lock in point. And I get distracted. And I find that is such a powerful reality..."[213]

A careful comparison of Bickle's teaching with that of Thomas Keating shows that he is completely in agreement with the practices of Roman Catholic mystics, past and present. The only difference is the addition of speaking in tongues.

In reality, this area of Bickle's theology much like every other area of his theology is developed more by his personal experience than Biblical study. In this same message, Bickle testifies extensively of his affection for the writings of Madame Guyon, who was the true source of this teaching for Bickle. He states that for nearly a month he didn't read anything but Madame Guyon and John G. Lake. Further, he states that he routinely buys and read every book on Contemplative Prayer that he can find regardless of who it is authored by. He says that many are good and some are not but his hunger in this area is so great that he will search for any nugget that he can find to help him in this area. So it becomes clear that Bickle did not develop this practice in his own life by determining that it was Biblical through a study of the Scriptures. Bickle began engaging in the practice first. The Bible verses are just tacked on in order to attempt to justify something that Bickle finds experientially satisfying regardless of whether or not the verses have anything to do with the subject at hand. In this same way, Bickle has deceived countless others into believing that they are engaging in an activity that is God-ordained when in reality, nothing could be further from the truth.

This practice is not even remotely Christian or Biblical. The Bible never instructs us to go inward to contact God. The Bible never instructs us to make our minds passive in order to encounter God. Biblical meditation is active not passive. The mind is actively thinking upon the Scriptures or the attributes of God. David wrote, "O how I love thy law it is my meditation all of the day." Or consider again the words of the Lord to Joshua, "And this book of the law shall not depart out of thy mouth but you shall meditate therein day and night for then you will make your way prosperous and then you will have good success." (Josh. 1:8) Christian contemplatives are unable to provide even one clear passage on the subject or one clear biblical example of the practice. Surely if this was, as Bickle claims, the "most dynamic pathway into the fullness of God", then we could expect that the apostle who prayed for the church to know such fullness would have provided instruction on the topic somewhere in one of his epistles. But such is not the case. In the face of the absolute absence of any biblical mandate, Bickle resorts to his all too familiar tactic of Scripture twisting in order to justify what he wants to do anyway. And sadly, it never occurred to Bickle to consider that the reason few Protestants have written on this subject or practiced it is because it is actually not found in Scripture. Once again the desire for experience trumps the desire to be Biblical.

E.W. Kenyon strikes again

In previous chapters we have discussed how modern prophetic teachers, borrowing from the errant views of E.W. Kenyon have been led into heresy. This is true in the area of their understanding of the atonement as well.

Remember, that in the scenario posited by Kenyon and his followers, God gave dominion over the earth to man. This was essentially an absolute dominion. When man fell, this dominion was turned over to Satan. God essentially lost dominion over the earth. The cross was then the means whereby God could once again gain legal access to the earth and regain the dominion that had been lost by man.

Ed Silvoso states, "Before Jesus victory at Calvary, God would not become a trespasser by challenging Satan directly in matters related to man and the world under his control. If he did so Satan would have called God a trespasser."[214]

Leaving for a moment the discussion of the faulty premise that God ever lost dominion over man or the earth, there is another issue. In Jesus ministry He frequently exercised authority over demons and directly challenged Satan in matters related to man. All of this was before Calvary. Not once did a demon reply, "Trespasser!" Instead, without exception they yielded to the sovereign authority of Jesus Christ.

The idea that the cross was somehow necessary for Jesus to have "legal right" and authority is a well-established dogma in the prophetic community.

Rick Joyner, for instance, writes, "Immediately after His victory on the cross and His resurrection, Jesus had legal authority to cast the devil into the lake of fire and to establish His kingdom on the earth."[215]

Shawn Bolz echoes this same sentiment when he says, "When Jesus paid the ultimate price on the cross, every force in the universe was subsumed under His jurisdiction. Every natural dynamic was forced to submit to God's spiritual laws. Jesus won back the keys to the kingdoms of earth."[216]

Once again, the supreme fallacy of this position can be demonstrated by noting that God never for one second lost control of or dominion over the earth. The entire account of the Scriptures reveal God as the sovereign ruler over all. And the atonement is never spoken of as giving Jesus the legal right to rule. Jesus did not have to die to gain legal right over the earth. Christ died in order to die as the substitute for sin and satisfy the divine wrath. But that's just not good enough for the modern prophets.

Perhaps the most frightening statement of all comes from Steve Thompson which we quoted earlier. He states,

> "Jesus, having one back authority on earth, could now mediate and rule in the affairs of earth. However, Jesus did not stay on the earth to rule it. He ascended to the Father and is seated at His right hand. So who now is responsible to rule and reign in the earth? Believe it or not, the church, which is the body of Christ."[217]

Thompson begins with the standard idea that Jesus won back authority on earth. Then he digresses even further into false doctrine. First Thompson assumes that because Jesus is not present on the earth in His physical body that He is not reigning and ruling over the earth. However the apostle Paul would disagree for he writes concerning Christ, "For He [Jesus] must reign [present tense] until He has put all His enemies under His feet." (1 Cor. 15:25 comments added) Jesus is now reigning and will do so until He has defeated the last enemy, death and turns the kingdom over to His Father. The physical presence of Christ is not required in order for Him to reign. But Thompson is not done for he now continues building his house of cards by asserting that it is the church that is to exercise dominion over the earth. This is how he builds support for his belief in dominion theology.

The most frightening aspect of this however comes when one reconsiders the entire scheme. God gave Adam dominion. Adam turned his dominion over to Satan through sin. Jesus regained dominion through His death on the cross. Jesus now gives this regained dominion over to the church. Is it therefore possible that the church could once again give dominion back to

Satan through disobedience the same way that Adam did when he rebelled against God? Could God find Himself back in the same sorry state that He was after the fall, unable to move on the earth without trespassing on Satan's property?

Fortunately, since the reign belongs to Christ and not the church we don't have to worry.

Become the Melchizedek Priesthood

Another teaching being perpetrated by the new prophets that misunderstands the atonement, diminishes the uniqueness of Christ, and brings the church closer to the kingdom of the cults, is the idea that the church will become the Melchizedek priesthood.

One of the earliest of the modern prophets to articulate this doctrine is Bob Jones. In an interview conducted by Mike Bickle at Kansas City Fellowship discussing the New Breed (sometimes also called the "elected seed"), which is just a modified version of dominion theology, Jones stated the following:

> "Not only will they have the word of God in them, that's the **foundation – apostles and prophets** – but they will have the word of God in them and they will have the **power** with the word – the Spirit. And the barrenness of the church will be over and the **foundations** of the church will be raised up. The walls will be raised up. You will see the glorious church begin to come in and you will begin to **birth** it. It will take probably another 15-20 years to get some of you into some level of maturity. There will be neither male or female in this. There will be maturity – what God is seeking. And He will be raising the saints up – to that level. First He will bring the **five-fold [ministry]**, but there is a ministry after the five-fold called the Ministry of Perfection – the Melchisedek Priesthood."[218]

Earlier, in the same message, Jones explains the role and purpose that this "Ministry of Perfection" will have in the end-time plan of God.

> "They themselves will be that generation that's raised up to put death itself underneath their feet and to glorify Christ in every way. And the church that is raising up in the government will be the head and the covering for them. So that that glorious church might be revealed in the last days, because the Lord Jesus is worthy to be lifted up by a church that has reached the full maturity of the God-Man!"[219]

We will discuss the idea that the church could be the Melchizedek priesthood momentarily, but for now it should be pointed out that Jones' statements that this generation of Christians will be the ones who put "death itself underneath their feet" and that reaches the "full maturity of the God-Man" come very close to the doctrine of immortalization taught by Latter Rain/Dominion Theology teachers. Bickle repeatedly claims not to be a proponent of Dominion Theology however, the deeper one looks into the doctrines he teaches, and the ministries he supports, the more apparent it becomes that Bickle's own eschatology is dominionist to the core despite all of his protests to the contrary.

Paul Keith Davis is another in the prophetic community proclaiming that the church, or at least a segment of the church, is the Melchizedek Priesthood. Davis writes,

> "This apostolic reformation will ignite the reestablishment and functioning of the Church in genuine spiritual power and authority. From this foundation, the Church will be able to soar to even greater places in God that await us—the Melchizedek Priesthood and a deeper apprehension of being sons and daughters who have overcome and discovered rest in God."[220]

Kirk Bennett, the man responsible for training prophets at IHOP for several years states the following:

> "…The Messiah was the forerunner of a different priesthood according to the order of Melchizedek and we were to enter into a whole priestly order with Him. And we are all under that priestly order even now. We are all part of that order of Melchizedek."[221]

There is no hint anywhere in the pages of Scripture that the Messiah came as the forerunner of a different order of priesthood or that believers enter into the priestly order of Melchizedek along with Jesus. This is Bennett reading IHOP theology back into the pages of Scripture. The book of Hebrews is repeatedly very clear that the Melchizedek priesthood belongs to Jesus. No one else qualifies for this order. Jesus stands alone as the eternal High Priest. Note what the Scripture actually does say about this Priest.

> "During the days of Jesus' life on earth, he offered up prayers and petitions with loud cries and tears to the one who could save him from death, and he was heard because of his reverent submission. Although

he was a son, he learned obedience from what he suffered and, once made perfect, he became the source of eternal salvation for all who obey him and was designated by God to be high priest in the order of Melchizedek." (Heb. 5:7-10)

Hebrews 6 is even more clear:

"We have this hope as an anchor for the soul, firm and secure. It enters the inner sanctuary behind the curtain, where Jesus, who went before us has entered on our behalf. He has become a high priest forever, in the order of Melchizedek." (Hebrews 6:19-20)

Some translations here state that Jesus entered as a forerunner for us behind the veil. But the meaning here is clearly not that Jesus is the forerunner so that we too can become the Melchizedek Priesthood but rather that Jesus has become the forerunner for us behind the veil, that is into the Holy of Holies the presence of God. Jesus entered into the presence of God on our behalf so that we too may come into His presence. The priesthood belongs to Jesus not to us.

As we come to Hebrews chapter seven the author explains to us how it is that Melchizedek pictures the priesthood of Christ. He writes,

"He is without father or mother or genealogy, having neither beginning of days nor end of life, but resembling the Son of God he continues a priest forever." (Hebrews 7:3)

The author of Hebrews continues,

"For it is clear that our Lord descended from Judah, and in regard to that tribe Moses said nothing about priests. And what we have said is even more clear if another priest like Melchizedek appears, one who has become a priest not on the basis of a regulation as to his ancestry but on the basis of the power of an indestructible life. For it is declared, 'You are a priest forever, in the order of Melchizedek'.......But because Jesus lives forever, he has a permanent priesthood." (Hebrews 7:14-17, 24)

The purpose of this discussion in Hebrews is to show that Jesus brings a better priesthood than the Levitical priesthood. Those priests served for a limited time because each of them died. They ministered with a sacrifice that could never fully take away sin because the sacrifice must be repeated again and again. But Christ has brought a better covenant through a perfect sacrifice and is a priest forever because He never dies. He maintains His priesthood through the power of an indestructible life. Therefore as the Scripture says, "He is able to save to the uttermost those who come to God through Him for He ever lives to make intercession for them." (Hebrews 7:25).

It is clear then that the Melchizedek priesthood belongs to Christ and Christ alone. None other has qualified nor ever will and there is no need for any other priest of this order because this Priest will never cease His intercession on our behalf. Never does the New Testament speak of the church as the Melchizedek Priesthood. No one else qualifies for this priesthood since it is on the basis of an indestructible life.

The teaching of the modern prophets is clearly unbiblical in this area. This teaching once again exalts man and minimizes the uniqueness of Jesus Christ. Once again the call of the modern prophets is to focus on how great man is rather than the glory of the Redeemer.

Certainly the Bible also speaks of believers as a nation of priests but we have no right to claim for ourselves that which rightfully belongs only to Jesus.

CHAPTER TEN

Onward Christian Monarch?
Modern Prophets and Dominion Theology

For the creation waits with eager longing for the revealing of the sons of God.
Romans 1:19

"In essence, the Father says to the Son, 'Once You have purchased redemption for mankind, You will sit at my right hand. You will have done Your part on earth 'till I make Your enemies Your footstool.' You will remain up here as the Head, and Your body on Earth will crush Your enemies. The last generation will be the 'foot generation and will rule on Earth over Your enemies. Until they do so, You are not going back to rescue, rapture, save, or anything else. Your body, in fact, will not be a beautiful bride until she has accomplished this crushing of Satan.'[222] Johnny Enlow

The modern prophetic movement is patently dominionist in their approach to eschatology. In this they are consistently following the pattern set by their predecessors William Branham and John G. Lake. For instance, Lake wrote:

"Beloved, God is calling men and women to a holier consecration, to a higher place in God, and I am one of God's candidates for that holy place in God. I want to get to the throne of God....And that is the experience that is going to make the sons of God in the world. That is the reason they will take the world for Jesus Christ, and the Kingdom will be established, and they will put the crown on the Son of God, and declare him, 'King of kings and Lord of lords".[223]

If you are paying attention at all to the modern prophetic movement, you are aware that Dominion Theology, also known as Kingdom Now theology or the Manifest Sons of God teaching has permeated this branch of Christendom.

Dominion theology is not new. Its roots go back to Franklin Hall and William Branham in the late 1940's, though, as already demonstrated, some of the doctrines predate Branham and can be found in the writings of John G. Lake and others. The doctrines of the Latter Rain were particularly developed by some of Branham's followers, most notably the Sharon Brethren.

The teaching was declared to be heresy by the Assemblies of God and was essentially marginalized on the fringes of the Pentecostal/Charismatic movement for a time but began to be resurrected in the 1980's. It now influences a major segment of the Christian population through teachers like Bill Hamon, Mike Bickle (despite his protests to the contrary), Rick Joyner, Paul Cain, Francis Frangipane, Kim Clement and literally a host of others. While some of these teachers may not endorse all of the teachings that generally comprise Latter Rain or Dominion Theology, all have major dominionist aspects to their teaching.

Major Tenants

Latter Rain Theology comes in a variety of forms and is therefore at times difficult to categorize in a general way. Tricia Tillin of Banner Ministries has done as thorough a job as anyone and we will work through her categories. She lists the following doctrines as being integral in the Latter Rain.

- the Church must be restored and equipped to rule by the five-fold ministries.
- it must come to perfection and complete visible UNITY.
- out of the purified church will come a spiritual elite corps, a Corporate Christ who possess the Spirit without measure
- they will purge the earth of all wickedness and rebellion
- they will judge the apostate Church
- they will redeem all creation, and restore the earth
- they will eventually overcome death itself in a counterfeit of the Rapture
- the Church will thus inherit the earth, and rule over it from the Throne of Christ.[224]

These doctrines are blatantly man-exalting. It is man who purges the earth, man who redeems creation, man who overcomes, man who gives the throne to Christ. The proponents of these doctrines spend a vast amount of time proclaiming how great this generation of Christians will become. No longer is the church looking to the return of Christ as the blessed hope. Instead the church becomes enamored with its own power and glory.

The Assemblies of God declared Latter Rain doctrines to be a heresy back in the 1940's because they believed that these teachings denied much of the truth about the return of Christ. In fact some early Latter Rain proponents denied a physical return of Christ, believing instead that Christ came again IN the church but not for the church.

In today's prophetic leaders one hears the echoes if not the outright declarations of the doctrines of the Latter Rain.

Restoration of the Church

Most readers will notice right away that many of these doctrines have already been documented and dealt with elsewhere in the book. The dubious Biblical basis for the Five-Fold ministry doctrine was dealt with in chapter 2. We further discussed the restoration concept within the apostolic and prophetic movement. As was demonstrated at that time, if the church was ever truly lost then Jesus failed in his mission. Further, Jesus is guilty of falsehood for He stated that the gates of hell would never prevail against the church.

We will look in-depth at the specific claims made by the modern apostles and prophets in the next chapter. For now suffice it to say that the modern apostles and prophets are adamant that the church must come under their leadership in order to be restored and fulfill its end-time mandate. They are the final restoration and culmination of what God is doing in this age.

An interesting practice that has developed as a corollary to this belief that the church must be lead and equipped by the modern apostles and prophets is the development of "Training for Reigning" Schools across the country. These schools are primarily to teach young people in aspects of spiritual warfare and the prophetic that will enable them to be a part of the end-time army that will claim the earth for Christ.

The Perfection of Unity

There is no doubt that the unity of the body is a major concern of the New Testament. Jesus prayed that his followers would be one (John 17:21). Furthermore, there is no doubt that the church has not taken this seriously enough. Paul commanded the believers in Ephesus to "endeavor to maintain the unity of the Spirit in the bond of peace." (Eph. 4:3) But it must also be noted that this peace we are to maintain is grounded in the great truths of the faith; one Lord, one faith, one baptism, one God and Father of us all. It is the relationship with Christ and the great truths of the common faith that bring believers together in unity. Unity does not come at the expense of doctrinal truth but rather is the natural result of clinging to it. Interestingly, it was the same apostle who commanded the Ephesians to maintain unity who commanded the church in Rome to mark those who caused division by bringing a doctrine contrary to what the church had been taught (Rom 16:17). In similar fashion, Paul declared to the church in Corinth that some factions (disunity) must exist in order that those who are genuine among them might be recognized as such. (1 Corinthians 11:19) These passages and many others like them do not seem to lend credibility to the doctrine of universal unity of the Body apart from the return of the Lord Jesus. Unity is extremely important but it does not come at any price. There are limits set upon unity by the Scriptures.

This emphasis on unity at all costs can be seen in the writings of Rick Joyner. In his book, "The Final Quest", which is a record of a series of visions he had, Joyner speaks about going to higher levels in God. He writes,

> "On the mountain there were ledges at different levels for as high as we could see. At each higher level the ledges became narrower, and more difficult to stand on. Each level was named for a biblical truth. The lower levels were named after foundational truths such as 'Salvation', 'Sanctification', 'Prayer', 'Faith', etc., and the higher levels were named after deeper biblical truths. The higher we climbed, the larger both our shields and our swords grew, and fewer of the enemy arrows could reach our positions....
>
> When we reached the level called 'The Unity of the Brethren', none of the enemy's arrows could reach us."[225]

So we see that in Joyner's scheme unity is one of the deepest truths because at that level the attacks of the enemy are no longer able to reach believers.

It is interesting to see Joyner writing in such a way about unity for he is one of the modern prophets who has been the most vocal in prophesying a coming civil war to the church. Elsewhere in "The Final Quest" he writes,

> "Then I turned and saw the army of the Lord standing behind me. There were thousands of soldiers, but they were still greatly outnumbered. I was shocked and disheartened as it seemed that there were actually many more Christians being used by the evil one than there were in the army of the Lord. I also knew that the battle that was about to begin was going to be viewed as The Great Christian Civil War because very few would understand the powers that were behind the conflict."[226]

It is more than a little ironic that Joyner believes that most Christians will be on the wrong side of the soon-coming civil war. These believers would actually be used by the evil one. So much for unity. One is beginning to get an idea of what the modern prophets really think about the rest of the church. But Joyner has clearer words than this. In another of his writings Joyner elaborates on this battle,

> "Like the American Civil War, the coming spiritual civil war will also be between the blue and the gray. In dreams and visions, blue often represents heavenly mindedness (the sky is blue), and gray speaks of those who live by the power of their own minds (the brain is often called 'gray matter'). This civil war will be a conflict between those who may be genuine Christians but live mostly according to their natural minds and human wisdom, and those who follow the Holy Spirit."[227]

Again we see what Joyner really believes about other brothers and sisters in Christ, especially those who are not inclined to be followers of the new movement. Joyner and those like him are heavenly minded. Those who oppose them may be Christians but they are at best living by their own wisdom and not following the Holy Spirit. At worst, they are demonized. This effort to demonize and disparage followers of Jesus with whom they disagree is rampant within the prophetic community. In their writings and messages, they rarely give believers who will not join their ranks the benefit of the doubt that they are convicted by the desire to be faithful to the Word of God as they understand it. No, almost without exception, believers who will not follow the modern prophets are depicted as prideful, dead, demonized or some other equally distasteful category.

Members of this movement like to claim a persecuted status whenever anyone dares to challenge them in regard to their false doctrines and extra-biblical practices. But the fact is that while they talk of unity, their writings and messages contain a great deal of venom and disdain toward the rest of the Body of Christ. Much like cults, they overstate the distinctions within the church that come with denominations and make it appear that these denominations have nothing to do with one another and are inherently divided. Joyner for instance writes,

> "In August 1993, I had a vision of the church that was represented as an island in the middle of a sea. Many different types of buildings were all over this island, each of which I understood to represent a different denomination or movement. These buildings seemed to clash with each other architecturally as very old ones were next to very modern ones. A war was going on between many of the buildings, and most of them looked like bombed-out shells. People were still living in the buildings, but most were starving and wounded."[228]

This prophecy continues for a great deal longer but Joyner's overall impression of different denominations has been made. He portrays them in much the same way as cults like Mormonism do, steeped in division and constantly in warfare with one another. Such is not truly the case, though it is certain that there are examples of this kind of denominational arrogance. In reality, most Christians find a great deal of unity with believers of other labels though they may feel strongly enough about secondary issues that they prefer to regularly worship in congregations that share their theology. They do not seem themselves as battling other believers. They freely join together in causes such as the pro-life movement, Christian concerts, community worship services, college campus organizations and many other activities. It has been the privilege of the author of this book to stand beside many brothers and sisters in Jesus from a variety of denominational backgrounds in evangelistic efforts and other ministry activities and never once did I feel like I was in the presence of an enemy. In fact, the leader of the apologetics ministry for which I work and I are from different denominations. While denominationalism within the church may not be the ideal condition, it does not contain the spirit of animosity attributed to it by Joyner and others like him. This warlike, divisive mentality is primarily on the side of the new prophets.

Joyner is also adamant that the unity he seeks is not based around doctrine or truth. He writes,

> "We must first understand that our unity is not based on doctrines. Such unity is superficial at best. Our unity can only be found in Jesus. To focus on Him and learn to love and cover one another is far more important than agreeing on all doctrines. Having like doctrines in not a basis for unity...it is a basis for division."[229]

We discussed in our chapter on the dumbing down of the church, the importance of doctrine. Statements like the previous one from Joyner are simply smoke and mirrors. Which Jesus are we to focus on? The answer given is doctrinal in nature. What are we to see when we focus on Him? This will involve doctrine. It is to be agreed that we do not have to agree on all doctrines but there are areas of no compromise.

Another example of this teaching of the necessity of complete unity within the body is Francis Frangipane. He writes,

> "The result of this new spiritual fullness will be a new level of unity. Fault-finding and gossip will disappear. In their place will be intercession and love. Wholeness will return to the Church. This also means that the ambition and division we see today between congregations will be identified as sins, which will be repented of before Jesus returns.
>
> The truth of this message must be made clear, for most Christians consider oneness within the body inconceivable before Jesus returns. They have not discerned nor warred against the enemy's lies, which have conditioned believers to accept strife and sectarianism in the Church. It is my passionate conviction that the Church which will ultimately be raptured will be free of strife and carnal divisions -- it will be a bride "without spot or wrinkle" made ready for her bridegroom."[230]

In addition to the call for a perfect unity within the church that comes without consideration of doctrinal purity, we notice the emphasis in Frangipane's writings of a church that is essentially glorified before the second coming of Christ. This leads us into our next example of dominionist teaching.

The Rise of the Bride Church

Dominion theology teaches that the church, or at least a portion of the church will rise to a level of perfection or near perfection before the coming of Christ. It is taught that Christ must be incarnated within the church before He can return. The church will literally become the fullness of Christ. Some early Latter Rain teachers denied an actual literal second coming of Christ in favor of the glorification of the church. While avoiding this most serious heresy, Francis Frangipane writes of this glorified Bride Church. He begins by stating,

> "Secure this thought in your mind: when the Spirit of Christ comes into the physical world, He must enter through a physical body"[231]

One must wonder what Frangipane means when he states that the Spirit of Christ must enter the world through a physical body. The Spirit of Christ as used in Scripture is another name for the Holy Spirit. The Holy Spirit has always been active in the world since the time of creation and He has never required a physical body. If Frangipane means Christ Himself then it must be remembered that Christ still has a physical body since the body that was crucified was raised again and glorified. Either way, the coming of Christ does not require a glorified church. But Frangipane continues on the next page,

> "When Christ first entered our world as a child, it was Mary whom God chose to give Christ birth. **Mary's life symbolized the qualities the church must possess to walk in the fullness of Christ.**"[232] (bold text in the original)

Frangipane is building to his description of the end-time church that will walk in the complete fullness of Christ. He goes on,

> "Indeed, our purity, our spiritual virginity as the body of Christ, is nothing less than God preparing us as He did Mary to 'give birth' to the ministry of His Son. Even now, in the spiritual womb of the virgin church, the holy purpose of Christ is growing, awaiting maturity; ready to be born in power in the timing of God!"[233]

Frangipane is now ready to tell us about this perfected church to which the body of Christ is going to give birth. He writes,

"Even now, hell trembles and the heavens watch in awe. For I say to you, once again, the 'virgin is with child'. Before Jesus Himself returns, the last virgin Church shall become pregnant with the promise of God. Out of her travail, the Body of Christ shall come forth, raised to the full stature of its Head, the Lord Jesus. Corporately manifested in holiness, power and love, the Bride of Christ shall arise clothed in white garments, bright and clean."[234]

So let us understand. The Spirit of Christ must enter the world through a physical body and that body is the Church. So God is preparing the church to be a pure virgin which Frangipane defines earlier in the chapter as being wholly devoted and untouched from the traditions of men. This virgin church will then be brought to a place of travailing and out of her travail a glorified Bride Church will emerge that is raised to the full stature of Jesus Christ. This must all happen BEFORE Jesus Christ can return.

Frangipane's statement, though powerfully and beautifully written, is simply theological nonsense. But notice again that out of the larger church's travail, a "man-child" church, the true Bride of Christ shall arise. It would appear that in Frangipane's theology not all of the church belongs in this special Bride class.

Frangipane is merely echoing the words of William Branham. Branham stated, "In them days it was God in a man, His Son, Jesus Christ. ...It was God In Christ, God, in a man, the fullness of the Godhead bodily In a man. God, in a man; now, it's God in men. See? The fullness of God in the Godhead bodily in His entire Church, manifesting Himself, fulfilling His Word."[235]

Purging Evil and Judging the false Church

We have already noted the prophecies concerning the great civil war which must come upon the church and through which those believers who are not open to the new revelation must be defeated. Therefore our attention will turn to the idea of purging evil from the earth itself.

Much, though not all, of the modern emphasis on spiritual warfare has its root in dominion theology and the concept of purging the earth, even if that specific language is not used. In order for God to move, the heavens must be cleared and opened. It is therefore necessary for believers to discern the territorial demons over their cities, engage in spiritual mapping, claim the gates of their cities, bind these demonic forces, etc, etc. The list is endless. One of the many versions of this is a teaching by Jill Austin, Mike Bickle and others that the church must pray for a "breaker anointing" defined as a *"catalytic deposit of the Holy Spirit where eternity breaks through into the natural realm. It is a holy invasion where the gates of heaven are opened*"[236] This teaching is based on a bizarre interpretation of Micah 2:13. It is just another example of prophetic teachers reading their own doctrines back into the Scriptures. One also wonders how it is possible to have a "catalytic deposit" of a person such as the Holy Spirit.

Elsewhere Bickle continues to show his dominionist theology. In a message supposedly based on Revelation 10, Bickle finds a mandate for the raising up of 10,000 apostolic preachers. Of these end-time apostles Bickle writes,

> "These preachers will walk in such a strong prophetic mantle that they will fulfill Amos 3:7: 'God will do nothing unless He reveals His secrets to His servants the prophets.' They will possess true friendship with God, as they stand in the counsels of the Lord. They will walk with such authority in the courts of heaven that they will be invited to partner with God in His end-time judgments. Their lives will shake heaven and earth. Creation will bow to the Word of the Lord." [237]

So we see that it is these new end-time apostles who will execute the judgments of God on the earth. In the messages in this series and other sermons as well Bickle is adamant that the words of these prophets that will activate the divine judgments against sin. Additionally, the lives of these last-days apostles will shake heaven and earth and creation will bow to the word of the Lord. This last phrase leads directly into the next aspect of dominion theology that is demonstrated consistently by the modern apostles and prophets, that of earthly conquest.

Redemption of Creation and Earthly Conquest

Some of the clearest examples of the Kingdom Now doctrine of earthly conquest come from the writings of Bill Hamon. Hamon states,

> "There is one final restorational move of God that shall fill the earth with the Church of the Living God, and cause all the kingdoms of this world to become the kingdoms of our Lord Jesus and His anointed, joint-heir, co-laboring Church. (Rev. 11:15)"[238]

Elsewhere in the same book Hamon writes,

> "God is preparing His Church to become an invincible, unstoppable, unconquerable, overcoming Army of the Lord that subdues everything under Christ's feet."[239]

It is clear that in Hamon's theology it is not Christ in His coming who subdues the kingdoms of the earth as the Scriptures indicate in Revelation 19:19. No instead it is the church that conquers for Christ. It is the church that "causes the kingdoms of this world to become the kingdom's of our Lord Jesus". It is the church that subdues everything under Christ's feet. This would seem to contradict the apostle Paul who stated that Christ would be the one who put all His enemies under His feet. In 1 Corinthians 15:25, the apostle states, "For He [Jesus] must reign until He has put all His enemies under His feet."

Johnny Enlow is another of the modern prophets proclaiming that the church must conquer the kingdoms of the world for Christ before He comes. He writes,

> "When they [the beast and the false prophet] are crushed, we will come to the Lord and say, 'The kingdoms of this world have become the kingdoms of our God' (Rev. 11:15). We will present the nations of the world to the Lord as His possessions. They will be the dowry that the Father is providing for us to present to the Bridegroom. Lovesick for His bride, Jesus will no longer be able to restrain Himself and will burst through the clouds to come sweep us off our feet. Our Prince Charming will come on a white horse to take us away."[240]

In earlier chapters we saw the bridal paradigm distorting the cross to become the dowry paid for the bride. Now the bridal paradigm is used to envision the conquest of the earth being performed by the church in order to have a dowry to give to the bridegroom. This conquest of the earth by the church will cause Jesus to become so lovesick for his bride that He can no longer restrain Himself and comes to claim His own. It is our actions that conquer the earth. It is our actions that make us beautiful to the "lovesick" Lord. No hint of a sovereign God who is working all things according to the counsel of His will and for His own glory who comes at the time predetermined and foreknown from eternity past. In short, there's no room for the Biblical view of God whatsoever. There's just not enough drama in that story for the modern prophets. They rewrite the story so that man, not God, assumes the lead role and takes center stage.

Joyner likewise writes of this unstoppable, conquering super- Church of the last days.

> "Angelic appearances will be common to the saints and a visible glory of the Lord will appear upon some for extended periods of time as power flows through them. There will be no plague, disease, or physical condition, including lost limbs, AIDS, poison gas, or radiation, which will resist the healing and miracle gifts working in the saints during this time. "[241]

Please do not miss the emphasis of Joyner's statement. It is all about us. The focus is on our greatness, our glory, our power. Angelic appearances will be common. Nothing will stand against us or be able to resist us. It is the height of what Martin Luther would call "glory theology". This is not the theology of the cross. This is not the attitude of the apostles of Scripture. Paul wrote, "God forbid that I should glory save in the cross of our Lord Jesus Christ by Whom the world was crucified unto me and I unto the world." (Gal. 6 :14)

More and more throughout the writings of the modern prophets, Esther is being perceived as a type of the end-time glorified Church. Steve Shultz states the following:

> "Throughout the Old Testament are different revelations of the Church which are concealed in types with figurative language. In the Book of Esther are prophetic pictures of the Church, her relationship with the Holy Spirit and her commitment to the Kingdom. Esther was not only a queen as a figurehead only, she made laws that governed a kingdom. Having endured a twelve-month process which involved the bathing in oils, spices, and perfumes, Esther was positioned to not only become the "chosen" one, but she was also empowered to shift her family into safety and prosperity as well as shifting the entire destiny of a nation.
>
> Prophetically, Esther represents the Church being directed by the Holy Spirit into a process of becoming an anointed vessel. We as the Church are becoming properly positioned to rule and reign with Christ and establish the Kingdom of God on this earth. Through her faith and determination, Esther was able to touch Heaven and accomplish Kingdom destiny.

Each of us, when we approach the King with expectancy, can become set ablaze with a passion for His Kingdom and be fulfilled in His divine presence. Come expecting an impartation to become the very fragrance of myrrh, aloes and spices which will allow continual entrance into His presence. As a result, in this appointed time, you can bring Heaven's purposes to earth."[242]

So according to Shultz we can receive an "impartation" to "become the fragrance of myrrh, aloes and spices" that will allow us to have continual access into the presence of God." Shultz seems to forget that we, as believers, already possess such continual access through the blood of Jesus Christ. It is this new and living way that provides access to God. We do not need anything else. We do not need a special impartation. The work of Christ is sufficient. Once again we see the modern prophets bypassing and overlooking the sufficiency and glory of the cross and what was accomplished by grace alone on behalf of unworthy sinners to invent a theology of their own that centers in the works of man to make himself into something pleasing to God.

But more to the point of this chapter, notice also that it is ultimately the church in Shultz's theology that is responsible for establishing the Kingdom of God on this earth. According to Shultz, we can "bring Heaven's purposes to earth." Once again the emphasis is on man. It really is all about us. We are powerful. We are glorious. We are the anointed ones. Mike Bickle has attempted in recent years to distance himself from dominion theology. The website for International House of Prayer includes carefully worded disclaimers stating that they do not support the doctrines the Latter Rain or Kingdom Now theology which go beyond Scripture. Their website states,

> **"We Deny** the distinctive doctrines that go beyond Scripture that are often associated with the Latter Rain theology that was popularized in the 1950s.

> Explanation: Some have wrongly identified our ministry today with the false teachings that were popularized by some in the Latter Rain movement. At no time in the past did we have any relationship with this movement."[243]

So it is everyone else's fault for connecting IHOP with the Latter Rain. The statement carefully notes that IHOP "at no time in the past" had any "relationship with this movement." Exactly what would be necessary to have a "relationship" with this movement is not explained. Apparently trumpeting the writings and ministry of William Branham doesn't constitute a relationship. Nor does providing a national platform for Branham associate Paul Cain to teach his "Joel's Army" doctrine.

But relationship is not the issue. Doctrine is. Nowhere does the statement specify which "distinctive doctrines" from the Latter Rain IHOP is disavowing. In reality one can find the writings of dominionist leaders such as Hamon, Joyner, Wagner and Frangipane featured prominently in the IHOP bookstore. IHOP conferences frequently feature speakers who blatantly promote dominion theology.

And Bickle himself, through his own teachings and his support of prophets Bob Jones and Paul Cain has promoted a version of dominion theology known at various times under the titles, New Breed, Elected Seed, Joel's Army, Apostolic Premillenialism and the Uniqueness of the End-Time Generation. Bickle frequently changes the titles when a particular teaching comes under fire. In this way, he can continue to teach the same doctrines while claiming to have changed or even to have never believed the controversial doctrines in the first place. In reality, the changes are merely window-dressing. The root teachings are dominionist to the core. In fact, according a foundational prophecy given to Mike Bickle in March of 1984 which he claims is his most comprehensive prophetic word called the Blueprint prophecy, the Lord stated,

> "The Out-Pouring of the Latter Rain shall be released in this area and upon this city. It shall be noised abroad even world-wide."[244]

This prophecy was never made public until 2002 and then only in an edited form. Bickle has never produced an unedited version of this word. He claims that he edits out those things that he doesn't understand yet or that he feels might be confusing. The quotation above is from the 2006 edition of this prophecy which is included on the IHOP website and which differs in significant areas from both the 2002 and 2009 versions. Ironically, the IHOP website also contains the 2009 edition of this same prophecy in which the phrase "of the Latter Rain" has been removed.[245] Is one to assume that this is something else that Bickle didn't understand or is it because he knew it would be controversial?

The following is a transcript of a recorded interview between Mike Bickle and Bob Jones that introduces the New Breed doctrine. This message is full of the Latter Rain doctrines that have been discussed in this chapter including that of earthly conquest.

"NEW BREED" Transcript

Bob Jones, relating a vision that he had: . . . "And as I was looking at that, he said, "Come, I want to show you something else." And so I went and I seen the Lord and it was like He was lookin' at little yellow things – little round yellow things like a spirit of God itself. And there were **billions** of them. And it was like Him and all the angels were looking through these and every once in awhile they'd say, 'Hey, here's an end-time one; get it down here on the end. This is a perfect one. Here's another good one.'

"I said, 'What are you doing?'

"He said, 'Oh, we're collecting those who are foreknown and predestinated for the end-times, for you see they'll be the best of all the seed that's ever been. And we're looking through the seeds and this'll be your grandkids. This will be the **end generation** that is foreknown and predestined to **inherit all things**. And these will be like grandchildren to you – even those that you minister to won't be this generation. Their children will be. You are to write into their minds – as they write into the children's minds. You're to bring them to a place to allow my Spirit to rule in their life where they can begin to **set the church on the proper foundations** – as they will. **They'll birth the church,** but their children will attain levels of the Holy Spirit that they will not. Although their parents will reign over them and be the **leaders of the last day church** – their children will possess the Spirit without measure – for they are the **best of all the generations** that have ever been upon the face of the earth. And the best of all generations are those **elected seeds** that will glorify Christ in the last days. That's the purpose so that Jesus in the last days has the **seeds** that will glorify Him above any generation that has ever been upon the face of the earth. They will move into things of the **supernatural** that no one has ever moved in before. Every miracle, sign and wonder that has ever been in the Bible – they'll move in it consistently, they'll move in the power that Christ did. Every sign and wonder that's ever been will be many times in the last days. They themselves will be that **generation that's raised up to put death itself underneath their feet** and to glorify Christ in every way. And the church that is **raising up in the government** will be the head and the covering for them. So that that glorious church might be revealed in the last days, because the Lord Jesus is worthy to be lifted up by a church that has reached the full maturity of the **God-Man!**"

Mike Bickle: "I'm going to sum that up real well. And you add to it or subtract from it, if it is not just what you shared it with me or how you remember it. What the Lord did, I'm just gonna put that in real tight there, the Lord took him to this beach before an ocean and this beach spoke of the sands of time and the ocean spoke of the nations of the world in all of history. And he saw these men and they put their hand in the sand and pulled out this box and they were empty. And then a little bit later, another guy did and it was empty. And then a little bit later, another guy did and it was empty – another did and it was empty. The Lord came to Bob and said, 'You do it right here." Bob said, 'Lord, they've all put their hands in and got empty boxes. They came up empty-handed – without a box. Why should I do it?' The Lord said, 'Put your hand in here.' He pulls it out and he sees this **box full of draft notices for the end-time army.** And he said the Lord told Him there was **300,000 enlistment notices** that he was going to send out across the **nations** in this **next generation.** It wasn't all going to be sent out then. **300,000 that would be the main leadership over one billion converts in the earth.**"

Bob Jones: "Amen"

Mike Bickle: "He said, 'I'll cause **300,000** to bear a **distinct anointing of leadership over the one billion.**' 300,000 sounds like a lot of **leaders,** but a **billion** is a thousand million. I calculated that out and that is 3 anointed vessels in that distinct way for 10,000 people.

That is nothing.

"He said, 'I'm going to cause **300,000 like Gideon's 300 [Army]** in Israel. I'm going to have 300,000. That will be a small number for the **nations** of the earth. But they will have like that **apostolic anointing** and the **signs and wonders** of the early church will be on 300,000. The Earth will have it. The rest will move in the miraculous, but I will have 300,000 that will have a **special measure of the Spirit** like the leaders of the New Testament.'

"Like they had even more than the people did. And so then he pulled out this box, he sees the 300,000 names, he actually reads a number of them and he says, 'Lord, who are these guys?'

"He looked back, 'Those were the leaders of past generations like John Wesley, Charles Finney, Martin Luther, who thought their generation was the chosen generation.' And every time they pulled their hand up

214

they came up empty-handed because the chosen generation – because there is **one generation that will enter into that which is beyond all the others in power.** They thought it was theirs. It is not.

"'Put your hand here.' So he sees the 300,000 and the Lord looks at Bob and says, 'From out of the sands of time I have called the **best of every blood line** in the earth unto this generation.'

"He said, 'Even the **blood line** of Paul. Even the **blood line** of David, the **blood line** of Peter, James and John, the best of their **seed** is unto this generation. They will be **superior** to them in heart, stature and love for me.'

"He says, 'For out of the sands of time, I have elected to bring them forth in this hour.' And he said, 'This **generation** of the young people that are coming' – their children is the **elect generation.'**

"And he said, 'As the thing grows,' he says, 'this **generation** will see the inception of this move. It will begin in their time. They will be as children in the Spirit.'

Bob Jones (much later) . . . "Not only will they have the word of God in them, that's the **foundation – apostles and prophets** – but they will have the word of God in them and they will have the **power** with the word – the Spirit. And the barrenness of the church will be over and the **foundations** of the church will be raised up. The walls will be raised up. You will see the glorious church begin to come in and you will begin to **birth** it. It will take probably another 15-20 years to get some of you into some level of maturity. There will be neither male or female in this. There will be maturity – what God is seeking. And He will be raising the saints up – to that level. First He will bring the **five-fold [ministry]**, but there is a ministry after the five-fold called the **Ministry of Perfection – the Melchisedek Priesthood.**

"You that are here now, you'll be moving into the five-fold ministries, but your children will be moving into the **ministries of perfection.** Coming to that characteristics – **coming into that divine nature of Jesus Christ.** Not having to come out of the wilderness, but being birthed natural into the Spirit. All their days movin' with the Spirit. Movin' in the ways of – that the Holy Spirit does. There is a **purpose.** It takes awhile – you've gotta get out of religion, or Egypt or death and then it takes awhile of dying out in the wilderness and **getting the next generation into the warfare** – that's where you are now – **you're in the warfare, start to take the promised land** – and then you raise up the generation to possess it. Well the children that are coming forth are to possess the promises of God. It is the **last day generation.** . . .

215

> *Mike Bickle:* "I want to say one things about this. The Lord said to Bob we were like the **David generation** that had many **wars** because there is going to be **great transition** in the body. Many misunderstandings, gossip, slanders, persecution – even within the house of God. He said that's why we won't enter into the fullness ourselves, but like **Solomon** who built the temple – because the Lord gave him permission to build the temple because he was not a man of blood – or a man of **war**. But He said **this generation in the next 10 or 15 years is a time of war and transitioning of whole new orders in the body** – but our children will be **kings and priests of peace** and not of wars and that's why they will go beyond where a lot of us are. . . ."[246]

Notice the astounding claims made for this final generation. They will be the best of all bloodlines and will be drawn from all the best bloodlines in the past. They will move in great signs and wonders. They will birth the church. They will place the church on its proper foundation. They will put death itself under their feet. And finally they will attain to the priesthood of perfection, the Melchizedek Priesthood. They will come to the full stature of the God-Man. This is dominion theology, pure and simple, despite the attempts to hide behind alternate titles.

It must be pointed out that several of these claims belong to Jesus alone. It is Christ who established and built the church. Christ placed the church on its proper foundation and continues to exercise headship over the church today. And it is Christ alone who is a priest forever after the order of Melchizedek. (See Hebrews 6:19-8:13) Once again we see modern prophets minimizing Christ and exalting this generation of believers. The drumbeat continues, "We're so great! We're so special! We will be so powerful!"

Similar statements can be found in messages by Paul Cain and interviews between Cain and Bickle. In one CD in particular, when Cain complains that they won't even let him bring the Joel's Army teaching on TBN, Bickle responds by animatedly instructing Cain to "tell it" because he [Bickle] wants his sons to hear it.[247] Bickle's attempted disclaimers ring hollow as long as he continues to promote the teachings of prominent dominionists in his bookstore, through his conferences and to teach a version himself albeit under different titles. Dominion theology by any other name is still dominion theology and it is still heresy.

Immortalization

Some dominionist teachers even go so far as to claim that the church will conquer death and receive glorified bodies before the return of Christ, a doctrine known as immortalization. Bill Hamon represents one of the most influential modern teachers of this particular heresy. He writes,

> "A greater measure of revelation, faith and overcoming grace is being released in the Church. The mortal Church is in transition and preparation for becoming the immortal Church. The resurrection-translation of the saints that brings about the redemption of their bodies into immortal, indestructible bodies will take place so that God can fulfill His greater purpose for and through His Church. There is a last-day ministry designed for the overcoming Church to accomplish in the heavenlies and on earth that will require the saints to have their bodies redeemed."[248]

Elsewhere Hamon declares that this bodily redemption will cause a chain reaction that brings redemption to all of creation. He states,

> "The Earth and all of creation is waiting for the manifestation of the sons of God, the time when they will come into their maturity and immortalization... When the Church receives its full inheritance and redemption then creation will be redeemed from its cursed condition of decay, change and death... the Church has a responsibility and ministry to the rest of creation. Earth and Its natural creation Is anxiously waiting for the Church to reach full maturity and come to full sonship. **When the Church realizes its full sonship, its bodily redemption will cause a redemptive chain reaction throughout all of creation.**" [249]

Earlier in the same work, Hamon writes,

> "The Church will gain victory over the last enemy, death. Victory speaks of a battle being fought. The last day saints will wage and win a warfare against death. The last generation saints will come to translating faith in preparation for participation in the translation."[250]

But for the apostle Paul, victory over death was something that the church looked to the coming of Christ to bring. It is not until the last trumpet that we are changed in a moment in the twinkling of an eye. It is only then that death is swallowed up in victory. (1 Cor. 15) Hamon's teachings are just one more example of the glorification of man and the minimization of the work of Christ. The last generation of saints, in Hamon's theology, are so special that they come to a "translating faith" that brings them the final victory over death on their own. It is the saints that win the last battle against death. Death is defeated by the church not the Lord. The role of Jesus is once again marginalized.

Now is the Time

To heighten the expectation even further, prophetic teachers add to the hype by repeatedly declaring that this season of power, glory and conquest for the church is now right around the corner. Of course, those who have either been in the movement or watching the movement for some time are aware that this rhetoric has been going on for decades without results. Still it is powerful in capturing the young and/or naïve. Ryan Wyatt typifies the current message when he declares:

> "We have had whole decades in the 1900's that were devoted to the restoration of the **Ephesians 4:11**, five-fold ministry gifts of apostle, prophet, evangelist, pastor, and teacher. All of this has been so that the saints can be equipped and reconnected with the Head in Heaven. When the Church reconnects with the Head in Heaven (Jesus Christ), then there will be an unhindered release of Heaven on earth. I believe we are entering into the time where we won't just see Heaven touch earth in seasonal revivals that come and go, but rather a time where **the saints of God manifest a continuous expression of Kingdom Glory and Power.** The continuous, sustained expression of the Kingdom of Heaven on the earth is the only thing that will truly establish and advance the government of God in our lives and regions.[251]

Wyatt draws from the dubious five-fold ministry well in order to explain what God has been doing in the past in the hope of preparing us for the unprecedented work that is about to begin. Notice that Wyatt indicates that this is so that the church can be "reconnected with the Head in Heaven" which will bring the unhindered release of Heaven on earth. Wyatt of course doesn't tell us when the church became disconnected from the Head in Heaven. Nor does he explain how it is possible for the body to become disconnected from the head in view of the fact that Jesus Christ has committed Himself to holding on to those who are His. If the body became disconnected from the Head then the entire church died and Jesus failed. It is simply impossible that the true church, comprised of those who are truly born again by the Spirit of God and indwelt by this same Spirit, could ever be separated from the Head. But in Wyatt's understanding not only did this separation occur at some unspecified time in the past but now in this generation the reconnection is just about complete and once that work is done the church will see a continuous expression of Glory and Power. And it is just around the corner. We are entering into it now. The modern prophets know that what they are doing at the present time is a hollow shell compared to both the activity of the New Testament apostles and the boasts they have made about the greatness of this generation of modern apostles. To keep their followers from abandoning them wholesale in the face of their unfulfilled claims they must continue to dangle the carrot that the real outbreak of power is just ahead of us. As Wyatt continues, he cannot keep from declaring how special this generation is. He writes,

> "The spirit of the warrior is coming upon the Church. Many believe that when you press into your promise land that all the warfare will cease. This is not true! **It's when we press into the promise land of God's Glory that the warfare goes to a whole new level.** The warfare in the promised land is CONSTANT. And we are the generation that can handle it! We are the generation that will become bold as lions and take this world for God! However, it will require a dramatic shift in our wineskin of life and ministry."[252] (bold text and capitalization in the original)

The arrogance of Wyatt's message is striking. "We are the generation that can handle it! We are the generation that will become bold as lions and take this world for God!" Other generations presumably couldn't handle it. And how fortunate God is to have a generation like us that can take the world for Him. We just have to make sure that we are ready to make the obligatory required dramatic shift in our wineskin of life and ministry. The prophets regularly retreat to the idea of new wineskins whenever they are attempting to get their followers to believe or practice something that clearly cannot be justified by Scripture.

The Prophets React

This return to the heretical teachings of the Latter Rain and the virtual deification of man has not gone without notice and opposition. Numerous websites have sprung up attempting to bring a corrective voice to this abandonment of sound doctrine. Both inside and outside the Pentecostal/Charismatic movement, faithful ministers and Christians have attempted to call attention to the heresies being advanced by the modern apostles and prophets. Their efforts have forced the prophets to respond. Rather than address the Biblical concerns raised by these discernment ministries, the modern apostles have, for the most part, responded with smoke and mirrors or the demonization of their opponents.

For an example of the smoke and mirrors approach one need look no further than Francis Frangipane as he attempts to obfuscate the issue in his newsletter. He writes,

> "So, you decide: Is the doctrine of worldwide evangelism a heresy? Or is Christ-centered unity among believers a false doctrine? Is reaching for Christ-like purity and power a deception?"

He continues,

> "My friends, the enemy has put a blockade of false warnings, fear and accusation around one of the most powerful end time realities: *the final work of the Holy Spirit to bring the gospel worldwide!* I am not saying we should be naive or blind to all that is wrong in the church, but neither should we be blind to what God is doing.
>
> To have faith for this outpouring is not heretical, even if it seems like heresy to those in unbelief. Therefore, do not fear being labeled a "heretic" when you speak of your vision. Pray for your nation with confidence, without intimidation, knowing that the reality of the latter rain is occurring even as we speak."[253]

This is a classic straw-man argument. Frangipane knows full well that the dimensions of Latter Rain or Kingdom Now Theology that he lists here are not where most Evangelicals part company with him. No one is opposed to world-wide evangelism, Christ-centered unity or Christ-like purity. It was not over these issues that the Assemblies of God rejected Latter Rain Theology as heretical. As this chapter has attempted to demonstrate, there is much more to this doctrine than these issues and Frangipane knows this because he, himself has written about it. This article is supremely disingenuous.

And Frangipane can't help but demonize those who would disagree with him. They are doing the enemy's work. They are the tool of the evil one to "put a blockade of false warnings, fear and accusation around one of the most powerful end time realities". Frangipane cannot allow that those who oppose the doctrines of the Latter Rain would do so because of Biblical conviction or a passion for the truth of Christ. He will not address himself to the Biblical arguments that are put forward against these doctrines perhaps because he cannot refute them. Instead he results to the last defense of the man without an argument, attack your opponent. Call their character into question. This is standard fare within the prophetic.

Their View of Other Believers

We have already discussed Joyner's claims that much of the church is actually on the side of the enemy and must defeated in a great civil war. As if this weren't bad enough, Joyner elsewhere states that most of the church is under the subjection of an Antichrist spirit that substitutes for Jesus. Joyner declares,

> "The change that is coming to the body of Christ is so profound that the world will have a new definition of Christianity...Those who submit to Him in truth...will be the most dangerous and powerful people on earth, and will be the greatest threat to the Antichrist spirit that now sits in the church as a substitute for Him."[254]

Modern prophets will not allow anyone to evaluate their doctrines or teachings that are a matter of public record. Yet these same teachers find themselves capable of rendering the severest judgments on the private motives and hearts of those who oppose them. In message after message, book after book, email after email, these self-appointed apostles castigate those who would challenge them as being pharisaical, prideful, having a Jezebel spirit, antichrist spirit, Judas spirit, or as only wanting to protect their own positions and power structures. Never is it even considered possible that someone might not be willing to follow the modern prophets because of a sincere desire to cling to the Word of God.

These men and women are above accountability and examination but they denounce their detractors in the severest of terms.

Jesus Can't Come Until the Church Gets It Right

Over and over the modern prophets proclaim that Jesus simply can't come until the church does its job. The language may vary but the message is consistent. The kingdom of heaven hinges on us. If this generation won't do it then our children or our children's children will. It is all up to the church. Consider again the words of Enlow when he maintains that the Father has declared to the Son,

> "The last generation will be the 'foot' generation that will rule on Earth over Your enemies. Until they do so, You are not going back to rescue, rapture, save, or anything else."[255]

Christ must sit on His hands and wait until the church gets it right and finally asserts its dominion.

Ryan Wyatt declares this same nonsense when he writes,

> "The Bible says in **Acts 3:19-21, "Repent therefore and return, that your sins may be wiped away, in order that times of refreshing may come from the presence of the Lord; and that He may send Jesus, the Christ appointed for you, whom Heaven must receive until the period of restoration of all things about which God spoke by the mouth of His holy prophets from ancient time."**
>
> I believe this literally means that Jesus Christ is "retained" in the Heavens "until" there is a restoration of all things on the earth. Restoration of what? It's the restoration of God's original plan and intent for His people on the earth. **God's original purpose for Adam was to be a carrier of the fullness of His glory, to be an ambassador of the Kingdom of Heaven, and to bring Heaven to earth daily.**[256] (bold text in the original)

Space will not permit including the entire "prophetic" word by Mr. Wyatt but one more section deserves special notice. Wyatt takes time to explain to us how important it is for us to have a body.

> "The fact that every human being has a body is very important--I believe no "spirit being" can function on the earth without flowing through a "human being" who has given that spirit permission to function. In **Genesis 1:26,** God delegated the authority over the earth to human beings. This means that humans have authority over the earth and spirit beings flow through them to further their purposes. This is true both for the Kingdom of God and the Kingdom of darkness. I believe demons need humans with bodies to flow through in order to function in the natural realm.

In the same way, the Holy Spirit is looking for a person who is yielded to Him in order to fill that person and flow out through them. This is the reason why our prayers are effective because as delegated authorities on this earth, we open up our lives by asking the Lord to come and flow through us in the earthly realm.

We give this authority either to God or the devil very easily. Our bodies are gateways. Gateways are opened for spirit beings to flow through us because of what we set our five natural senses on. What you set your eyes upon gains entry into your soul, your mind, and your heart. The same goes with your other four senses. Have you ever heard the expression, "You are what you eat"? Well, what you open yourself up to is what comes into you and flows and functions through you."[257]

In words similar to those of Frangipane quoted earlier, Wyatt asserts that no spirit, including the Holy Spirit, can function on the earth without flowing through a human. The Sovereign God the Holy Spirit has to have human permission to function on the earth? Really? Did Adam give permission for God to "flow through him" when he was being tossed out of the garden for disobedience? Must God simply wring His hands until He can find a man willing to cooperate with Him? Is this really the teaching of Scripture? We must answer with a resounding, "NO!" And it does not matter what Mr. Wyatt believes.

Conclusion

Certainly a great deal more could be said in this chapter and a host of other examples given but hopefully what has been presented is enough to establish beyond reasonable doubt that the leaders of the modern apostolic and prophetic movement have resurrected the discarded heresies of the Latter Rain Movement and reintroduced them into a new generation of believers who sadly lacked the discernment of their forefathers who rejected these doctrines for being unbiblical. Indeed many of the current leaders are not even shy about identifying themselves with Latter Rain or Dominion Theology. Those who attempt to distance themselves from these movements can be shown to teach the very heresies they claim to disown.

The doctrines of Dominion Theology diminish the work of Christ and exalt man. They are fully man-centered. Man does the real work. Man is the central focus. For all of the talk about Jesus and love for Him within this movement, the real longing that comes across in the writings and messages is a desire for power and signs. The repeated theme is our own greatness, our own power, the world will recognize us, hell will tremble before us, all of heaven longs to meet us. This message is surely readily received by a narcissistic church that has been tutored to believe that the greatest need of man is healthy self-esteem.

The message of suffering for Christ, of taking up one's cross, of dying to self is exchanged for one of self-exaltation and near deification. Once again the message of the modern prophets seems to have more in common with the spirit of the age than the Spirit of Christ.

Jesus does not appear to be sought for who He is as God and Savior but for the power He can bring to the church. He is merely the means to an end. The real goal appears to be earthly power and greatness.

The church no longer looks to the return of Christ as the blessed hope and the time of deliverance but rather to its own triumph and conquest as Jesus sits as a spectator on the sideline waiting for His people to establish His reign.

The doctrines of the Latter Rain need to be returned to dumpster of discarded theological fallacies as the church repents of its self-absorption and returns to the Bible as the authority for doctrine instead of new revelations.

May God grant such a revival.

CHAPTER ELEVEN

A New Doctrine a Day Keeps the Truth Away
Modern Apostles and New Revelation

"I must state emphatically that I do not believe that any kind of prophetic revelation is for the purpose of establishing doctrine." Rick Joyner

We have attempted to demonstrate that the modern apostolic and prophetic movement is at the same time marginalizing and undermining the central truth's of Christianity. However the problems do not stop there. The movement is also introducing a flood of new doctrines and practices into the Body of Christ that have never been a part of the church's teaching and which cannot be established Biblically. The words of the prophets themselves become the basis for establishing doctrine.

It should be pointed out that the prophets themselves warn against establishing doctrine with modern prophecy. Rick Joyner, for instance, writes, "I must state emphatically that I do not believe that any kind of prophetic revelation is for the purpose of establishing doctrine. We have the Scriptures for that."[258]

Despite the warnings from modern prophets against using prophecy to establish doctrine, it seems that this is not as easy to practice as it is to say. The fact is that modern apostles and prophets are introducing new doctrines into the church on an almost daily basis. The difficulty may come from the relationship between doctrine, teaching and practice. Teachings and practices all, by necessity, have a doctrinal root or rationale. Therefore when these prophets introduce practices such as spiritual mapping into the church they may not realize that they are establishing doctrine. But the reality is, that spiritual mapping (and other prophetic practices) require an entire series of doctrines in order to support them. For example, in order to believe in spiritual mapping one must hold to certain assumptions about the nature and organization of demons, the nature of spiritual warfare, the nature of prayer, the power or lack thereof of the gospel message, divine election, the sovereignty of God and a number of other things. The same could be said of the rest of the new practices and teachings (such as breaking spiritual curses) that are being introduced by the various apostles and prophets. One must believe certain doctrines or the practices themselves make no sense.

The following is just a small sampling of the new and exotic doctrines that are being taught by the prophets and established by prophetic revelation.

Demon-possessed Christians in Satan's End-Time Army

Rick Joyner in the Final Quest, gives this shocking revelation which teaches plainly that Christians who are opposing this new prophetic movement are being influenced by demons. After describing Christians who had demons riding on them, Joyner moves to describing Christians who he called, "prisoners".

> "Occasionally the weaker prisoners would stumble and fall. As soon as they hit the ground, the other prisoners would begin stabbing them with their swords, scorning them as they did this. The vultures would then come and begin devouring the fallen ones even before they were dead. The other Christian prisoners stood by and watched approvingly, occasionally stabbing the fallen one again with their swords.

> "As I watched, I realized that these prisoners thought that the vomit of Condemnation was truth from God. Then I understood that these prisoners actually thought they were marching in the army of God! This is why they did not kill the little demons of fear, or the vultures—they thought these were messengers from God! The darkness from the cloud of vultures made it so hard for these prisoners to see that they naively accepted everything that happened to them as being from the Lord. They felt that those who stumbled were under God's judgment, which is why they attacked them the way they did—they thought that they were helping God!

> "The only food provided for these prisoners was the vomit from the vultures. Those who refused to eat it simply weakened until they fell. Those who did eat it were strengthened for a time, but with the strength of the evil one. Then they would weaken unless they would

drink of the waters of bitterness that were constantly being offered to them. After drinking the bitter waters they would then begin to vomit on the others. When one of the prisoners began to do this, a demon that was waiting for a ride would climb up on him, and would ride him to the front of the divisions.

"Even worse than the vomit from the vultures was a repulsive slime that these demons were urinating and defecating upon the Christians they rode. This slime was the pride, selfish ambition, etc., that was the nature of their division. However, this slime made the Christians feel so much better than the condemnation that they easily believed that the demons were the messengers of God, and they actually thought this slime was the anointing of the Holy Spirit.

"I had been so repulsed by the evil army that I wanted to die. Then the voice of the Lord came to me saying, *"This is the beginning of the enemy's last day army. This is Satan's ultimate deception. His ultimate power of destruction is released when he uses Christians to attack one another. Throughout the ages he has used this army, but never has he been able to use so many for his evil purposes as he is now. Do not fear. I have an army too. You must now stand and fight, because there is no longer any place to hide from this war."*[259]

It is very difficult to square Joyner's revelation of these demon-possessed Christians who provide much of Satan's army in the last days with the proclamation of Scripture. For instance Paul writes, "He has delivered us from the kingdom of darkness and translated us into the kingdom of the Son of His love." (Col. 1:13) Joyner establishes the doctrines that many believers are demon-possessed and comprise a large segment of the enemy's end-time army purely on the basis of his revelation. So while, in theory, Joyner claims that doctrine must be established by Scripture, in reality doctrine is established by Joyner's revelations.

Unclaimed Spiritual Inheritances and Assignments

Shawn Bolz teaches that there are unclaimed, unused or abandoned spiritual inheritances and assignments left from previous generations that are waiting in the spirit realm (like unclaimed salvage and freight) that can be claimed by today's believers. He writes,

"Literally, there are spiritual inheritances and assignments that have been abandoned and unfulfilled—but are available to be picked up again. In the days ahead, the Lord is going to direct many on how to

access the unused treasures......We need to understand the concept of
the unfinished commissions lying idle in the spirit realm that are waiting
to be picked up by those who have a right to them. Sometimes these
mandates are unfinished because the person died prematurely;
sometimes the person who was walking with the Lord fell into
disobedience or sin and left an unfinished assignment. On the other
hand, a spiritual inheritance is left behind by those who have gone on to
be with the Lord. God wants to open our eyes to see our divine
birthright to the spiritual inheritances and unfinished commissions
surrounding us.[260]

During an interview for the show, "It's Supernatural", concerning his book,
Bolz informs viewers that they can also receive the spiritual inheritances
that belonged to aborted babies.[261]

Consider the doctrines that are introduced here.

1. There are spiritual commissions and inheritances in the spirit realm.
    (This is a new doctrine which cannot be established by Scripture but
    rests exclusively on the revelation of Bolz.)
2. These inheritances can be claimed by other believers.
3. Some people die outside of God's sovereignty. (This is a natural
    deduction from the teaching that people died prematurely and left
    behind work God intended them to do. Apparently God is not
    sovereign over the issues of life and death.)
4. There are specific activities that we can do to claim these inheritances
    for ourselves.

This is just a sampling of the doctrines that must be true if Bolz's revelation
is to be accepted. Bolz is establishing doctrine prophetically whether or not
he intends to do so.

Doors to Heaven

For another example of prophets establishing doctrine, one only needs to
look a little further in the same work. Now Bolz introduces us to the
concept that there are doors in heaven through which believers may pass to
receive particular blessings. Bolz writes,

"When the Minister of Finance [the angelic figure who is giving Bolz all
of this revelation] left the room the second time and flew up to Heaven,
he disappeared through a doorway. I saw a huge gate located in the

middle of the heavenly sky. The nameplate across the top of the top of the gate read: THE DOORWAY OF FAVOR. It was also the doorway to Isaiah 62:

> 'You shall no longer be termed Forsaken...
> You shall be called Sought Out,
> A City Not Forsaken.

--Isaiah 62:4,12 NKJV

> I knew that this was a doorway that, when passed through, would cause divine favor to be released in Heaven and on earth. Those who entered this door would capture Heaven's attention. They would be sought after and filled with His abundance."[262]

Despite Bolz's insertion of a Biblical text, there is nothing truly Biblical in any part of the previous quote. All of this information is to be received purely on the basis of Bolz's revelation. Once again notice the doctrines that are established.

1. There is an angelic being called the Minister of Finance.
2. There are doorways in heaven through which believers may pass.
3. Passing through these doorways releases various activities in heaven and on earth.
4. One of these doorways is the Doorway of Favor.
5. Passing through this doorway will get Heaven's attention and bring abundance.

These are all doctrines. The prophets may not be intending to establish doctrine but this is the result of these revelations. If one is to accept Bolz's revelation, one must accept the doctrinal baggage that comes along with it.

It should also be pointed out that, true to the norm of the modern prophets, the emphasis of this revelation is both on what we must do for God to release His activity and the greatness that will accompany the believer. There is nothing in this revelation that exalts Jesus Christ. It is thoroughly man-centered.

Paul Cox is another prophet who informs us that there are multiple doors in heaven. In typical prophetic fashion he attempts to establish a scriptural basis for his new revelation by jerking verses out of context. He writes,

"Revelation 4:1,"After these things I looked and behold, a door standing open in heaven" (NKJV) It is clear from this passage that these doors are in heaven. Ephesians 2:6 declares that we are seated with Christ in heavenly places. When we go through the doors, we go into the heavenly places."[263]

Cox regularly leads people in counseling sessions to go through various doorways into heaven to receive the ministry he perceives them to need. He then lists 80 different rooms that people he has ministered to have entered including the swimming pool, stables, Bone Room, Sewing Room, Family Photos, Vault, and the Gymnasium.

Once again, despite the effort to establish this doctrine Biblically, the Scripture in the book of Revelations simply will not support the interpretation that there are permanent doors in heaven that believers may walk through at any point they choose to move from this earth into a part of heaven to receive ministry. These doctrines are established by Paul Cox through his personal revelation. The fact that this is a new doctrine can readily be detected by realizing that no one in the Bible attempted to minister to by leading someone through a heavenly doorway.

Spiritual Portals

Not to be outdone, John Paul Jackson, also has a teaching of a similar nature. Except in Jackson's theology, there are portals to heaven at various geographic locations throughout the earth. By going to these particular locations, a person may receive open heaven revelations. The following prophetic vision is quoted extensively to stave off the charge of taking John Paul out of context and because it provides an excellent example of the length to which the prophets will go to attempt to justify their new revelations Biblically. Jackson writes,

"God delights in revealing Himself to those who love His appearing and to those who watch for His coming.

One of the marvelous mysteries of God is the existence of portals-- doors and passageways--leading to and from the heavenly realms. When you are standing in a portal, it feels like an open Heaven.

A heavenly portal is a spherical opening of light that offers divine protection by which angels and heavenly beings can come and go, without demonic interference. God has designed portals to begin in the third Heaven, travel through the second Heaven, and open upon Earth.

Throughout Scripture, we see the existence of doorways or portals:

"Lift up your heads, O you gates! And be lifted up, you everlasting doors! And the King of glory shall come in"--Psalm 24:7.

"He commanded the clouds above and opened the doors of heaven"--Psalm 78:23.

"Blessed is the man who listens to me, watching daily at my gates, waiting at the posts of my doors"--Proverbs 8:34.

"Most assuredly, I say to you, hereafter you shall see heaven open, and the angels of God ascending and descending upon the Son of Man"--John 1:51.

"After these things I looked, and behold, a door standing open in heaven. And the first voice which I heard was like a trumpet speaking with me, saying "Come up here, and I will show you things which must take place after this. Immediately, I was in the spirit"--Revelation 4:1-2a.

The "door" in Revelation suggests God's invitation for us to have access to His heavenly realm. As His friends, the Lord wants to open the portals of Heaven and release an unparalleled visitation of heavenly hosts.

Jacob Discovered a Heavenly Portal

Jacob spent the night in a place where his forefather Abraham had "called upon the name of the Lord"--Genesis 12:8. As he rested his head upon a covenant stone, a portal opened. Jacob saw a vision of a ladder with angels ascending and descending on it. When he awoke from sleep, he said,

"Surely the Lord is in this place, and I did not know it...How awesome is this place! This is none other than the house of God, and this is the gate of Heaven!" Genesis 28:16-17

Eager to mark the specific location where he had encountered the stairway to heaven, Jacob erected a monument and named the place, "Bethel" or "dwelling place of God." Several times after this, the Lord told Jacob to return to Bethel, where He would speak to him."[264]

Later in the same teaching, Jackson states the following:

"Sadly, while many in the New Age movement recognize the existence of portals, the portals they recognize are those of the second Heaven. Many erroneously think they are hearing from God when actually they are being deceived by the counterfeit.

While living in Babylon, the prophet Daniel encountered angels who had battled with principalities. However, since the prince of Persia ruled the nation, the portal to the third Heaven was stopped up, much like a kitchen sink that is clogged with debris, so that nothing can flow from the source. But the Lord is calling us to take back these places full of divine destiny, so that His angels can come and go unencumbered in our midst.

Often, the Keys to Open these Heavenly Portals Reside in the Actions of Our Hearts

At Pentecost, the key to unlocking the portal was the unity of the believers. Gathered together, Scripture says they were "in one accord," when suddenly, a portal opened. A sound from Heaven was heard that resembled a mighty rushing wind, filling the whole house. A supernatural manifestation that looked like flames of fire appeared on the believers and filled them with the Holy Spirit--Acts 2:1-4."[265]

Jackson is correct that the teaching that there are geographic locations that provide access to the sacred realm is a pagan concept. It is related to the idea that deities or spirits were territorial and could be contacted in sacred groves, mountains and other natural locations. What is alarming is that Jackson takes this admittedly pagan view and attempts to superimpose it upon the Word of God. None of the passages he quotes actually teach the doctrine he is advancing. The idea that believers must visit a portal or open a portal to communicate with God is ridiculous. No true apostle or prophet of God in the Scripture ever taught on the keys to opening a spiritual portal. Nothing in the Scripture describes these portals as spheres of light that begin in the third heaven and open on earth. Nothing in the

Scripture teaches that a portal was opened on the day of Pentecost. Jackson is reading his own revelations back into the text. If Jackson's revelation is truly from God then it establishes a veritable host of doctrines that cannot be found in the pages of Scripture.

The God of the Bible is the sovereign ruler of the entire earth. He works wherever He chooses. He communicates with man wherever and however He chooses.

As one encounters the writings of the various prophets one finds that they frequently borrow revelations from one another. Once a particular doctrine catches hold within the prophetic community, one will find a number of prophets repeating the doctrine.

For instance, Chuck Pierce joins the "portals" mania when he declares, "As we ascend in worship, we also know that a portal opens for angelic visitation."[266]

Likewise, prophetess Kathie Walters informs her followers that there is a major spiritual portal at Niagara Falls that is guarded by over 100 angels.[267]

Through this process of borrowing one another's revelations and expanding upon them, errors that might have otherwise remained localized and largely unnoticed, are propagated like internet viruses throughout the Christian church worldwide. Prophetic internet hubs like the Elijah List and Identity Network also greatly contribute to the worldwide dissemination of error.

Apostolic Love Covers Sin from God's View

In another example of prophets establishing doctrine, Danny Steyne informs us that apostolic love can actually cover a city from God's view. After citing Genesis 18:16-22 Steyne writes,

> "Love Covers...
>
> When God has to visit a place in order to see it, Apostolic Love has covered it! Often I have heard people say that Lot had no business living in Sodom and that he was a compromiser! I believe Lot was a righteous man (2 Peter 2:7) distressed by the world around him. Lot

was nevertheless touched by the hand of God to love those around him to the degree that his love for them "covered" their sins to such a degree, that God couldn't see them from Heaven, but had to take a road trip to find out the truth! Love covers..."[268]

Denny Steyne makes the mistake of literalizing a metaphor or personification. The God of heaven did not have to literally visit Sodom and Gomorrah in order to ascertain the level of their sin. This was a communication to Abraham of the impending judgment on the cities. The metaphor was for Abraham's benefit. It is not meant to be taken literally. Further, it is also difficult to see how Lot could have been an apostle since he lived several thousand years before the time of Christ. This is a perfect example of one of the modern prophets taking a passage and distorting its meaning in order to advance his agenda. Steyne then introduces a completely new doctrine, that of apostolic love building a covering over a city or geographic region.

Critical Speech Releases Demonic Activity

Victoria Boyson through revelation establishes the doctrine that our negative or critical words cause demonic activity in the lives of those we criticize. She states,

> "Our words release hell's destructive power on earth. When we judge others we activate demons against them."[269]

Of course, once one accepts the doctrinal assumption that negative, judgmental or critical words do, in fact, release demonic activity, one has to determine some course of action to counteract negative words spoken by someone else upon oneself. This then leads to doctrines like breaking off curses. The entire situation leads to a spiritual paranoia for one can really never be sure if someone else might have spoken critically of you today. Therefore it becomes necessary to daily break the curses spoken against you. This is exactly what is taught by many within the prophetic community and it has no Biblical justification whatsoever. Never do we see anyone in the Bible going through some ritual or praying to have the curses spoken against them broken. These doctrines have more in common with the occult practice of spell casting than with anything from a Biblical worldview.

Storehouse Cities

In a remarkable addition to traditional eschatology, Paul Keith Davis finds in Genesis 41:41 a mandate that in these last days, God is today raising up overseers who will be stationed in particular cities around the globe (Kansas City being one of them). These overseers will have the right, just as Joseph could go into the wheat fields of Egypt and demand 1/5 of the harvest, these overseers will have the right to go into the fields of men around their cities and demand that 1 in 5 will be saved. These new believers will be brought into the storehouses in these cities and will be trained until the time of disaster on the earth. This will be a time when the whole world will begin to be hungry spiritually just like the world was hungry physically in the days of Joseph. At this time these storehouses will be opened and these believers will be sent out and will bring in the end-time harvest prophesied by so many of the modern prophets of a billion souls. They will defeat the enemy completely in the final hours of this earth and will win the day for Christ.[270]

Once again notice that multiple new doctrines are being established on the basis of the revelation of the modern prophet and not on Scripture. Scriptures do not establish the doctrines of "storehouse cities", end-time overseers, the billion-soul harvest or any of the other doctrines taught in this revelation. Again we see the man-exalting attitude of the movement on full display. Man will completely defeat the enemy and win the day for Christ. How different than the picture presented in the Scriptures where Christ comes as the conquering one who puts down all rule and authority. The book of Revelation states,

> "Then I saw heaven opened, and behold, a white horse! The one sitting on it is called Faithful and True, and in righteousness he judges and makes war. His eyes are like a flame of fire, and on his head are many diadems…From His mouth comes a sharp sword with which to strike the nations, and he will rule them with a rod of iron. He will tread the winepress of the fury of the wrath of God the Almighty." (Rev. 19:11-12a,15)

The apostle Paul concurs writing that Jesus,

> "is revealed from heaven with his mighty angels in flaming fire, inflicting vengeance on those who do not know God and on those who do not obey the gospel of God." (2 Thess. 1:7b-8)

The Scriptures declare that it is Christ that finally defeats the enemy. It is Christ that wins the day.

Judicial Intercession

In 2004 Jim Goll gave the body of Christ a new intercessory assignment directly from the mouth of the Holy Spirit. It was called Judicial Intercession. In this unique teaching, believers are instructed to, in prayer discern the name of the demon or demons afflicting ones household. Then one asks to go before the judgment bar of God in the courtroom of heaven. At this point then, one presents the specific charges against the demon in question and demands reparations. The demon is found guilty by God and must then pay restitution for all of God's blessings that it has blocked. This then will release a tremendous flow of healing and prosperity upon one's house. Goll said it this way.

> "These powers will have a name such as the generational spirit of infirmity, poverty, rejection, abandonment, death etc....After identifying and capturing the thief, then we can bring these criminal demonic forces into courtroom hearing to be judged....First of all, we present our case of the injustices received, and we ask the judge to release the penalty due the offender. The case is heard and the thief is then brought before the judge for sentencing. Secondly, we then file for the appropriate amount of compensation that is due to the same degree of the offense. If we would truly do this with a pure heart and clean hands (Psalms 24:3-6), then the recompense of restored relationships, healing of damaged emotions, stolen health, finances, hope, purpose, prophetic destiny and calling and so much more would be enormous."[271]

Where has this teaching been for the 2,000 year history of the church? It's too bad that Jim wasn't around earlier to teach the church about this method of prayer, this panacea that removes all barriers and opens the floodgates of all blessings! Sarcasm aside, please remember that there are definite doctrinal implications concerning the source of difficulty and disease as well as the solution to these difficulties that must be established and accepted if this revelation is in fact from the Holy Spirit. This revelation has definite doctrinal content.

Cleansing the Land

On October 17th, 2005, the Elijah List offered teachings on how to cleanse one's house and the land upon which the house sets from demonic influences from the land's history and from curses spoken against the current residents. This teaching included a kit that one could use in the process of spiritual cleansing the property.[272]

Prophetic Decrees

Making prophetic or apostolic decrees is another area of new doctrine and practice advocated by many of today's apostles and prophets that has become in vogue in recent years. In this teaching, one is to discern the will of the Lord and then man must bring that will to fruition by declaring it out loud, declaring or commanding it to be so. The prophetic decree then activates the court of heaven to bring the will of God to pass. Once again, man is the key to the process. Apostle Chuck Pierce states the following concerning prophetic decrees,

> "Only God can reveal Himself to us by His Spirit. (Matt. 16). Once we receive revelation, we should begin praying that revelation. Then we move from 'praying to saying'. Prophetic declaration is very important to change the atmosphere of the heavenlies. We become the trumpet of the Lord in all the earth. We are that human shofar."[273]

Todd Bentley demonstrates how to make these decrees. He writes,

> "God, we are going to make a decree: Exaltation will come! Restore! Restore! Restore! God we loose it in heaven. Restore! Restore! Restore! Divine order coming now. In every area where there has been stealing and killing and destroying we speak the word of the Lord. We say over that loss, Restore! Devil give it all back! The thief and the liar, give it all back! God, we believe You will restore and we claim it! God, we ask for it! We declare it!
>
> God, we proclaim the day of your vengeance. We proclaim that this is the year of your favor! This is the year of the Lord's favor! This is the year! This is our acceptable year, liberation, and Jubilee! Lord, I say it over the people today: Favor! Favor! Favor! Divine Favor! I proclaim and I decree: Favor! Favor! Favor! The vengeance of God! The vengeance of God! Ho!"[274]

One simply wonders why, if this is so important in order to "change the atmosphere of the heavenlies" why one cannot find a single word about it in the New Testament. There is not one single example of this kind of proclamation anywhere in the ministry of the apostles. This just seems to be one more man-centered doctrine that enables us to feel extremely important as we assist God in creating his rule over the world.

The Season of the Basilisk

In one of the more bizarre examples of prophets establishing doctrine, Bob Jones (the prophet, not the University president) and Paul Keith Davis, over the course of several years, unfolded a revelation about a particular demonic spirit that is given authority during a particular three-week period to wreak great destruction in the earth. This demon, which they identify as the Basilisk, is most powerful during the period from the 17th of Tammuz through the 9th of AV (remember that God operates on the Jewish calendar according to many of the prophets). This revelation began back in 1996 but culminated in a teaching released on June 21st, 2007, entitled, "The Season of the Basilisk". In this teaching, Davis, the primary author, identifies a number of historical events that have happened during this time period from the smashing of the tablets by Moses to the expulsion of Jews by Ferdinand and Isabella to the declaration of World War I and attributes them all to the work of this demon. The purpose of this revelation was to call the church to heightened spiritual warfare during the "Season of the Basilisk" in 2007 (July 3-24). Davis writes,

> "On July 23, 1996 and again on July 23, 1997, Bob was given visions from the Lord displaying this powerful demonic spirit He is desiring that we understand and oppose. It was clear in the visions that this spirit did not expect to be uncovered nor revealed. This evil spirit is accustomed to operating in secret without being detected or obstructed. This great enemy of the Cross has authority to release extensive destruction and misery in the Earth, especially if unopposed by the praying Church. This evil spirit is identified as Basilisk."

Davis continues,

> "Apparently, during certain cyclical seasons, a tremendous increase in power is given to this spirit to cause death and destruction."[275]

So apparently, the Holy Spirit takes a three week vacation every year from His restraining activity and allows this super-demon to run amok. The only hope for controlling this monster is the praying church. Davis and Jones identify activities attributed to this spirit that go all the way back to Moses but, even though the praying church is vital to the restraint of this demon's destructive activity, God didn't reveal the identity of this spirit to anyone until 1996 and didn't give the full revelation until 2007. So for approximately, 3,500 years, depending on the date on uses for the Exodus, God has given this demon free reign for three weeks every year! Of course, if one picked any three week period and looked down through the pages of time, one would be able to find a number of bad things that occurred and one would not have to postulate the existence of a super-demon who was given heightened authority. All Davis and Jones have uncovered is that man has consistently been sinful since the Fall.

True to form, Davis and Jones attempt to establish this teaching biblically by taking a number of verses that speak of poisonous snakes and applying them to this demon. But it is clear in the article that the real basis for this teaching is the prophetic revelation given to Bob Jones.

2011 the Year of the Lion

Another bizarre prophecy was given by Bob Jones shortly before the beginning of 2011. Speaking at a prophetic gathering, Jones stated that 2009 was the year of the ox. 2010 was the year of the eagle and 2011 would be the year of the Lion. Jones states that the year of the Lion is a year of authority. He states,

> "The Year of the Eagle will end on September the 10th, for I go with the Lord's calendar, which the Jews claim is theirs; but it's really not theirs, it's the Lord's. On September the 10th, the New Year begins. It's the Year of the Lion, so **it's time that the Lion begins to roar.** When the lion roars, he roars into the earth; he doesn't roar into the air, he roars into the earth. **He says, 'This is my territory,' and the vibrations will go out for miles and miles.**
>
> **So, we're coming to the Year of the Lion. We're coming to authority.** Get ready to see authority like you haven't seen before." (emphasis in the original)

He goes on to state that 2012 will be the year of the man and that all of this activity is to prepare for the harvest.[276]

Jones' prophecy makes God appear to work on some type of Christianized version of the Chinese calendar. Nowhere in Scripture does God make these types of declarations. Nowhere does God indicate that He is working in one way throughout the entire earth for the season of a year. This word is purely from Bob Jones' imagination. This has no ring of Biblical truth anywhere in it. And once again, like so many other prophecies that we have already seen, this word is completely man-exalting and man-centered. "We are coming to authority. Get ready to see authority like you haven't seen before." My, aren't we special.

This litany of examples has been given in order to demonstrate that the practice of prophetically inventing new doctrine is not limited to a few obscure and isolated ministries but is rather rampant within the movement. And the examples given in this chapter are just the tip of the iceberg. Space constraints will not permit a discussion of the breaker anointing, Jezebel spirit, soaking or marinating in the Holy Spirit, the Josiah generation, etc., etc. ad nauseum. It would take a virtual encyclopedia to document all the new doctrines and practices moving through this community on a daily basis.

At this point, I suspect that the response of those in the prophetic community to the preceding material would be to say, "But these things aren't doctrines!" This is not written out of sarcasm. After reading more than 6,000 individual prophetic messages, spending hours reading books and listening to sermons by leaders in the movement and interviewing many who are currently as well as formerly in the movement, I truly believe that most members of this community do not have a good understanding of what a doctrine is. It is the only plausible explanation that I can give for how the prophets can claim not to establish doctrine on the one hand while filling the body of Christ with new doctrines on the other hand.

I am convinced that the modern prophets understand doctrine in terms of what might be termed denominational distinctives, in other words doctrines that define particular movements within the larger body of Christ. While these are certainly doctrines, the word is actually much broader in meaning than that.

Webster's Dictionary defines doctrine as "something that is taught". That's it. A doctrine is something that is taught. We might say that a doctrine is something that is believed to be true.

Now it is patently obvious that these prophetic messages contain a great deal of teaching. One can only assume that the prophets themselves believe these teachings to be true. The prophets intend that these teachings be taken seriously by their listeners or readers. They intend that their readers believe these teachings to be true. In most instances, the prophets advocate some form of behavior change on the part of their hearers in order for those individual's lives to line up with the new revelation whether that be to engage in a new form of intercession or the use of a ritual to cleanse their property. They are therefore doctrines. Further many of these teachings come with the authority of being a word from the Holy Spirit or an open heaven visitation and we know that God expects His word to be taken seriously and that such words are binding upon all believers. Since none of these teachings have any clear support in Scripture, which is why the church has never taught them until now, the real basis for establishing these doctrines is the revelation of the modern prophet. Period. So despite all the protests to the contrary, modern prophets are writing doctrines.

Of course the question that immediately springs to mind though is, "Why shouldn't these prophets establish doctrines?" If the apostles and the prophets of the past established doctrines and if this is truly the greatest generation of apostles and prophets that has ever lived then why shouldn't these apostles and prophets establish doctrines as well?

The fact is, that despite all the exalted claims and the bravado this group of ministers knows that what they are doing is far less than the revelation of Isaiah, Daniel or Paul. Despite all the smoke and mirrors, these teachers know that if they are compared with the New Testament apostles or the prophets in the Old Testament, they will pale in comparison. This is why they run from the tests given in the book of Deuteronomy. They can't pass them and they know it. Furthermore, they know that if they were to overtly claim to be bringing revelations on par with Scripture that even people as doctrinally weak as their average followers would recognize instantly that they are frauds. Such a claim would open them up to the charge that they are cult leaders because they would have an authority other than the Bible. So they must tip their hat to the Scriptures as the final authority for truth all the while undermining that same authority by introducing teachings of their own that stand in addition to or even in contradiction to the Word of God. In this way, they may appear to be orthodox all the while promoting every form of heresy.

And all of this new revelation does come with a cost.

All of these doctrines and activities distract the church from the pure milk of the word, from the doctrine that is able to build up and that will prove to be a sure foundation in times of trouble. These practices divert the church from truly God-honoring and God-ordained methods for spiritual growth and evangelism. They move the church into activities that are at best frivolous and at worst animistic and occultic. They are man-centered rather than Christ-centered and cause their adherents to become prideful and self-exalted. The result is a group of followers, especially young people that are very passionate and excited but that are easily defeated. The church is weaker not better.

CHAPTER TWELVE

Oops! They did it Again
Modern Apostles and False Prophecy

There will be rapidity, and there will be acceleration so that America will suddenly have five new sources of energy. Kim Clement[277]

The Old Testament Scriptures are very clear that a true prophet of God did not have the luxury of being wrong. (Deut. 13 & 18) As we have discussed previously Old Testament prophets and New Testament apostles could be identified by the fact that they spoke the very words of God and these words came to pass.

As previously discussed, New Testament scholar Wayne Grudem makes a strong case for a level of prophecy in the New Testament that is much lower than that of the Old Testament prophets and the New Testament apostles. This would amount to merely impressions that should be introduced with a humble, "I sense the Lord might be leading us to......"

Whether one agrees with Grudem's conclusions or not, the fact is that if this were all today's prophets were doing, a book like this would be unnecessary. But the sad truth is, as this book has already demonstrated repeatedly, they are doing and claiming a great deal more. These prophets and apostles claim to be carrying Elijah's mantle and filling a role greater than the apostles of the first century church. As discussed earlier, they make these outlandish claims until they miss.

In this chapter, we will examine the most common responses of those in the prophetic movement to the overwhelmingly large number of failed prophecies given regularly. In addition we will examine a few instances of these failed prophecies. Lastly, we will discuss the impact that such failed prophecy has on the church as a whole and on individual believers.

It should be noted that none of the modern apostles and prophets deny that there is a great deal of failed prophecy in the movement. Even the best of their number only claim to be 66% accurate. While it is doubtful that they could even support this claim of accuracy, if one accepts their own numbers that means that nearly one third of all the prophetic messages being given are complete misses! Given the incredibly large amount of prophetic activity occurring in today's church, this would mean the amount of false prophecies numbers well into the thousands. While the greatest problem within the movement is still the false doctrines being promulgated, surely the issue of failed prophecy is not a minor issue.

But, in listening to the defenders of the movement, one is given a completely different picture.

It's No Big Deal

Perhaps the most common response among members of the apostolic/prophetic movement to the mass of failed prophecies is to deny the seriousness of the issue. While they magnify their claims about their own status and ability, they consistently minimize the significance of placing words in the mouth of God that He did not say. They fail to appreciate the awesomeness of claiming to speak for God. The following comment by Francis Frangipane is typical of this attitude. In an interview with Charisma magazine regarding Rick Joyner and his failed prophecy concerning the destruction of California, Frangipane stated,

> "The idea that a prophet should never make a mistake assumes that teachers, evangelists and pastors also never make mistakes," says author and pastor Francis Frangipane. "All are speaking for the Lord, yet who has not admitted that they either taught something wrong or at least publicly repeated wrong information?"[278]

The problem with Frangipane's statement is that the Bible itself never makes this same association. The Bible does not equate the level of revelation being given in the teaching ministry with that which is claimed in the prophetic ministry. The fact is that there is a higher level of accountability for the person who speaks, "Thus saith the Lord" than for other types of ministry. With the teacher, evangelist and pastor there is, or should be, an understanding that the person is taking from the Word of God and interpreting it, explaining it and applying it to the congregation. It is implied that there is a mixture of the human and the divine. The possibility for error is acknowledged and indeed, as Frangipane correctly points out, all honest pastors would have to admit that at some point in the past they have been wrong. But a prophet speaking "thus saith the Lord" is supposedly speaking from direct revelation. It is an immediate word directly from God. This does not allow for the same mixture of divine and human activity because the Word of God cannot be wrong. There is a higher level of accountability for someone who is claiming direct revelation than one who is teaching from the Scriptures. The Scriptures indicates that it is a serious thing to claim to speak directly from God. It would seem today's apostles and prophets do not truly appreciate this issue.

But consider the word of the Lord through the prophet Jeremiah concerning those who prophesy falsely in the Name of the Lord:

> "I have heard what the prophets have said who prophesy lies in my name, saying, 'I have dreamed, I have dreamed!' How long shall there be lies in the heart of the heart of the prophets who prophesy lies, and who prophesy the deceit of their own heart, who think to make my people forget my name by their dreams that they tell one another, even as their fathers forgot my name for Baal? Let the prophet who has a dream tell the dream, but let him who has my word speak my word faithfully. What has straw in common with wheat? Declares the LORD. Is not my word like fire, declares the LORD, and like a hammer that breaks the rock in pieces? Therefore, behold, I am against the prophets, declares the LORD, who steal my words from one another. Behold, I am against the prophets, declares the LORD, who use their tongues and declare, 'declares the LORD". Behold, I am against those who prophesy lying dreams, declares the LORD, and who tell them and lead my people astray by their lies and their recklessness, when I did not send them or charge them. So they do not profit this people at all, declares the LORD." (Jeremiah 23:25-32)

These are serious words and must be weighed heavily by anyone who dares to speak a word in the name of the Lord. The modern prophets may not feel that their errant predictions are serious but that will not help them escape their accountability before the Lord.

Baby Prophets

If dismissing the entire topic of failed prophecy as one not worthy of serious consideration does not work, a second line of defense is to claim that these are baby prophets and babies make messes. In this scenario, the prophetic gifting is treated like any other spiritual gift. We expect that a pastor will become better at his ministry over time. We allow for growth and development in all the other gifts and the prophetic, so the argument goes, is no different. We could see a version of this in Shultz's statements regarding Deuteronomy 18 quoted in chapter 2. A prophet who makes false prophecies is merely a person who is still learning to hear from God.

The problem with this line of reasoning is similar to the previous one. The fact is that the Scriptures themselves do not allow for this development, if one is speaking of the same level of prophesying done by the Old Testament prophets or New Testament apostles. The argument appears logical at first but it simply cannot be supported biblically. There is no caveat. There is no exception. There is no gray area.

And how could there be? If a person is truly having an "open vision" then there can be no ambiguity. If a person is truly taken to heaven and hears the Lord speak to them personally, then that word must by definition be accurate. If they heard the internal, audible voice of God and heard the very words themselves then these words must be true for God neither lies nor makes mistakes. There is no room in these types of claims for a learning curve. Either these people are hearing directly from God or they are not. If they continue to claim that they are, then their words must pass the test.

Once again, the modern prophets want to have it both ways, they want to claim a status and privilege equal to the prophets of Scripture but do not want to accept the same level of responsibility and accountability. If they are carrying the same mantle as the prophets of Scripture then they should meet the same standard. If they are unable to do so, then they need to stop all the self-aggrandizing statements and outlandish claims and admit that what they are speaking are at best impressions on their hearts and minds.

God would have to kill us

"Prophet" Bob Jones gives one of the most interesting, and ludicrous explanations attempted by a member of the apostolic/prophetic community. Jones claims that if the prophetic words were 100% accurate then God would have to kill those who disobeyed like he did Ananias and Saphira. The following discourse is from an interview with Bob Jones conducted by Mike Bickle. (It should be noted that Jones frequently has to have his revelations mediated by another prophet like Bickle or Paul Keith Davis because, like the oracle of Delphi, Jones's words are frequently incoherent if taken by themselves. The discerning individual might keep that fact in mind when evaluating the claims of Jones's startlingly accurate predictions in the past. One must seriously consider whether some historical revision has occurred.)

> (Jones) 'The Rhema (*the spoken word as opposed to the logos or written word. While the bible does not really make a hard distinction between these two words, Charismatic leaders frequently do.*) will be two-thirds right on. Not quite time for Ananias and Sapphira yet.'

> (Bickle) 'The Lord actually said that sentence to you?'

> (Jones) 'Yeah, I mean what he was really showing me was: I'm going to release the Rhema to where that many begin to move two-thirds right on with their words, and the other third will be like poppin' a bullet at the enemy and he wouldn't fire. It was a blank. And he (God) said: I'm the one that's loading the gun, so there's going to be some blanks there . . . the blanks is (sic) pointed in the general direction of the enemy anyway, . . . If I (God) release the 100% Rhema right now, the accountability would be so awesome and you'd have so much Ananias and Sapphira going on the people couldn't grow.'[279]

So apparently, if the Lord gave the church a pure word, the level of accountability would be so great that God would have to kill people left and right and the church would stagnate. Had Jones read the story of Ananias and Sapphira in context, he might have noticed that their problem was not that they didn't listen to God's prophets. Ananias and Sapphira were killed because they pretended to give all the proceeds of the land they sold to the church when in fact they kept some for themselves. They attempted to deceive not only men but God Himself. But, as we have repeatedly demonstrated throughout the course of this book, context is irrelevant for a prophet in need of a verse that appears to substantiate his opinion.

But the idea that God Himself would load "some blanks" into the guns of these prophets is also extremely problematic. Essentially, this makes God directly responsible for false prophecy. This is hard to reconcile with a God who, according to the New Testament, cannot lie (Titus 1:2, Heb. 6:18)

Additionally, the idea that the church can grow better under a mixture of true and false words is ridiculous. Peter told the believers to earnestly desire the pure milk of the word for their spiritual growth. The apostles repeatedly admonished the church to shun false teachings.

Lastly, even though one would be hard-pressed to find a modern prophet who was 66% accurate, the Biblical standard remains 100%. God did not equivocate. He did not lower the standard. Jones and Bickle may wish to dance around the standard and attempt to lower the bar in order to justify what is happening in today's church but God's word remains firm.

So despite the best efforts of its leaders, the prophetic community fails to reasonably, convincingly and most importantly, biblically explain how they can, at the same time be speaking the very words of God and give false prophecies. They fail to explain how they should be given status equal to biblical prophets without having to pass the biblical test. Despite the popularity of the song, it would appear that these are not the days of Elijah but something altogether different.

Chronicle of failed prophecies

The list of failed and false prophecies proclaimed by the modern apostles and prophets is exceedingly long. Space will only allow for a small sampling of the examples in this area.

It should be noted again that there is a significant difference between the failed prophecies of the modern prophets and those of the Biblical prophets that were reversed by God and therefore did not come to pass. As was noted earlier, the Lord has clearly said in Jeremiah 18, that judgment pronounced upon a nation might be avoided upon the repentance of that nation. Indeed there are examples in the Bible where the prophecy itself was the means that God used to bring about such a repentance. The city of Nineveh is a classic example. The prophecy of Jonah led to repentance to which God responded by foregoing the cities destruction. In these cases, the Bible is very specific to demonstrate that it was a change in the heart and behavior of the people standing under the threat of imminent judgment that led to the averting of the disaster. This is markedly different from a prophetic word that simply fails to materialize. It is this last issue that is rampant within the apostolic and prophetic movement.

The cleverest among the modern day prophetic practitioners make prophecies that are unverifiable. They prophesy great increases for the kingdom of God or seasons of breakthrough for God's people. These words are so vague as to be essentially meaningless though they sound impressive. One would never be able to know when and if they were ever fulfilled. These words constitute the vast majority of what is being published today as prophecy. In some ways it is difficult to chronicle the success or failure of many of the modern prophets because their words are not testable.

But one guy that can always be counted upon to go out on a broken limb is Kim Clement. Clement is proof positive that modern prophets can be wrong more often than a bad weatherman and still garner a following. (My apologies to all meteorologists for the unjust comparison.)

For instance, in early 2004, Clement supposedly received a word from the Lord about the upcoming capture of Osama Ben Laden. He stated,

> "Osama Ben Laden said that in 35 days, America, he was prophesying, predicting, that this country would be abolished basically, wiped out, because he has a plan for 35 days. And the word of the Lord came to me...the spirit of the Lord said to me, 'You prophesy that the very thing that he said and predicted for this nation, tell him, prophesy, that that is reversed, and I'm going to bring him out in 35 days!'"[280]

When this prophecy failed to materialize, the prophetic community attempted a number of valiant explanations but none were convincing. Most readers will surely know that the demise of Ben Laden did not occur until 2011, and he was killed, not captured.

In the same prophecy, Clement also proclaims,

> "Alzheimer's has come against too many of God's people...The word of the Lord, the prophetic word of the Lord is coming to you tonight. Alzheimer's, diabetes, Parkinson's disease, a rare bone disease and lung, God says, these five things will suddenly come to the surface with incredible discoveries and it will begin this year...God is going to bring it to pass because of your prayers...We declare it is done, in the Name of Jesus..."[281]

One first notices that while God can specify to the prophet Alzheimer's, diabetes and Parkinson's diseases, God becomes very vague about the bone disease to be healed and the phrase, "and lung" could mean almost anything. It appears that the "prophet" is simply speaking off the cuff. But still more pertinent is that the prophecy was given in 2004. Great discoveries were to begin that year. Today, as of the writing of this book none of these diseases have experienced the "incredible discoveries" Clement prophesied would begin to come to the surface. Clement simply got it wrong. As one with family members suffering from both diabetes and Alzheimer's I wish that he had been right about this but he wasn't.

But Clement wasn't done. He further stated,

> "On March the 11th and the month of March has been set aside by God for the church in the United States of America for something unbelievably wonderful to happen—so powerful...God just said to me, there's going to be one unusual event... almost like a renting of something, a curtain, a veil for the church."[282]

Once again, nothing came of this prophecy. March 11th, 2004 indeed the entire month of March came and went with nothing noticeable much less "unbelievably wonderful" happening for the church.

Bob Jones attempted to bail Clement out by saying that this prophecy was fulfilled in the Spiritual realm. According to Bob the glory of God had left the church in 1977 but returned to the church in the fulfillment of Clement's prophecy on March 11, 2004. So an unnoticeable, unverifiable event from 1977 was reversed by an unnoticeable, unverifiable event in 2004.[283] One is reminded of Jehovah's Witnesses who also must appeal to spiritual fulfillments of their failed prophecies concerning the return of Christ. Clement's prophecy clearly anticipates a physical, visible fulfillment. Jones's words are simply a weak attempt to cover the obvious miss.

Another example of Clement's errant track record can be found in his proclamations concerning the Christmas season of 2006.

November 19, 2006 - Humble, TX

An Unfolding of Many Things through the Christmas Season

"This is Your Year of Jubilee"

The Spirit of God says, "It is My desire and My intention to take unnecessary debt away from My people. It shall come to pass that in the New Year, supernatural intervention shall drive you," says the Lord. "This is your year of Jubilee."

God says, "There will be an unfolding of many things through the **Christmas season** that will cause **volcanic eruptions**." The Spirit says, "There will be eruptions of a great kind, where the Kingdom has been stifled by men's blindness, because sight has come, and men have seen the glory of the King."

God says, "A spirit of acceleration shall bring about rapidly, like a **volcano**--wondrous things from My Spirit. I have chosen things **every month of next year**--every month to come to you as a treasure." God says, "There will be one breakthrough for every person that has seen and perceived the glory of God's Kingdom. I will give you one miracle a month," says the Spirit of the Living God.

"In your **Christmas**, I shall bring something during that season to this nation, and to the nations that have cried out." God says, "Do not say that Christmas is not the celebration day. This Christmas, I will bring about changes so massive, that the Church shall no longer even look like the Church has looked before. I will invade the **marketplace**. I will take **Texas**, and I will honor you. I will buckle the **Bible belt** again, and bring honor back to you," says the Lord.[284]

Again, nothing earth shaking or volcanic occurred over the Christmas season unless one considers the death of a 90 year old former president particularly remarkable for the kingdom of God. What was this change that was "so massive" that the church was supposed to no longer look like it did before? This massive change simply did not occur. Nor did anyone seem to notice the things that were to come to the church as a treasure in "every month" of 2007. The only thing "massive" here is the way this prophecy failed to come to pass.

Bill Yount is a folksy guy with a grandfatherly face and a unique visionary style. His prophecies are normally of the unverifiable kind, i.e. "I see a joining of the old and new generation of believers" or "Angels imbedded in church walls are being activated" but occasionally, he goofs and actually prophecies something that can be tested. Consider the following example:

> "I Heard the Father Say...'I am Beginning to Prophesy Through Commercials, Candy and Clothing—Especially Over the Holidays!"

> "I sense the Father saying, 'I will begin to meddle in the candy industry.' I sense the Lord is going to begin to name some new candy bars. When these are named they will release a prophetic anointing every time the name of the candy is mentioned. These names will have the power to call forth life and salvation. I am sure this prophetic candy is bound to have a heavenly taste to it that will be out of this world! People will end up tasting and seeing that the Lord is good! I saw angels anointing candy bar wrappers like God anointing prayer cloths of the Apostle Paul. Names on popular candy wrappers will speak prophetically to whomever reads or speaks their names. Candy wrappers will become like anointed prayer cloths throughout the land."[285]

Just what were those new candy bars whose names released a prophetic anointing? Where are the testimonies of people who were called to life and salvation by the mere mention of these names? Were large numbers of people healed by having candy wrappers laid on them like the cloths that were taken from the apostle Paul?

In the same prophecy Yount said that "Levi's" jeans were going to receive a prophetic anointing to call forth the spiritual Levites of this hour and that "Wrangler" clothing would be anointed to tame the tongue and give people the "tongue of the learned to speak a word to those who are weary."[286]

Yount ends this "word" with the statement:

> "Earth, Earth...hear the word of the Lord"[287]

This statement, whether intentional or not, places Yount's candy bar prophecy on par with the prophecies of Isaiah, Jeremiah and the rest of the prophets. Yount calls on all the earth to hear the word of the Lord in this prophecy. Yount either heard the Lord or he did not. There is no room for ambiguity here. If the prophecy did not come to pass, and clearly it did not, then Yount has spoken presumptuously and is a false prophet. He should repent and quit proclaiming nonsense to the body of Christ. To date, he has not done so.

Yount's prophecy is laughable and silly. It could probably be argued that, aside from the publishers at Elijah List, few people, if any at all, took Yount's prophecy seriously. Apart from the embarrassment that such prophecy brings to the body of Christ little lasting harm was probably done. Such is not always the case however.

One of the most devastating and potentially damaging of the failed prophecies was issued by Rick Joyner in conjunction with Bob Jones.

On December 31, 1997 Rick Joyner and Bob Jones prophesied that California was to be destroyed by earthquakes and nuclear bombs. The Mississippi river will be 35 miles wide. The timetable for this prophecy was nine months.[288] Obviously this prophecy did not occur. This is the failed prophecy which the Charisma article was referencing when it interviewed Francis Frangipane about failed prophecy.

This prophecy by Joyner is extremely important because it shows the danger of following these wandering stars. It caused near panic among some of their followers in California. People sold houses and left jobs in order to escape the impending doom. Somehow Joyner saying, "Oops, sorry", just doesn't seem to cover it. Though he admits now that he should not have released the prophecy (he says it was misunderstood but one struggles to see how this was possible nor does this feeble attempt at a cover explain why the misunderstanding wasn't corrected by the prophets immediately), there is no way to make restitution to those whose lives were disrupted because of this errant word. Even more seriously, there is no attempt to undue the spiritual damage and disillusionment that occurs in the lives of the naïve when these prophet's words fail to come to pass.

More recent examples of failed prophecies would be a couple by Catherine Brown. On March 27, 2007, Brown issued a prophetic word with the following title, "THERE WILL BE A SEVEN-YEAR PERIOD OF PLENTY, FOLLOWED BY A SEVEN-YEAR PERIOD OF FAMINE". In this prophecy, Brown claimed to have powerful words from the Lord spoken into her heart, including the following:

"There will be a seven-year period of plenty, followed by a seven-year period of famine. From 2007-2014, I am granting a window of grace and mercy to prepare for the seven years of famine."

"I am calling for the Kingdom economists and accountants, for without them, My Church cannot fulfill her global mandate on the earth. I am going to pour out My anointing upon them in unprecedented levels. It will be seen as a thousand-fold increase of the anointing that was upon My servant Joseph in the days of Egypt."

Notice that the season of plenty was to last for seven years. This was to give time to prepare for the harvest and the season of famine. Also notice that the anointing for this time of plenty was to be a thousand-fold increase of the anointing on Joseph in Egypt.[288] That is truly powerful stuff.

Of course, on September 15th of 2008, just one year into the prophesied time of plenty, the Dow Jones lost 500 points in a day. It was one of the worst financial crashes in recent history. The markets remained volatile for months afterward costing numerous jobs and prompting governmental leaders to institute a number of bail-out programs. As of the writing of this book the economy still has not even recovered much less had the type of increase that Brown called for in her prophetic word. Can we call this a failed prophecy now or do we have to wait until 2014? Of course by 2008 most people had forgotten all about Brown's false prophecy so she didn't have to face any real consequences for her failed prediction.

The point needs to be made again that Brown was claiming to receive the very words of God. She claimed first person communication. This wasn't a vision that she would have to interpret. If Brown actually heard these words from God, they would have come to pass. Since they did not, it is self-evident that this was not a word from the Lord.

Later in that same year, on June 22, 2007 Brown declared, "A Word about Revival in Sweden". In this prophecy Brown first gives us insight into how modern prophets get their words. She says that a friend called her who had been to Sweden and then she saw that the meatballs she was about to cook were in a package labeled, "Crown of Sweden". This of course was clearly an indication that the King of Kings had a word for Sweden. Those unfamiliar with the prophetic movement might think that this is an extreme example but that is not so. Modern prophets regularly receive prophetic promptings through ordinary daily events, alarm clocks, car odometers, calendars etc. The list is truly endless. These leaders of the mystical church of the twenty-first century can find prophetic significance virtually everywhere. They are omen seekers and tea leaf readers.

So what was the word from God concerning Sweden? He was about to bring revival. According to Brown this revival in Sweden was to last three years. She then goes on to say,

> "I see this revival in Sweden gaining national and international media attention. I see many children and youth being caught up in Heavenly visitations and a phenomenal outpouring of prophetic utterance on the Swedish people. **I see miracle meetings in the land with huge numbers of conversions and healings with creative miracles as part of the blessing.**" (emphasis in the original)[289]

We should now be coming to the end of the three year revival period. There has been no indication of great numbers of conversions or any of the other signs in Sweden. The "revival" of course has not gained any national or international media attention.

The revival simply did not happen. It became one more example in the litany of failed prophecies from today's prophets.

In similar fashion, on July 28th, 2007 Bobby Conner prophesied the following:

> "WE STAND ON THE VERGE OF THE LARGEST HEALING MOVEMENT IN THE HISTORY OF THE CHURCH!"
>
> I have experienced the outstanding privilege of being in ministry meetings when suddenly the entire room would be filled with the overwhelming smell of fresh baked bread. In most of the cases when this occurred, we would experience marvelous manifestations of divine healing. Jesus states that healing is the children's bread (see Mark 7:27). This bread for the sick and hurting is the Lord Jesus serving the bread of His Presence, for He is the Healer. The Holy Spirit is releasing an awesome anointing for healing in our day; this anointing is going to be placed upon the Body of Christ.

In a prophetic visitation the Lord said to me, "Tell the Church, ready or not here I come, and I have a gift in My hand--it is the gift of healing. It will be placed upon the Body, not just upon somebody." We have witnessed the marvelous gift of healing move and minister while resting upon somebody."[290]

Once again, it would seem that there is no possibility for misinterpretation of this word. Bobby received it in a prophetic visitation directly from the Lord. And this word seems to be unconditional for the Lord says, "ready or not here I come".

We are now three years later. The healing movement did not come. Really not much has changed. Many of the modern prophets are now saying that we have been in the wilderness in the last several years. Of course, most people have forgotten that Conner gave this message and have simply moved on to other things. One of the reasons that these prophets can continue to prophesy falsely is that they know few people, especially among those who are their followers, are actually keeping track of what they say.

Fulfilled prophecy?

It is interesting also to see the lengths to which members of the prophetic community will go in order to attempt to find a fulfilled prophecy. On July 2nd, 2004 the Elijah List published an email with the following title,

> "Peter Wagner Points to Accurate Prophecy by Chuck Pierce Over Colorado".

Wagner introduces the prophecy this way,

> "Here is a notable, accurate prophecy from Chuck Pierce that I believe Elijah List readers will like. The prophecy, given in October 2003, was that rain would come to Colorado. Here are three recent newspaper pieces reporting that, after four years of drought, this year we have been getting good rain so far."[291]

True to his word, Wagner does include recent newspaper articles discussing the rain in Colorado. While it must be remembered that one correct prophecy does not make one a prophet, this at first does look like a case where the prophet got it right. One can understand why the Elijah List, which has published so many false prophecies in its history, would be excited to show a success. But problems emerge when one actually reads the prophecy. Instead of actually prophesying rain, here's what Pierce actually said,

> "What I saw over Colorado was this: Watch the lightnings (sic) this year. The atmosphere is going to be charged here. The lightnings (sic) couldn't get to the ground, and you are to call the lightnings (sic) to the ground. I don't know what that means. In the past, the lightnings (sic) have stayed in the atmosphere but not gotten to the ground to really bring that connection from the heavenly strength of God into the very ground that we are in here. God wants the ground to connect with the lightnings (sic) of God this year whatever that means....The Lord says watch Colorado this year because it could go either way. Don't rationalize the drought that dwells above you and manifests in the earth realm, because it has not been decided yet how the overall State [Colorado] is going to embrace the covenant of God. You will be able to discern that better this year by the atmospheric change and how the rain that is in heaven above you touches the earth. It will be a sign to you this year. Cry out for the rain that is in the atmosphere to come down on the earth of Colorado as a sign because that says you are entering into a new dimension of tabernacle as a State."[292]

Moving past the cryptic statements that even Pierce admits he doesn't understand, one notices that Pierce doesn't really prophesy rain at all. He tells them to cry out for the rain because the rain or lack thereof will be a sign this year of Colorado's spiritual state. Pierce says it hasn't yet been decided which way it will go. So Pierce's notably accurate prophecy boils down to, "It will either rain or not rain over Colorado this year."

Wow. Thanks Chuck. This was a gutsy call.

One thing that the discerning reader can readily pick up on in the previous example is the significant editing that is done in the reporting of fulfilled prophecies versus what is actually said in the prophecies themselves. This example ought to be kept in mind the next time one hears of a prophet who is incredibly accurate in what they say or that one hears of great prophecies in the history of a movement that dramatically came to pass. There is a great deal of historical revision that occurs in the prophetic movement with regard to the fulfillment of prophecy.

Of course the easiest way to demonstrate "fulfilled" prophetic words is simply not to report them until after they have supposedly come to pass. One will frequently read that a particular prophet predicted something that recently happened without any accompanying documentation to show when it was that they made their prediction.

In light of the litany of failed prophecies with the modern prophetic movement the words of Richard Fisher seem particularly relevant, "today's modern prophets are like a child playing an instrument and making numerous mistakes all the while claiming to be a prodigy. We are just supposed to ignore all the sour notes." Today's apostles and prophets are truly wells without water. They boast great things but produce little results.

The Effect of Failed Prophecies

1. Personal damage- As was mentioned earlier, people who base critical decisions on the words given by these prophets may face serious personal damage when the word turns out to be wrong. One of the authors knew two young ladies who dropped out of college after receiving a personal prophetic word. They were determined to pursue a musical career together even though neither of them were particularly talented in that area. Despite the best attempts of both students and professors, the girls were determined because they were sure they had "heard from God". Another prophet who had taken up residence in the Kansas City area had many of the members of his church investing in food supplies and generators in preparation for a supposed invasion of the United States by Iraq that was to have occurred in the 1990's. When the prophecy failed to materialize the prophet simply moved on but the people were left with the personal results.

2. Spiritual damage- What happens to people spiritually when prophecies fail? In many cases they become discouraged. How did God let them down? What did they do that prevented God's Word from coming to pass? Severe confusion can result. If they were wrong about this prophet whom they had trusted so much, how can they know when it is ok to trust another minister? And if this word wasn't from God, how will they recognize when direction is truly from the Lord? Once again, the prophets rarely have to fix their own messes.

3. Loss of credibility to the church- But what about the credibility of the gospel message in the eyes of the world. The failed prophecies by these

prophets make the church appear gullible (which is sadly true in too many cases). Skeptics like the amazing Randi tend to project what they see in the modern prophets backward onto the Bible and assume Jesus and the apostles were playing the same shell games as the modern prophets but no one was able to catch them.

Additionally, the church comes off much like the boy who cried wolf. We have said, "thus saith the Lord" so much that the words now have a hollow ring. May God forgive us for cheapening His Word.

CHAPTER THIRTEEN

Must We Follow Modern Apostles and Prophets?
The Authority of Modern Apostles and Prophets

No ministry which rejects or avoids what is now happening in the restoration of the prophetic ministry will be able to truly fulfill its own calling and purpose in this hour.—Rick Joyner

There is a very practical question that emerges from this discussion of the apostolic and the prophetic. The question is, "What authority do these people have over today's church?" This is a very real concern. If one discounts the words of the modern apostles and prophets is he being disobedient to God? How should the church respond to these men and women?

In beginning this discussion it would be good to look at the authority of a prophet of God in the Old Testament and of the apostles in the New Testament. If today's apostles and prophets are the continuation of this gifting as they believe God states in Ephesians 4:11, then it would be reasonable to assume that they have similar authority. It would also be reasonable to expect them to meet certain Biblical criteria.

If, on the other hand, what they are doing is something quite different altogether, what should the response of the church be?

Old Testament Prophets Spoke with Absolute Authority

The words of the Old Testament prophet carried the complete authority of God Himself. Their words were to be obeyed without question. To fail to follow the words of the prophet in the Old Testament was to risk the judgment of God. God condemned the nation of Israel in Jeremiah's day for failing to listen to the voice of the prophet. Through His prophet God says,

> "I set watchmen over you, saying, 'Pay attention to the sound of the trumpet!' But they said, 'We will not pay attention.' Therefore hear, O nations, and know, O congregation, what will happen to them. Hear, O earth; behold, I am bringing disaster upon this people , the fruit of their devices, because they have not paid attention to my words; and as for my law; they have rejected it." (Jeremiah 7:17-19)

Once Israel had established that a particular individual was a prophet, his or her words were to have unquestioned authority. This makes perfect sense because God's Word has absolute authority. If a prophet is truly speaking for God then to disobey the prophet is the same as disobeying God Himself.

New Testament Apostles Spoke with Absolute Authority

Even a cursory study of the New Testament will demonstrate that the New Testament apostles saw themselves as delivering the Word of the Lord and carrying an authority that was in a similar vein with the prophets of old. They believed that they were speaking the very Word of God and that this word then was to be obeyed.

Paul claimed that his word was really in fact the very Word of God (1 Thess. 2:13). Since the word of the apostles was the Word of God, Peter called on his readers to remember the commandment of the Lord and Savior given through the apostles. (2 Pet. 3:2) Indeed the apostles felt free to give commandments to the church. Paul commanded the Thessalonians to stay away from a brother walking in idleness (2 Thess. 3:6). He commanded the church in Corinth to discipline and remove the brother walking in immorality (1 Cor. 5:3-5; 13). The Revelation of the apostle John was preserved by the church and placed in the canon for future generations to study as the Word of God.

All of these examples and so many more that could be produced demonstrate that the New Testament apostles saw themselves in the same tradition as the prophets of the old covenant. Their words were to be obeyed.

But as we have discussed in the early chapters of this book, there does seem to be a distinction with the New Testament prophets. Their words are to be judged and weighed. There are no prophecies from the Corinthian prophets that were preserved within the canon of Scripture. We know that Philip's daughters prophesied but we are not told anything about what they said. Their words clearly were not Scripture. This would seem to indicate that there is a lower form of gifting in the New Testament that amounts to "something God brings to mind", as Dr. Grudem would state it, that is less than the authoritative Word of God.

The pivotal question is then, "What kind of authority are the modern apostles and prophets claiming for themselves?"

It is the contention of this book that the modern apostles and prophets are claiming an authority for themselves that is equal to or greater than the authors of Scripture. They make great claims but are unwilling and unable to endure the level of accountability that comes with such claims. Let us consider the level of authority assert for themselves.

Speaking the Very Words of God

In some sense this assertion is made every time one of the prophets claims to be speaking the Word of God or speaks in first person from the Lord. Modern prophets do not seem to understand the seriousness of this.

For instance Mike Bickle writes,

> "For the most part, the same New Testament prophetic gift can operate in very different packages. Usually people have no problem with the woman in the prayer group who feels a burden to pray for someone, who senses the Holy Spirit leading her prayer, and who states that God is 'impressing' something on her heart. All of this is in a package that most people are familiar with and understand.

> "But if she speaks up during the Sunday morning service in her non-charismatic church and loudly proclaims her revelation interspersed with 'Thus saith the Lord', she could get a significantly different response. Here are the same words and the same message, but delivered in a very different package."[293]

As was stated in the introduction, Bickle's assertion that a person saying that the Holy Spirit might be impressing something upon her and the same person proclaiming loudly, "thus saith the Lord" are equivalent statements is simply wrong. By definition the phrase "thus saith the Lord" invokes the authority of God Almighty. The words of God cannot ever have less authority today than they did in the Scripture. If a proclamation is truly coming with "thus saith the Lord" authority then it is to be obeyed. In fact, to disobey or ignore a statement coming directly from God is to risk God's wrath and judgment. We are accountable to the Word of God to follow it. Claiming to be speaking in the first person for God is to claim the authority of a word with no mixture of error. This same thing would be true for prophecies claiming to come in open heaven revelations. These prophecies must be 100% accurate. They are claiming that level of divine import.

In the same manner, when a prophet like Bill Yount ends a prophecy with the words, "Earth, earth... hear the word of the Lord" as he did in his infamous candy bar revelation, he is echoing the manner of the Old Testament prophets. Not only so, but he is calling the entire earth to respond to the word of the Lord that he has just proclaimed. To place oneself in such a position is to claim the status of the Old Testament prophets. The corresponding accountability must accompany such proclamations. Once again, the prophets must not continue to have it both ways, high authority with no accountability.

But additionally, modern prophets do occasionally directly claim that they are speaking the very words of God. Once again we turn to Mike Bickle as he comments on Wayne Grudem's claim that the New Testament prophets spoke something God brought to mind and not the very words of God. Bickle states,

> "While affirming the value of the 'mixed lot', Grudem argues from 1 Corinthians 14:36 that no prophets can ever speak 'words of God'. Grudem has been very helpful in making a clear distinction between the authority of Scripture and prophetic utterances.

> "However, I do not believe he convincingly eliminates the possibility of a person speaking a prophetic word or words that are 100 percent accurate in every detail and, as such, are God's words....

> "On occasion God speaks to His servants in an audible voice. Clearly these are His 'very words' that may be reported with 100 percent accuracy.

"Additionally, open visions of the spiritual realm or of future events are familiar modes of communications to those who move in the prophetic realm with a remarkable degree of accuracy."[294]

Let's start with areas of agreement. If God truly speaks to a person in an audible voice then it would be agreed that these are his very words. The first issue of course then becomes that this person must be correct in everything they say for there is no room for a mixture of error in a word truly coming from God by direct impartation. This is the whole point. Modern prophets are consistently claiming this level of authority while, at the same time, proclaiming words that are Biblical heresy and prophecies that fail.

Further, it is agreed that if a person truly had an open vision of the supernatural realm that this is something that should be the very Word of God. However once again, if this is true, then these words must not have just "remarkable" accuracy but complete accuracy. The standard cannot be any lower than that. Once again, the burden is on members of the prophetic community to produce a prophet that speaks with this kind of accuracy.

But there is another issue as well that Bickle and those like him refuse to address, and it is probably the most serious of all. That is, the Word of God cannot have any less authority today than it has ever had. Therefore, if these prophets are actually speaking the very words of God, then there are some corollaries that come with that.

1. These words should be gathered up, collected, preserved and added to the Canon because they are, in fact, the very words of God and must be treated as such. They must be preserved for future generations to study. If what Joyner claims for the "Final Quest" is true, then this book comes, by his own admission, with greater authority than all of Paul's epistles, as well as those of Peter, John, James, Jude and the book of Hebrews. The "Final Quest" in Joyner's scheme should stand alongside the gospels and the book of Revelation in authority.
2. The Canon is still open for today's prophets are speaking the very words of God.
3. The entire church, not merely today, but in succeeding generations is absolutely bound by the authority of these words just as we are the words of Scripture for they would be the very words of God. We

may struggle with how to understand them but we ignore them and disregard them at our peril for God will not hold anyone guiltless who ignores His very words.

4. These words are no longer subject to the judgment of men. Just as we do not place ourselves in judgment of the word of God through Paul or Jeremiah, we must, if these prophets are in fact speaking the very word of God, bow before these words as an absolute authority.

As audacious as the claims of modern prophets are, and they are exceedingly audacious, when pushed they will all admit that they are not writing Scripture. Therefore, they are NOT prophesying in the same manner as the Old Testament prophets and the New Testament apostles. They are functioning on a lower level and need to quit claiming definite divine authority for their revelations.

Greatest Apostles and Prophets in History

Unfortunately, not only do today's apostles and prophets not admit to functioning in a lesser role than the authors of Scripture, they in fact take the opposite position and claim that they are part of the greatest generation of apostles and prophets that have ever lived. This is one of the most offensive aspects of the movement.

For example, Shawn Bolz, a prophet that has been examined repeatedly in this book because of his outlandish prophetic utterances writes the following:

> "Just as in John 2:10, the Father has saved the best wine for last, and we are about to witness a generation whom God will use to bring the most intense manifestation of Heaven to the earth."[295]

Lest it be assumed that this perhaps merely represents a slip of the pen and not a statement truly indicative of Shawn's belief system, consider the following:

> "God shall release an entire generation of people who live by His Spirit and love the object of the Father's desire—His Son. We shall behold wonders in Heaven and shall call them forth to attest to God's glory on earth. We shall start to move in the creative power of the Holy Spirit, imitating God:

266

.....the God who gives life to the dead and calls thing that are not as though they were. Romans 4:17"[296]

Notice that these prophets will call forth wonders and even be able to imitate God in their ability to give life to the dead and call things that are not as though they were.

In case you still didn't get how important and incredible these new prophets are, consider one more comment from Bolz:

"God is declaring our generation to be unlike any other generation on the face of the earth."[297]

By now hopefully you have come to understand just how significant and impressive Bolz believes that this generation of apostles and prophets is going to be. No generation compares to them.

As one reads the messages of today's apostles and prophets this is a common theme. While they will tip their hat to acknowledging Jesus and loving Him, the focus of their message is very frequently on how important, how powerful, how impressive, this generation of believers truly is. This movement is perhaps the most egomaniacal, man-exalting movement to come along in the modern era.

And Bolz is not the exception by any means in his assessment of the importance of the modern apostles and prophets. Consider some comments by Rick Joyner, speaking of the prophets of this hour (represented by the Eagles in his vision).

"We are the hidden prophets who have been kept for this hour. We are the eyes of those who have been given the divinely powerful weapons. We have been shown all that the Lord is doing, and all that the enemy is planning against you. We have scoured the earth and together we know all that needs to be known for the battle."[298]

So these prophets know all the strategies of God, all the plans of the enemy, and all that needs to be known for the final battle. Remember they don't get this information by the study of Scripture. No, Scripture can't tell you all that you need to know for the end times. They have received this knowledge by direct impartation from God.

In this same prophecy, Joyner eventually finds himself in heaven. As he makes his way to the throne, he notices that all the people in heaven that he passes bow to him in greeting. He finally inquires about this,

> "You are one of the saints fighting in the last battle,' a man close by responded. 'Everyone here knows you, as well as all of those now fighting on the earth. We are the saints who have served the Lord in the generations before you. We are the great cloud of witnesses who have been given the right to behold the last battle. We know all of you, and we see all that you do."[299]

Continuing in this same line of thought, Joyner finishes his approach to the throne of God and notes the following:

> "Everyone there [in heaven] showed respect to me, not because of who I was or anything that I had done, but simply because I was a warrior in the battle of the last days."[300]

So again we are impressed with how absolutely special this generation truly is for all of heaven bows before them. Multiple modern prophets have had visions where they saw the apostle Paul running to greet them or the saints of heaven standing in line to meet and question them because of the importance of this generation.

Interestingly, though Joyner says that his honor in heaven is not based on what he had done, elsewhere he gives a different tune. In one of the most amazing passages in the book, while still approaching the throne of God, Joyner speaks with the leader of a company of angels, this angelic being becomes very emotional as he states,

> "We have witnessed many wonders since the creation. But the voluntary suffering of men for the Lord, and for their fellow men, is the greatest wonder of all."[301]

One might have expected the angel to declare that the suffering of the Lord Jesus, the sinless Lamb of God on behalf of sinful, rebellious, unworthy, ungrateful, condemned mankind was the greatest wonder of all but no, on the contrary, what really amazes angels is the suffering of the saints on behalf of the Lord. I remind the reader that this statement came to Joyner in what he claims is the highest level of revelation and therefore must be the absolute truth. Angels are more impressed with our sacrifice than that of Jesus. This Christianized narcissism is considered deep prophecy.

Absolutely necessary to the church

The modern apostles and prophets do not consider their ministry optional. They boldly proclaim that no church today can be in proper alignment with the Lord if it rejects the ministry of the new apostles and prophets.

In a section under the heading, "Why we must emphasize the Prophetic", Rick Joyner makes the following declaration, "No ministry which rejects or avoids what is now happening in the restoration of the prophetic ministry will be able to truly fulfill its own calling and purpose in this hour."[302]

The message is pretty clear, "You can't really be the church in this hour without us. Better get on board."

Bill Hamon, a man who credits himself with really launching the modern prophetic movement writes, "...the Apostle is the covering and protecting cloud and the Prophet is the enlightening and directing fire. That is one reason why apostles and prophets must be restored before the Church can fulfill its predestinated end-time purpose on earth"[303]

Notice that prophets must be restored before the church can fulfill its end time mission.

Continuing in the same discussion concerning why it is absolutely essential that the church come under the authority and direction of the modern apostles and prophets, Hamon states the following:

> "The full restoration of apostles and prophets back into the Church will then bring divine order, unity, purity and maturity to the corporate Body of Christ......That will in turn bring about the end of this world system of humanity and Satan's rule. The fulfillment of all these things will release Christ, who has been seated at the right hand of the Father in heaven, to return literally and set up His everlasting kingdom over all the earth."[304]

Another leader who is not shy at all about the importance of the new apostolic and prophetic movements for the future of the church is International Coalition of Apostles President C. Peter Wagner. In an interview with CBN, Wagner made the following statement:

> "I believe that *the government of the church is finally coming into place* and that is the, the Scripture teaches in Eph. 2 that the foundation of the church is apostles and prophets, previous to this decade of the 80's and the 90's we practically ignored prophets and apostles and now we're seeing, that I believe is a major reason we're going to new levels in prayer we're going to new levels in spiritual warfare, we're going to new levels in healing and miracles we're going to new levels of deliverance, of demonic deliverance and so that's so this is the new era we are going into, I don't know if its coincidental or what but it's just as we are moving into the new millennium."[305]

One can certainly agree with Wagner that these new apostles and prophets are taking the church in new directions. However, it has been the contention of this book that these new directions include an abandonment of the historic Christian faith all the while professing to be restoring it.

You're what kind of an apostle?

One of the more obvious new directions in today's apostolic movement is in the expansion of the term apostle to cover activities never considered apostolic before. Wagner has identified a plethora of apostolic positions unknown in the history of the church. The following is from the International Coalition of Apostles, **"What is an Apostle?"** document, accessible on the ICA website,

> *What is an Apostle?*
>
> *"Definition*
>
> An apostle is a Christian leader gifted, taught, commissioned and sent by God with the authority to establish the foundational government of the church within an assigned sphere of ministry by hearing what the Spirit is saying to the churches and by setting things in order accordingly for the extension of the kingdom of God.

Gifts and Ministries

> Apostles, by definition have been given the spiritual gift of apostle by the grace of God. This gift is listed among many others in 1 Corinthians 12. The same chapter, however, indicates that not all of those with the same gift have the same ministry, and not all those with the same ministry have the same activity (see 1 Cor. 12:4-6)
>
> Many apostles minister primarily in the nuclear church, which takes the shape of congregations of believers that meet in church buildings or in homes or groups of such congregations, while others minister primarily in the workplace. The first would be termed "nuclear church" apostles as over against "extended church" or workplace, apostles.
>
> Some are territorial apostles to whom God has given authority covering a certain geographical area such as a neighborhood or a city or a state or a nation. Others have authority in a certain social arena such as government or finances or media, etc.
>
> Among those with the gift of apostle, some have the ministry of vertical apostle. This means that they are in an apostolic leadership position over a network of churches and ministries or a network of those who minister in a certain affinity sphere such as women or prayer or youth or worship, etc. Others are horizontal apostles who have a ministry of covering and connecting peers such as other apostles or pastors or prophets, etc.

Gifts and Offices

> The gift of apostle, as in the case of all spiritual gifts, is given to believers by God as He pleases (see 1 Cor. 12:11, 18). Spiritual gifts are given only by the grace of God.
>
> However an office, such as the office of apostle, is not given by grace alone, but given as a result of works that have demonstrated faithfulness in stewarding the gift."[306]

Moving past the ICA claim that receiving the office of an apostle comes as a result of one's works and faithfulness in stewarding the gift, (contrary to what Paul says in Scripture 1 Corinthians 15:8-10 where works come as the result of God's calling and grace) we now discover that the Body of Christ must have nuclear church apostles, marketplace apostles, territorial apostles, vertical apostles and horizontal apostles. We can add to that another category that has come into play called philanthropic apostles. And this is probably not an exhaustive list. Does anyone have a score card for all of this? How in the world could the average church leader know to which apostles he is supposed to be relating? And this mess of titles is supposed to somehow put the church in order and make things better? And what does one do when the apostles give different directions (a very frequent occurrence)? Does the vertical apostle outweigh the territorial apostle in one's area or is it the other way around? Of course, all of this is assuming that these extra-biblical categories of apostles are actually legitimate.

It has been well stated that the direction in which Wagner and others are taking the church leads to little more than a Charismatic College of Cardinals. The hierarchy of Rome is replaced by the hierarchy of Wagner's apostles.

Wagner elsewhere criticizes current church structures, which he calls old wineskins, for being too political and good-old-boys-networks. Yet Wagner seems to believe that his own network is unsusceptible to the same kinds of maneuverings and the tendency toward becoming mutual admiration societies. Yet ironically, in order to be accepted as an apostle one must be nominated by one of the other apostles (and pay a fee to the ICA of course). So in other words, we know that Chuck Pierce is an apostle because Peter Wagner says he is and we know that Wagner is an apostle because Dutch Sheets says he is. And we know that Sheets is an apostle because Chuck Pierce says he is. It seems that the qualifications for becoming an apostle have changed a bit from those set forth in Scripture. But this new system certainly does allow for a large number of people to feel very important and powerful.

Apostles and the Coming Golden Age

Now that the offices of apostle and prophet have been and are being restored the church is ready for the triumphant golden age that will usher in the return of Christ. This is one of the few consistent messages from the new spiritual elite. This is the birthright of the church. All that creation has been longing for has now arrived in this blessed generation.

In his book, "Engaging the Revelatory Realm of Heaven", Paul Keith Davis becomes almost euphoric in his descriptions of what is ahead for the church. He writes,

> "Receiving revelation from the Lord on a perpetual basis is not merely a gift. It's a part of who we truly are—spiritually minded people who receive their spiritual DNA from the Lord Himself. Through this priestly endowment, all those things our eyes have not seen, our ears have not heard, and our minds have not yet imagined God is unveiling with a deeper understanding to those who love Him, who hold Him in affectionate reverence, and who recognize His many blessings."[307]

Receiving revelation is not a gift but who we are. It's our DNA. All of the mysteries are about to be opened up to us. For Davis, this hodge-podge of heresy called the apostolic and prophetic movement is the evidence of a deeper understanding of the Lord. Davis will give the obligatory deference to loving the Lord and recognizing His blessings but the real message, the steady drumbeat of the book is how special and great we are. He continues,

> "We are presently entering a season of extraordinary enlightenment. We will experience the unveiling of Kingdom realities in an unprecedented way. Messages of truth and power will emerge with genuine authority to break strongholds and dominions within us, our churches, and our communities. We will be 'tasting the good word of God and the powers of the age to come.' "[308]

Extraordinary enlightenment, unprecedented, genuine authority, powers of the age to come. Heady stuff. But Davis' delusions of grandeur are just getting warmed up. He further states,

> "Our generation stands on the threshold of experiencing a spiritual restoration that will equate in prominence with the recovery of the Jewish people to the land of Israel."[309]

And finally,

> "This apostolic reformation will ignite the reestablishment and functioning of the Church in genuine spiritual power and authority. From this foundation, the Church will be able to soar to even greater places in God that await us—the Melchizedek Priesthood and a deeper

apprehension of being sons and daughters who have overcome and discovered rest in God."[310]

We have finally arrived. The church is reestablished in genuine power and authority. These new apostles and prophets form the foundation that allows the church to soar into even greater places in God. And then a theme that we have studied in previous chapters, the church becomes the Melchizedek priesthood as we have a deeper understanding of our role as sons and daughters of God.

This is the vision and it is all about the greatness of this generation of believers. No other generation has really had it the way that we will. This generation is really special. What arrogance.

One young man who spent a significant part of his upbringing in a church steeped in these messages told of a service in which the older members of the congregation gathered to wash the feet of the teens of the church, not to teach them about Christ-like humility and service but to pay homage to them because they were the anointed generation. His heart was broken as he recounted seeing elderly saints he knew had spent their lives serving Jesus bowing in servitude before young people who were being told that it was their birthright to be the greatest believers in the history of the church.

What is reality?

For all the exaggerated claims and hype, today's prophets and apostles bear little resemblance to the type of prophecy and apostolic ministries that occurred in the Bible with the Old Testament prophets and New Testament apostles. They do not walk in that authority. And they know it.

Bickle gives an account of what is far too common within prophetic circles when he states,

> "In a public meeting, a prophetic minister spoke the following prophetic word to a man whom he had never met: "You have a music ministry. You're called to be a singer." What they prophetic minister actually saw in a vision was musical notes around the person. So the prophetic minister thought the man was called by God to sing or play an instrument, but the person to whom the revelation was directed didn't play or sing at all. He was the owner of a music store.

"When we took the prophetic minister aside and questioned him, his response was, "Well, how was I supposed to know?""

"That is precisely the point—he wasn't supposed to know. It seemed obvious to him that the person would be in the music ministry as a performer. However, when he made an assumption about prophetic revelation based on what *seemed obvious*, he got into trouble. He could have said, "I see musical notes around you: does this mean anything to you?"[311]

This type of "revelation" is a far cry from anything we see in the Scripture. When do we ever see Jesus, one of the Old Testament prophets or a New Testament apostle engaging in a Q&A session in order to obtain the necessary information to give an accurate revelation? His question, "How was I supposed to know?" is enlightening. One might have thought the Lord who knows all things would have revealed this to him if he were truly receiving a revelation from God.

But there is something else that must be noted here. What is the difference between the information that this prophet supposedly saw and that of a psychic giving a cold reading? "I see musical notes around you: does that mean anything to you?". One could see the same type of activity watching any number of psychics on TV. In fact it can be done just as well by any second-rate magician. This reduces prophecy down to the level of a parlor game.

The fact is that the Biblical prophets did not have to engage in such tactics.

Conclusion: What is the Church's Responsibility?

There is no denying the sincerity and passion of most of today's modern prophets. There is no doubt that their call to prayer and fasting, their concern for the poor and their belief in a God who is still available to intervene on behalf of His people are messages that the church needs to hear.

However, as we attempted to show in this book, their lack of understanding of or refusal to follow basic rules of interpretation has led them, and consequently their followers, into all sorts of fanciful interpretations. These novel interpretations have in turn led to a number of new doctrines, false doctrines and unbiblical practices being introduced into the life of the church.

Additionally, many of the modern apostles and prophets are placing their own words alongside the Bible in positions of equal authority or even greater authority. Indeed some of the modern prophets have a very low view of Scripture generally.

Modern prophets frequently are guilty of taking isolated events from Scripture and attempting to build norms for the church today around them. They are also building norms for other believers based on their own mystical experiences.

Because of their general disdain for theological education, the new prophets and apostles are generally lacking in any sort of theological precision. This has allowed them to make statements about the different members of the Godhead and about the atonement that seriously depart from the boundaries of orthodoxy.

Today's apostles and prophets make great boasts of open heavens, heavenly visitations, appearances of angels and miracles. They are claiming to be the greatest generation of apostles and prophets that have ever lived. In a variety of ways, they are indicating that the rest of the Body of Christ cannot fulfill its mission without coming in line with them. Yet their record is a string of failed prophecies or prophecies that are so vague as to be meaningless. For all the hype they have produced very little despite the rock star status that some members gather. While they talk of a great harvest, most of their followers have come from other existing churches and ministries.

Lastly, today's prophets have been generally uncorrectable. Their statements in this regard are brazen and defiant. Christians who express concern over the unsoundness of their doctrine and practices are demonized in a variety of ways and threatened with the judgment of God. We, as the Body of Christ, are commanded to test those who claim to be prophets among us.

> "Beloved, do not believe every spirit but test the spirits to see whether they are of God, for many false prophets have gone out into the world." (1 John 4:1)

We are not being pharisaical when we are obedient to the clear command of Scripture. The Ephesian church was commended by Christ because they had "tested those who call themselves apostles and are not, and found them to be false." (Revelation 2:2)

The church is commanded to clearly mark out those who bring doctrines contrary to the message that we have been given and to avoid them completely, assuming they do not repent. (Romans 16:17) We must not continue to tolerate the intrusion of false teachers and false doctrines into our midst.

The church must once again love truth. We are commanded to worship in spirit and truth and our God is a God of truth. Passion apart from knowledge is not enough. We must pray for unity but a Biblical unity that is built around the truth not in contradiction to it or ignorance of it.

We must stop placing immature men in places of prominence quickly based on their charisma and apparent gifting. It is destroying the men and damaging the church.

The church must return to the passion for seeing Jesus exalted. Enough of these visions of self-aggrandizement. Enough of the messages that tell believers how great they are or are going to be. Enough hero worship. Point men to Christ. It is Christ who must be lifted up. He must increase and we must decrease.

It is time that the Body of Christ begin to demand accountability from those who would claim to speak for God. God does not give false prophecy. Our God does not change. He will not speak in contradiction to His Word. We must, as a church, hold fast to the apostle's doctrine or what we pass down to our children and grandchildren will be little more than emotional hype, a mere hollow shell of the true faith.

APPENDIX A

Patron Saints of the Prophetic

In the new apostolic and prophetic movements power is everything. The movement will endorse virtually anyone who has a testimony of unusual or supernatural occurrences within their meetings. However, without question there are two names that occur most frequently as examples of the type of ministries to which the modern apostles and prophets are aspiring. These two figures that continue to exert such tremendous influence are William Branham and John G. Lake.

William Branham

We begin with William Branham because, without a doubt, he is the greatest historical figure to whom the modern prophets refer. Disgraced prophet Paul Cain, who travelled with Branham for a time, calls him the greatest prophet who has ever lived. It is without dispute that when it comes to supernatural activity and words of knowledge, William Branham was, and is today, without parallel. Pentecostal historian Roberts Liardon lists him as one of God's generals in his book by the same title[312]. Though they may try to distance themselves from his erroneous doctrines, modern prophets today constantly point to him as a model for the type of power that this generation will be experience on a regular basis.

However, most people who refer to Branham's greatness have very little knowledge of who the man was beyond the claims of angelic visitations and the occurrence of healings and words of knowledge in his meetings.

Space will not permit a detailed discussion of his personal history. There are several good resources available to the person who wishes to go deeper.

There are, however, a couple of items of interest. First he claimed that all of his healings were done by his angel who always stood on his right side. For this reason, he always had people stand on his right so they would get a double blessing.[313] When questioned, he attributed his miracles to this angel and not to God. Secondly, he always required that people affirm their faith in him as God's prophet before he would heal them. This was consistent with an angelic message that he claimed to have received in 1946 that launched his healing ministry. (It should be noted that Branham gave very different accounts of this encounter and that testimony from his own family indicates he had begun his healing ministry at least five years earlier.) The angel told him, "If you will be sincere, AND CAN GET THE PEOPLE TO BELIEVE YOU, nothing shall stand before your prayer, not even cancer."[314] Neither attributing healings to an angel nor requiring a person seeking healing to confess their belief in the healer as a prophet of God were ever done by any apostle in the New Testament. Further, Branham detected diseases by a physical vibration in his left hand[315]. Once again, this has no parallel in Scripture but interestingly, does in occultism.

What is universally recognized is the false doctrine that William Branham began to teach. The following list of aberrant doctrines can all be found documented in Roberts Liardon's book, "God's Generals", in a chapter that is very favorable to the ministry of William Branham.

- He taught that the doctrine of the Trinity was a doctrine of demons and that anyone baptized in the trinitarian formula went into darkness.

- He taught that belonging to any denomination was the mark of the beast.

- He believed that the words that he spoke would begin to literally transform the bodies of his listeners into glorified bodies ready for the rapture. Because of this teaching and others, he is considered the originator of Dominion Theology.

- He taught the serpent seed doctrine that Eve had sex with the devil which produced Cain leading to a soul-less race of people destined to be damned.

- He had an extremely low view of women. He taught that men could divorce as often as they wished (a woman cutting her hair was grounds for divorce) as long as they married a virgin. Women were not free to divorce. He even stated in one sermon that he thought women weren't worth the price of a clean bullet to kill them.

- He denied that hell was eternal.

- He taught that all disease was demonic
- He taught the destruction of the United States would begin in 1977.
- He taught that healings could be lost if a person quit believing.[316]

There is more but that list alone should be sufficient for any believer to know that this man was not a prophet of God in any way. Amazingly, while admitting that these doctrines are all false, Liardon considers Branham to be one of "God's Generals".

While Christians should be distancing themselves as far as possible from this man, modern prophets, in their urgency for confirming signs and wonders, continue to assign great status to him. When confronted with his doctrine, they will usually respond along the line of Paul Cain and Roberts Liardon by claiming that they are speaking only of his power not his doctrine. But it must be remembered that power is not the test! For instance, the book of 1 John is devoted to enabling Christians to know that they are born again. In the entire book, not one time are miracles mentioned as confirming evidence of salvation or anointing. When instructing the church to test the spirits to see whether they are of God, the apostle John appeals to a doctrinal test not to the apparent power of the minister.

Many in today's church are seemingly completely unaware of the warnings of Jesus.

> "For false Christs and false prophets will appear and PERFORM GREAT SIGNS AND MIRACLES to deceive even the elect–if that were possible. See I have told you ahead of time." Matt. 24:24 (emphasis added)

> "Many will say to me on that day, 'Lord, Lord, did we not prophesy in your name, and in your name drive out demons and perform many miracles?' Then I will tell them plainly, 'I never knew you. Away from me, you evildoers!' " Matt. 7:21-23

It should be obvious from these verses that supernatural activity does not indicate that a minister is truly coming in the power of the Almighty God. It is interesting that members of a movement that gives so much credit to the devil in other areas will not even consider that Branham's miracles may have had a demonic source.

John G. Lake

The second figure that must be considered is John G. Lake. There has been a great deal of renewed interest in Lake in recent years, particularly in the Northwest. Curry Blake operates Lake's official on-line ministry and claims to be the fulfillment of a prophecy supposedly given to Lake about someone to come and renew Lake's ministry. He also operates healing rooms similar to Lake's. (It should be noted that the concept of healing rooms is completely different from the ministry of Jesus who healed instantly with a command or a touch. Jesus never established rooms for people to receive prayer day after day. These were actually the brainchild of Alexander Dowie who was Lake's mentor.) Cal Pierce claims that he is re-digging the wells of John Lake to recover his spiritual inheritance. Roberts Liardon includes a chapter on Lake in his book, "God's Generals". And one of the most prominent figures in the prophetic movement, Mike Bickle, says that John G. Lake has influened him *"more than any man other than Jesus."* This is certainly high praise even if the statement is hyperbole. The Complete Works of John G. Lake are available for purchase at IHOP. As with Branham, it is evident that many who reference Lake have never actually read him nor have they taken even a cursory look at his history beyond the claims of the miraculous.

False Doctrine

Lake's doctrine was clearly beyond the bounds of orthodoxy in many areas. Consider the following statements by John G. Lake which come from his own sermons as recorded in a book sympathetic to Lake published by Kenneth Copeland Publications.

Little gods

"The power of God, the Holy Ghost, is the Spirit of Dominion. It makes **one a god.**"[317]

"I want you to hear what Jesus said about himself. God was in Christ, wasn't He? An incarnation. God is in you, an incarnation, if you were born again. **You are incarnate**"[318]

"God's purpose through Jesus Christ is to **deify the nature of men**"[319]

Obviously all of these statements are false. Salvation does not make one a god. And while it is gloriously true that the third Person of the Trinity, the Holy Spirit comes to live inside the believer at salvation, we do not become an incarnation in the sense that Jesus was God incarnate.

Dominion Theology

Although, true Latter Rain or Dominion Theology did not come into a full-blown existence until the days of Branham, Hall and the Sharon Brethren, many of the beliefs can be seen in the writings of John G. Lake, especially the idea of Christians conquering the world in order for Christ to return. Consider carefully the following statement.

> "Beloved, God is calling men and women to a holier consecration, to a higher place in God, and I am one of God's candidates for that holy place in God. I want to get to the throne of God....And that is the experience that is going to make the sons of God in the world. That is the reason they will **take the world for Jesus Christ,** and the Kingdom will be established, **and they will put the crown on the Son of God, and declare him, 'King of kings and Lord of lords' ".[320]**

Notice that it is the church that will "take the world" and will crown the Son of God as King of kings and Lord of lords. It is not Jesus who returns to put down all rule and authority.

Communication with the Dead

One of the more bizarre teachings of John G. Lake was about communication with the dead, something strictly forbidden in the Bible. Lake taught that there was nothing wrong with communicating with the dead as long as you didn't call them up from hell. It was ok to call them down from heaven. In reality the Bible makes no distinction concerning where the spirit is coming from. It forbids communication with the dead in all forms. For instance Isaiah 8:19-20 declares,

> "And when they say to you, 'Inquire of the mediums and the necromancers who chirp and mutter,' should not a people inquire of their God? Should they inquire of the dead on behalf of the living? To the teaching and to the testimony! If they will not speak according to this word, it is because they have no dawn."

The New King James version translates the last phrase, "it is because they have no light in them". Isaiah makes a blanket condemnation of all communication with the dead.

In contrast note what John G. Lake taught,

> "Listen it is not dragging spirits up, and it isn't dragging some spirits down. There is nothing about calling spirits down from God in the Word; only about calling them up from the depths."[321]

Lake gives an account of his deceased wife speaking to him through a woman who had come for healing for a bad eye. (Today we call this "channeling") He says the Spirit came over this woman and then says the following:

> "She arose from her chair, her eyes quite shut, and came in my direction. I got up and moved my chair. She walked right around and came to me. She slipped her fingers down, gave me a little chuck just like my late wife wouild have done, and said, 'Jack, my Jack, God is with you all the time. Go right on. But my baby, my Teddy, I am so lonesome for him, but you pray so hard, you pray so hard."[322]

Again, Lake believed this was his late wife speaking to him which would mean that the Holy Spirit came upon this woman and enabled Lake's deceased wife to communicate with him from the grave in direction contradiction to the Word of God. Lake apparently never considered that another spirit might have been the source of this revelation.

More Strange Doctrine

But the aberrant doctrines of John G. Lake do not stop there.

> Lake taught that you could receive sin impulses from other people if they laid hands on you. [323]

He believed that God doesn't appreciate disabled people. "Do you know when my legs straightened out it taught me the beginning of one of the deepest lessons that ever came in my life. **It taught me God did not appreciate a man with crooked legs any more than He does with a crooked soul.**"[324]

Notice that Lake considers this statement one of the "deepest" lessons that ever came in his life. Once again, Lake's message stands in direction contradiction to the Scriptures that teach that God is sovereign over the human physical condition and can actually use disabilities for His glory. For instance, when Moses attempted to shy away from his calling by claiming that he was slow of speech, the Lord responded,

> "Then the LORD said to him, 'Who has made man's mouth? He makes him mute, or deaf, or seeing, or blind? Is it not I, the Lord?" (Exodus 4:11)

God indicates that He is the one who determines who is born disabled and who is not. This would include such disabilities as crooked legs. God further tells Moses to go to pharaoh and that God will be his mouth and teach him what to say. God is able to use men through their disabilities. In fact, such weaknesses may be exactly what causes the man to be more dependent on God. But there is no place for this in Lake's theology.

Fraud

In addition to all the false doctrines, when one looks at the newspaper articles of the day, one finds that John Lake was a documented fraud. His personal ethics are extremely suspect.

According to the July 24th, 1921 issue of the Oregonian and subsequent issues. John Lake was arrested, charged, and forced to settle out of court for a blue sky scam in which he promised members of his congregation stock in a mining company if they paid their tithes in a lump sum. The stock was never delivered.

On Nov. 21, 1933 in the Oregonian, Lake advertised the appearance of an Arab healer, Abdul Ben Shinandar at his church. On Nov. 25 the same paper uncovered that the Arab healer was actually Lake dressed in costume.

One of the strangest incidents came on August 25, 1921 when the paper reports that Lake was arrested and had to post $100 bond for impersonating a police officer.

The May 24, 1920 issue of the Oregonian and subsequent issues chronicle the arrest of John G. Lake after the death of Hanna Anderson who died of neglect when attempts to heal her of the flu failed. Not only did Lake not heal her but he also failed to report the illness to the CDC which was required by law at the time. He was found guilty of laxity and fined.

These are not the actions of a man of God but that of a charlatan.

Inability to Heal

The Hanna Anderson story is not the only example to show that Lakes claims of tremendous healing power were exaggerated. Consider the following headlines.

"Miracles Not Seen"- The Morning Oregonian, May 24, 1920

"X-Ray Belies Healing"- Oregonian 11/27/21. This particular story is of a 7 year old girl with a severely fractured thigh whose parents denied her proper medical care and took her to Lake instead. Lake pronounced her healed, however when the girl still didn't recover she was finally taken to physicians and the fracture was discovered. Doctors indicate that she would have been crippled for life had she not received proper treatment.

"Grandma says girl made to Hear Wasn't Deaf"- Spokane Press 7/16/24 (This article does have a story of another woman who claimed to be healed and able to walk. There is also an interesting account in the same story of a woman who was "healed" by Lake 5 times but the "pain keeps coming back.")

"Miracles Fail, Imp of Tragedy Stalks in Tent" Spokane Press 7/23/24

The reason John Lake became so popular is that, like Benny Hinn and others today, he had a very active public relations machine. Many of the positive articles that appear about him were written by him. The reality is that he is long on claims and short on documentation.

Once again reality fails to match the hype. Lake was a man of false doctrine and poor personal ethics. He is no one to emulate.

I readily acknowledge that most of the teachers who praise him have probably never read the newspaper stories that document his fraud, however his false doctrine should have been evident as they read his works and sermons. But once again, we see that false doctrine doesn't concern the modern apostles and prophets as long as one can claim miraculous power. The fact that his messages continue to influence modern prophetic teachers and their followers is frightening.

APPENDIX B

The Occultic Mindset of Spiritual Warfare

Early in my Christian walk, I came in contact with some of the more prominent teachings of spiritual warfare through the writings of Mark Bubeck, Neal Anderson, John Dawson and the fictional works of Frank Peretti. For a season early in my ministry I became deeply immersed in this teaching. I declared things in the heavenlies, attempted to discern the demons over my city, drove around my city claiming it for Jesus, anointed the chairs in our sanctuary on a regular basis, and bound Satan daily. I would be lying if I said that there wasn't a part of me that really got in to this whole experience. I felt very important and very powerful. It was very exciting. Until one day a very simple question refused to let go of me. "When did anyone in the Bible do this?"

That was the question that started me on an investigation of this teaching. Today I am confident that not only is this teaching not Biblical, it is actually occultic in nature. I don't make that statement lightly. I have studied and written on the subjects of the New Age, Wicca and even tribal religion. The modern teaching on spiritual warfare has more in common with these practices than anything that can be found in the pages of the New Testament (that book that is supposed to teach us, among other things, how Christians are to live).

I should hasten to emphasize that this is not an exclusively Charismatic issue. Writers like Neal Anderson and Mark Bubeck (incidentally one of the nicest guys you could ever hope to talk to) are considered Evangelical and yet they have done much damage to the body of Christ in this area. Bubeck's books even include prayers for the Holy Spirit to search your blood stream, gastro-intestinal organs and other body systems for demons.[325] No such instruction is ever given in the Scriptures.

Space will only allow for a small number of examples to support my thesis of the occultic nature of modern spiritual warfare teachings but perhaps these will cause readers to dig even further to determine if these teachings are truly from the Lord.

1. *Manipulation of spiritual forces.* One of the underlying assumptions of the occultic worldview is that all of life is connected by a spiritual force, a belief known as monism. The practice of magick is based on the belief that one is able to manipulate this force in order for the practitioner to create his own reality. Modern Word Faith teachers and spiritual warfare teachers unknowingly have bought into the same mindset. For Word Faith teachers the monistic force is faith itself. Kenneth Copeland has frequently stated that faith is a force that even God uses to accomplish His purposes. David Yonggi Cho has stated that this force can even be used by non-believers which is why Buddhist monks sometimes get results. Many of the modern prophets have stated the same thing about the New Age. For many in the spiritual warfare community the force is more personal in the form of angels, demons and the Holy Spirit. While this may seem more biblical, the fact remains that much of their efforts are in actuality ritualistic actions aimed at manipulating these beings to their own ends. Giving the monistic force personal and Biblical names doesn't make the underlying belief any less false.

It is out of this foundational belief that many other ancillary beliefs and practices arise. For instance words are seen as extremely powerful. Once again, in Word Faith circles, words are the containers of the force. What I confess I possess. If I say that I am going bald I will get more baldness. But if I confess that I have a full head of hair then that is what I will receive. This is what leads Word Faith preachers to teach their followers to, "Say to your wallet. Why you big fat wallet. You're so full of money." Of course, apparently it doesn't work for them because they have to keep asking for donations. Similarly, as discussed previously in this book, prophetic teachers like Victoria Boyson and Mike Bickle teach that when we criticize someone we are releasing and activating Satanic activity upon them and if we bless them we are releasing Holy Spirit activity.

This authority that is supposedly in words then leads to the increasingly popular binding and loosing and warfare in the heavenlies teachings. In this practice Satan and his forces are actually addressed and commanded in prayer. Their "strongholds" over cities are pulled down. Their strategies are foiled. They must leave the region. Authority is claimed by the Church and the Spirit is loosed.

Now, I hate to spoil the party. But is this really what Jesus was teaching in Matthew 16 when He said that whatever you bind on earth is bound in heaven? The answer is a decided "no". Before discussing what binding and loosing really means, the evidence that modern spiritual warfare teachers cannot be correct in what they are teaching is easy to detect from the New Testament. The fact is simply this, NOWHERE IN THE NEW TESTAMENT IS SATAN EVER ADDRESSED IN PRAYER. Prayer is made to God. We do not have one single example of anyone in the New Testament ever engaging in this type of prayer. The only time that Satan or a demon is ever addressed by a believer is when they are being cast out of an individual. The historical fact is that binding and loosing were rabbinical terms that the apostles would have been familiar with that had to do with forbidding and permitting certain practices and which speaks to the apostle's authority in laying the foundation for the practices of the church.

Christians are spending too much time shouting at the devil. And can someone please tell me, "What is the statute of limitations on binding the devil?" He seems to continually get loose! How long does it take to bind a demon and clear the heavenlies? These practices have been occurring in my hometown, Kansas City, for nearly 30 years with no verifiable or discernable results.

2. *Ritual Magick.* In the occult worldview, rituals can be performed in the physical that have ramifications in the spiritual. So a pin stuck in a voodoo doll can cause spiritual forces to work against an individual that can result in bodily injury. Alarmingly, many of the modern teachings and practices within the spiritual warfare camp operate on the same principle as ritual magick. One of the most disturbing segments of the film, "Jesus Camp" was to see a teacher hand a hammer to children and tell them to go to the front and smash cups labeled "abortion", "homosexuality" etc. etc. The children attending the camp were led to believe that by commanding the heavenlies and smashing the cups things would be broken in the spirit realm. Much of the same thing can be seen in many of the practices of anointing. Rebecca Brown teaches people to anoint the doors and windows of their homes so that demons don't have any points of access to their

homes. Most of the teachings on cleansing the land also have more in common with ritual magick than with anything found in the pages of Scripture. The church is mimicking the pagan world.

3. *Power Centers.* In the occultic mindset, certain grounds are sacred. They may be possessed by either good or evil spirits. Some of these power centers may be taboo to all but the most highly initiated or they may be places to gather for worship because the power is strong. We have seen over the last two decades a number of these power centers emerge and diminish, Toronto, Pensacola, Smithton, etc. People have travelled across the country to go to the place where God was manifest in order to get in the river or acquire an anointing. The Bible knows of no such practice. When extraordinary miracles were done by Paul in Ephesus there is no indication that the rest of the first century church believed they had to get to Ephesus in order to acquire the anointing. No early leaders began to travel the country claiming that they were operating in the mantle of the Ephesus anointing. An omnipresent God can be encountered anywhere.

Additionally, the modern teaching of spiritual portals by prophets like John Paul Jackson, Kathie Walters, Paul Keith Davis and many more has more in common with the occult than the Bible despite the way they butcher the story of Jacob's Ladder to try and make it fit.

4. *The Devil Made Me Do It.* The occultic world is all about spirits. Animism is all about spirits. Spirits are responsible for everything. Spirits must be placated. While it is certainly true that the Western mind tends to ignore the spiritual dimension and tends almost toward Deism, the modern spiritual warfare teachings are certainly an over-correction. If it rains on a church picnic it is the devil's fault. Every sin is evidence of a "stronghold" that must be pulled down.

The problem is that this silver bullet approach to holiness keeps the individual from dealing with what is often the true source of the problem; a carnal, rebellious heart. It lacks a call to serious repentance. It does not teach the believer to use the means of grace that God has provided for the mortification of the flesh and growth in godliness.

5. *Shamanism.* In the occult the shaman is the expert in the things of the spirit. He has visions of the spirit world and brings back information to the

followers. Many of today's so-called prophets are nothing more than shamen. People flock to them to hear of their visits to the otherworld and to act on the information that they bring back. This has opened a literal Pandora's box of new practices.

What is particularly disturbing in the spiritual warfare scenario is that many of these practices were supposedly learned by interviewing demons! Bubeck, while acknowledging that demons are "inveterate liars like their leader Satan", instructs readers that when they interview a demon they should ask, "Will this information stand as truth before the throne of the true and living God?"[326] For some reason Bubeck believes that a demon can't lie if addressed in this fashion. But why would we ever seek to learn about the things of the Spirit from a liar and the father of lies?

There are many more examples that could be given but I hope that this short essay will cause the reader to begin to seriously re-examine many of the spiritual warfare teachings that are rampant within the church today in the light of Biblical revelation. Occultic practices are being brought into the church under the guise of spiritual warfare. Doctrines and practices within the church should be based solidly on the Word of God either by direct commandment or precept, example or necessary logical deductions (For instance the doctrine of the Trinity is a necessary logical deduction from the Scriptural teachings that there is one true God and three distinct Persons who are called God).

Remember the question that I said started it all for me. "When did anyone in the Bible ever do this?" It's a good question. It's worth pondering the next time you are thinking about jumping into a new thing.

End Notes

Introduction

[1] Bickle, Mike, "Growing in the Prophetic", 1996 Charisma House (Lake Mary, FL) page 101
[2] Hamon, Bill, "Prophets and the Prophetic Movement", 1990 Destiny Image Publishers (Shippensburg, PA) page 94
[3] Elijah List website "About Us", http://www.elijahlist.com/ourhistory.html
[4] International Coalition of Apostles website, "Introduction" http://www.apostlesnet.net/index.asp?action=introduction
[5] Ibid. "Members" http://www.apostlesnet.net/images/Directory.pdf
[6] Ibid, "What is an Apostle?" http://www.apostlesnet.net/images/What_Is_an_Apostle.pdf
[7] Bickle, Mike "Kansas City Prophetic History", Disc 2, Track 2
[8] Ibid
[9] Ibid

Chapter 1

[10] Gundry, Stanley N. and Wayne A. Grudem general editors. "Are Miraculous Gifts for Today?" 1996 Zondervan (Grand Rapids, MI) pages 10-13 I have attempted to give a fair summary of their more lengthy descriptions of the positions.
[11] Grudem, Wayne "The Gift of Prophecy in the New Testament and Today". 1988 Crossway Books, (Westchester, IL) page 67. Actually Dr. Grudem spends chapters 3-5 outlining and defending this premise.
[12] Ibid chapters 1 and 2
[13] Ibid page 111
[14] Ibid page 75 emphasis in the original
[15] Ibid page 113
[16] Ibid pages 119-120
[17] Zarit, Romy published on the Elijah List on 4/21/04 www.elijahlist.com/words/display_word_pf.html?ID=2102
[18] Brown, Catherine published on the Elijah List on 6/21/04 www.elijahlist.com/words/display_word_pf.html?ID=2225
[19] Clement, Kim published by the Elijah List on 9/9/2004 www.elijahlist.com/words/display_word_pf.html?ID=2445
[20] Goll, Jim published by the Elijah List on 5/2/2004 This prophecy is particularly interesting because it calls believers to a new form of praying where they accuse demons harassing them before the throne room of God in order to receive reparations of healing, prosperity et. al. that the demon has been stealing from them.

Chapter 2

[21] Pierce, Chuck, "The Worship Warrior: How Your Prayer and Worship Can Protect Your Home and Community", Regal Books, (Ventura, CA) page 117-118

[22] Bowman, Robert- "The Five-fold Ministry" article appears on the website www. Apologeticsindex.org

[23] "Endtime Revival-Spirit-Led and Spirit-Controlled; A Response Paper to Resolution 16" General Council of the Assemblies of God, 2000 page 3

[24] Storms, Sam- Article found at the author's personal website www.enjoyinggodministries.org

[25] Grudem, Wayne, "The Gift of Prophecy in the New Testament and Today", pages 275-276

[26] Ibid

[27] Grudem, Wayne, "Systematic Theology", published jointly by Inter-Varsity Press (Leicester, Great Britain) and Zondervan Publishing House (Grand Rapids, MI) page 911

[28] Steinkamp, Orel, "The New Apostolic Reformation" found at www.deceptioninthechurch.org

[29] Wyatt, Ryan, Elijah List March 7, 2007 www.elijahlist.com

[30] Randles, Bill "Weighed and Found Wanting" page 48

[31] Eastman, Dick "Heights of Delight: An Invitation to Intercessory Worship" as cited in "The Worship Warrior" by Chuck Pierce, Regal Books (Ventura, CA) page 117

Chapter 3

[32] Sullivant, Michael, "Prophetic Etiquette" 2000 Charisma House Publications (Lake Mary, FL) page 138

[33] Deere, Jack, "Surprised by the Voice of God" 1996 Zondervan Publishing House (Grand Rapids, MI) page 323

[34] Joyner, Rick, "Maturing in the Prophetic" February 22, 2011 posted on the Elijah List at http://www.elijahlist.com/words/display_word.html?ID=9614

[35] Gentile, Ernest B. "Your Sons and Daughters Shall Prophesy" 1999 Chosen Books (Grand Rapids, MI) page 314

[36] Ibid 317-327

[37] Ibid 321 The quote from Blattner is taken from "Pitfalls of Prophecy and How to Avoid Them" printed in "Equipping the Saints 3:4 (fall, 1989) page 19

[38] Robertson, O. Palmer, "The Final Word" 1993 The Banner of Truth Trust (Carlisle, PA) page 8

[39] Fee, Gordon, "Paul, the Spirit, and the People of God" 1996 Hendrickson Publishers Inc. (Peabody, MA) page 173

Chapter 4

[40] Joyner, Rick "A Prophetic Vision for the 21St Century" 1999 Thomas Nelson Publishers (Nashville, TN) pages 38-39

[41] Joyner, Rick "The Final Quest" 1996 Whitaker House Publishers (New Kensington, PA) page 21

[42] Ibid page 108

[43] Joyner, Rick "Overcoming Evil in the Last Days" 2003 Destiny Image Publishers (Shippensburg, PA) pages 144-145

[44] Ibid 133

[45] Ibid 133

[46] Bickle, Mike "Contending for the Power of God" CD #1

[47] Harmon, Cedric "God's Lightening Rod" Charisma Magazine, April 2001

[48] Joyner, Rick "Overcoming the Religious Spirit" 1996, Fourth printing in 2002 MorningStar Publications (Charlotte, NC) pages 21-22

[49] Frangipane, Francis "The House of the Lord" 1991 Creation House (Lake Mary, FL) page 131

[50] Joyner, Rick "A Prophetic Vision for the 21st Century" 1999 Thomas Nelson Publishers (Nashville, TN) page 148.

[51] Sheets, Dutch The Shift for 2006--Ministries will Restructure, as will Churches, Businesses, Individuals, and Families" Found at http://www.elijahlist.com/words/display_word/3723

Chapter 5

[52] "Metaphysical Bible Dictionary" , Unity School of Christianity 1931 (Unity Village, MO) page 211

[53] Lemke, Steve, Areopagus Journal Jan-Feb 06, page 8

[54] Reeves, Kevin, "The Other Side of the River", Lighthouse Trails Publications page 100

[55] Bickle, Mike "Contending for the Power of God" CD #4 FOTB

[56] Ibid

[57] Ibid (It should be noted that Jill Austin and many other of the prophets have similar teachings.)

[58] Bennett, Kirk "Prophecy and the Arts" CD #1

[59] Hood, Allen "The Playfulness of God" CD #1

[60] Bickle, Mike "Thunder from Heaven" CD #2 Much of this can also be obtained from the back cover of the set.

[61] Bolz, Shawn "Keys to Heaven's Economy: An Angelic Visitation from the Minister of Finance" 2005 Streams Publishing House (North Sutton, New Hampshire) page 88

[62] Ibid page 125

[63] Pierce, Chuck D. "The Worship Warrior" 2002 Regal Publishing (Ventura, CA) page 53

[64] Ibid 121

[65] Shultz, Steve November 18, 2006 quoted from an ad for Voice of the Prophetic magazine. This ad is no longer on the internet.

[66] Storms, Sam "Convergence: The Spiritual Journeys of a Charismatic Calvinist" 2005 Enjoying God Ministries (Kansas City, MO) page 118

[67] Ibid page 118

[68] Hodge, Charles, "Systematic Theology" as cited by Keith A. Mathison, "The Shape of Sola Scriptura" 2001 Canon Press (Moscow, ID) page 147

[69] Grudem, Wayne "Systematic Theology" 1994 a joint publication by Inter-Varsity Press (Leicester, England) and Zondervan (Grand Rapids, MI) page 105

[70] Joyner, Rick "The Final Quest" 1996 Whitaker House (New Kensington, PA) page 10

[71] Ibid page 11

[72] Grudem op. cit. page 73

[73] Tenny, Tommy "The God Chasers" 1998 Destiny Image Publishers (Shippensburg, PA) This quote is found on the second page of the Introduction. These pages are unnumbered.

[74] Alec, Wendy "Journal of the Unknown Prophet" 2002 Warboys Media   page 84

[75] Joyner, Rick "A Prophetic Vision for the 21st Century" 1999 Thomas Nelson Publishers (Nashville, TN) page 241

[76] Pratt, Richard L. "Hyper-Preterism and Unfolding Biblical Eschatology" chapter 3 of the book, "When Shall These Things Be?" Keith A. Mathison editor 2004 P&R Publishing (Phillipsburg, New Jersey) page 139

[77] Op.Cit Joyner "Final Quest" page 134

[78] Thomas, Choo "Heaven is So Real" 2003 Charisma House (Lake Mary, Fl) page 168

[79] Ibid page 177

[80] Ibid page 124

[81] Baxter, Mary K "A Divine Revelation of Hell" 1993 Whitaker House (New Kensington, PA) This quote is taken from the second page of the introduction. These pages are unnumbered.

[82] Ibid pages 13- 14

[83] Ibid page 15

[84] Deere, Jack Sermon given at the National School Of The Prophets Mobilizing The Prophetic Office May 11, 2000 11:30 AM tape #3

[85] Edwards, Jonathon "The Works of Jonathon Edwards"   Vol. 2 page 260

[86] Op. Cit Joyner "The Final Quest" page 13

[87] Op. Cit Bickle "Growing in the Prophetic" page 64 (Unfortunately, prophets may still establish new doctrines even when they are associated with a local church unless that church is determined to test all things according to the Word of God.)

[88] Op Cit Joyner "The Final Quest" This claim can be found on both page 89 and page 112.

[89] Pierce, Chuck elijahlist.com August 28, 2007

[90] Ibid (September 28, 2008)

[91] Ibid (October 10, 2008)

[92] Otis, George Jr. "Informed Intercession" 1999 Renew Books (Ventura CA) page 67

[93] Ibid page 204

[94] Ibid page 205

[95] Bennett, Kirk "The Prophetic Seer Training Course" module 1 CD1

[96] Op. Cit Bickle "Growing in the Prophet" pages 117-118

[97] Ibid page 118

[98] Bickle, Mike "Kansas City Prophetic History", Disc 2, Track 2

[99] Op.Cit Grudem "The Gift of Prophecy in the New Testament and Today" page 244

[100] Op Cit Thomas page 153

[101] Ibid page 129

[102] Bolz, Shawn www.elijahlist.com 7/3/2004 Throne Room Encounters: Are You Ready to See Heaven?

[103] Ibid

[104] Bickle, Mike, The Prophetic History, Disc 7, 2002. All grammatical errors and emphasis are from the original.

[105] Davis, Paul Keith "Engaging the Revelatory Realm of Heaven" 2003 Streams Publications (North Sutton, NH) page 57

[106] Bennett, Kirk The Prophetic Seer Module 1 CD 2

[107] Panich, Tom "Third Heaven Vision Anointing Oil" Elijah List December 26, 2005
[108] Sullivant, Michael "Prophetic Etiquette" 2000 Charisma House (Lake Mary, FL) page 101

Chapter 6

[109] Frangipane, Francis, "The House of the Lord" Creation House (Lake Mary, FL) page 36
[110] Wienbaum, Dan KMBC evening news as found at www.religionnewsblog.com/17207/caleb-horner-6
[111] Moreland, J.P. "Kingdom Triangle" 2007 Zondervan (Grand Rapids, MI) page 131
[112] Ibid page 132
[113] Sullivant, Michael, "Prophetic Etiquette", Charisma House, (Lake Mary, FL) page 118
[114] Ibid page 119
[115] Bickle, Mike, "Contemplative Prayer" CD 2 FOTB
[116] Storms, Sam "Convergence: Spiritual Journeys of a Charismatic Calvinist" 2005 Enjoying God Ministries (Kansas City, MO) page 127
[117] Bickle, Mike, "Growing the Prophetic" Chrisma House (Lake Mary, FL) page 50-51
[118] Ibid page 63
[119] Ware, Bruce "Father, Son, & Holy Spirit" 2005 Crossway Books (Wheaton, IL) page 16
[120] Ibid page 17
[121] Ibid page 77
[122] Frangipane, Francis, "The House of the Lord" Creation House (Lake Mary, FL) page 36
[123] Ibid page 84
[124] Joyner, Rick "There Were Two Trees in the Garden", 1986 Morningstar Publications (Charlotte, NC)   page 31
[125] Frangipane, Francis article dated August 21, 2005 "Repairers of the Breach" Elijah List
[126] Op Cit Bickle page 63
[127] Wagner, Peter C. Guest Commentary "Goodbye, Theologians" Ministry Today Magazine September 6, 2006 www.ministrytodaymag.com/blog/2006/09/guest-commentary-goodbye-theologians
[128] Ibid
[129] Wagner, Peter C. "Dominion!" 2008 Chosen Books (Grand Rapids, MI) Chapter 3 states that Dominion Theology is the new paradigm for the church. Chapter 4 discusses Open Theism and affirms that it is the best model for understanding God's working in the world.
[130] Op Cit Wagner "Goodbye Theologians"
[131] Ibid
[132] Op Cit Wagner "Dominion!" page 58
[133] Ibid
[134] Wilson, Douglas "Easy Chairs, Hard Words", 1991 Canon Press (Moscow, ID) page 138
[135] Joyner, Rick "There Were Two Trees in the Garden" 1986 Morningstar Publications (Charlotte, NC) page 1
[136] Ibid italics in the original
[137] Davis, Paul Keith "William Branham: A Forerunner Ministry and Prototype of the Bridal Company" Elijah List www.elijahlist.com/words/display_word_pf.html?ID=7420
[138] Bickle, Mike "Contemplative Prayer" CD series. CD #2
[139] Pierce, Cal "The Kingdom Healthcare System: The Marriage of Health and Healing in the Body of Christ" Published on Elijah List on October 30th, 2009. This information is from the biographical blurb at the bottom of the article by Pierce.

[140] Ibid

[141] Tozer, A.W. "The Knowledge of the Holy" 1961 Harper and Row (New York, NY) page 6

Chapter 7

[142] Ibid page 9

[143] Gruden, Wayne "Systematic Theology" 1994 InterVarsity Press (Leicester, England) and Zondervan (Grand Rapids, MI) page 226

[144] Ware, Bruce "Father, Son, & Holy Spirit" 2005 Crossway Books (Wheaton, IL) page 17

[145] Carol Arnott as quoted in Counterfeit Revival by Hank Hanegraaf 1997 Word Publishing (Dallas, TX) page 111 Incidentally, both authors are acquainted with a minister who was present at this conference and verified that the statement occurred essentially as reported.

[146] Steyne, Denny "Apostolic Love, The Gospel of Love that Demonstrates True Apostolic Authority" posted on Elijah List 11/23/06

[147] For a much more thorough discussion of this subject the reader is referred to "God's Lesser Glory", "God's Greater Glory" and "Their God is Too Small" all by Dr. Bruce Ware, as well as "Beyond the Bounds" by Piper, Taylor and Kjoss.

[148] Boyd, Gregory "Letters from a Skeptic" as quoted in "Beyond the Bounds" by John Piper, Justin Taylor and Paul Kjoss Helseth 2003 Crossway Books (Wheaton, IL) page 10

[149] Wagner, Peter C. "Dominion!" 2008 Chosen Books (Grand Rapids, MI) page 76

[150] Ibid page 77

[151] Ibid page 79

[152] Jones, Bob and Paul Keith Davis "Shepherd's Rod 2006" published in Nov. 2006 on the Elijah List

[153] Bickle, Mike, "Contending for the Power of God" CD Series ,FOTB

[154] Op Cit Jones and Davis "Shepherd's Rod"

[155] Yount, Bill Elijah List Feb. 12, 2007

[156] Bentley, Todd "Making Decrees to Activate the Heavenly Court, Elijah List Oct. 31, 2004

[157] Ibid

[158] Ibid

[159] Op Cit Wagner page 65

[160] Ibid page 71. Wagner is quoting from Steve Thompson, "Your Authority in Christ" published by MorningStar Journal, the ministry of Rick Joyner

[161] Anonymous document- "Authority of the Believer: Prophetic Decrees", Roman numeral II "How God's Power is Released in the earthly Realm" This document has been used as a part of the training program for those in the IHOP prayer rooms. I attribute responsibility for it to Bickle as the head of this ministry.

[162] Ibid

[163] Bolz, Shawn, "Keys to Heaven's Economy: An Angelic Visitation from the Minister of Finance", Streams Publishing House (North Sutton, NH) page 72

[164] Ibid

[165] Ibid page 73

[166] Ibid pages 74-75

[167] Ibid page 94

[168] Hicks, Scott Elijah List August 21, 2006 "God's Collection Agency—Your Debt has been Paid!"

[169] Sheets, Dutch "Intercessory Prayer" as quoted in "Worship Warrior" by Chuck Pierce 2002 Regal Books (Ventura CA) pages 211-212 This book is interesting because, without intending to be, it is actually a fine compilation of the errant teachings of a number of members of the prophetic movement.

[170] Otis, George Jr. "Informed Intercession" 1999 Renew Books (Ventura, CA) page 55

[171] Willimon, William as quoted in "Christless Christianity" by Michael Horton, 2008 Baker Books (Grand Rapids, MI) page 47

[172] Hamon, Bill "Prophets and the Prophetic Movement" Fifth printing 1999 Destiny Image Publishers (Shippensburg, PA) page 59

[173] Op Cit Ware page 57

[174] Phillips, Theresa "Arise America and Take Your Place: Prophetic Words for America and the Nations" posted on Elijah List February 21, 2011

[175] Hood, Allen "The Playfulness of God" CD #1 The section is very lengthy which is why I did not give a direct quote.

[176] Op. Cit Ware page 21

[177] Bennett, Kirk, "The Prophetic Seer Training Course" Module 1, CD2 IHOP

[178] Hood, Allen, "The Cross of Christ: The Tenacious Pursuit of the Bridegroom" CD 2, FOTB

[179] Bennett, Kirk, "Prophecy and the Arts", A training course from IHOP CD #1. This no slip of the tongue because "Bennett makes the same assertion in his "The Prophetic Seer" Training course on CD #2

[180] Bolz, Shawn, "The Throne Room Company", Streams Publishing House (North Sutton, NH) page 69

[181] Op Cit Tozer page 12

Chapter 8

[182] Joyner, Rick "There were Two Trees in the Garden" 1992 Whitaker House, (New Kensington, PA) page 59

[183] Grudem, Wayne "Systematic Theology" 1994 InterVarsity Press (Leicester, England) and Zondervan (Grand Rapids, MI) page 543

[184] Bolz, Shawn, "The Throne Room Company", Streams Publishing House, (North Sutton, NH) page 26

[185] Op Cit Grudem page 551

[186] Bolz, Shawn, "Keys to Heaven's Economy: An Angelic Visitation from the Minister of Finance", Streams Publishing House, (North Sutton, NH) page 35

[187] Ibid page 78

[188] Op Cit Bolz "The Throne Room Company" page 68

[189] Ibid page 59-60

[190] Ibid page 60

[191] Thomas, Choo "Heaven is so Real" 2003 Charisma House (Lake Mary, FL) page 200

[192] Bickle, Mike "The Pleasures of Loving God" 2000 Creation House (Lake Mary, FL) page 30

[193] For an example of this teaching see Allen Hood's series "The Playfulness of God" CD #1 Hood specifically uses the term dowry and says that it is paid by the groom for the bride. Typically in cultures engaging in this practice, this is called the bride price not the dowry. However since this is the term used by Hood and others like him, we have chosen to use it as well.

[194] Sutton, Matthew Avery "Aimee Semple McPherson and the Resurrection of Christian America" 2007 Harvard University Press (London, England) page 55

[195] Ibid page 57

[196] Ware, Bruce "Father, Son, & Holy Spirit" 2005 Crossway Books (Wheaton, IL) page 21

[197] Connor, Bobby "2007 Shepherd's Rod" published on Elijah List January 8, 2007

[198] "Divorce Decree from Baal" This version is attributed to Dutch Sheets. However, there are several versions in circulation and several members of the prophetic movement are given credit for this. This particular version can be accessed at http://blogs.myspace.com/index.cfm?fuseaction=blog.view&friendID=135190141

[199] Thomas, Choo "Heaven is So Real" 2003 Charisma House (Lake Mary, FL) page 131-132

Chapter 9

[200] Thomas, Choo "Heaven is So Real" 2003 Charisma House (Lake Mary, FL) page 133

[201] Ibid page 46

[202] Ibid page 249

[203] Horton, Michael "Christless Christianity" 2008 Baker Books (Grand Rapids, MI) page 61

[204] Jones, Bob Prophetic.TV episode #9 2006 Larry Randolph has to appear on this interview with Bob Jones in order to "interpret" him. Bob frequently has to be interpreted by others because his prophecies sound more like the oracle of Delphi than a Biblical prophet.

[205] Hood, Allen from the series The Cross of Christ: The Tenacious Pursuit of the Bridegroom. CD #3 2003 FOTB

[206] Bickle, Mike "Fellowshipping with the Holy Spirit" session 1 1983. I refer to this as a foundational teaching because it can still be found in podcast form on many of the House of Prayer websites around the country.

[207] Ibid emphasis added

[208] Ibid emphasis added

[209] Ibid emphasis added

[210] Tyrell, Michael Posted by Patricia King on the Elijah List Feb. 3, 2007

[211] Keating, Thomas from the book "Open Heart, Open Mind" pages 139-141 as posted at http://www.kyrie.com/cp/explanations_cp_TK.htm

[212] Bickle, Mike, Contemplative Prayer CD #2 FOTB ministries. All of these references to Bickle's teaching on this subject can be found on this CD.

[213] Bickle, Mike "Contemplative Prayer" CD #4

[214] Silvoso, Ed "That None Should Perish: How to Reach Entire Cities for Christ Through Prayer Envangelism" Regal Books (Ventura, CA) 1994 page 195

[215] Joyner, Rick Taking the Land Part LIV Morningstar weekly bulletin week 48, 2006 This is an email bulletin sent out weekly to subscribers. It can be accessed at http://www.morningstarministries.org/Mobile/default.aspx?group_id=1000013670&article _id=1000013228

[216] Bolz, Shawn "The Keys to Heaven's Economy" Streams Publishing House (North Sutton, NH) 2005 page 82

[217] Steve Thompson as quoted in the book, "Dominion" by C Peter Wagner Chosen Publications (Grand Rapids, MI) 2008 page 71

[218] Mike Bickle and Bob Jones, "Visions and Revelations" Kansas City Fellowship 1989 The transcript can be read at http://herescope.blogspot.com/2006/02/new-breed-defined.html

[219] Ibid

[220] Davis, Paul Keith "Engaging the Revelatory Realm of Heaven" Streams Publications (North Sutton, NH) 2003 page 56

[221] Bennett, Kirk Prophecy and the Arts CD #1 IHOP Training Course

Chapter 10

[222] Enlow, Johnny "The Seven Mountain Prophecy" Creation House Publications (Lake Mary, FL) 2008 page 24 The seven mountains spoken of in this book represent the seven areas of culture that the church must come to control which are: media, government, education, economy, religion, celebration and family.

[223] Lake, John G "John G. Lake: His Life, His Sermons, His Boldness of Faith" Kenneth Copeland Publications (Fort Worth, TX) 1995 page 510

[224] Tillin, Tricia "The New Thing" internet article available at http://www.intotruth.org/res/newthin2.html#BELIEFS

[225] Joyner, Rick "The Final Quest" Whitaker House Publishing (New Kensington, PA) 1996 page 26-27

[226] Ibid page 22

[227] Joyner, Rick" A Prophetic Vision for the 21St Century" Thomas Nelson (Nashville, TN) 1999 page 184

[228] Ibid page 168

[229] Joyner, Rick "There Were Two Trees in the Garden", Morningstar Publications (Charlotte, NC) 1986 page 31

[230] Frangipane, Francis article dated August 21, 2005   "Repairers of the Breach" Elijah List

[231] Frangipane, Francis "In the Presence of God" New Wine Press (West Sussex, England) 1994 page 154

[232] Ibid page 155

[233] Ibid

[234] Ibid 157

[235] Branham, William "The Mighty God Unveiled Before Us" page 20

[236] Austin, Jill "The Breaker Anointing-A Holy Invasion where Eternity Breaks Through" found at www.elijahlist.com/words/display_word.html?ID=2083

[237] Bickle, Mike, "Thunder from Heaven" CD series. This statement is actually found on the back cover of the set in addition on CD #4.

[238] Hamon, Bill "Apostles, Prophets and the Coming Moves of God" Destiny Image Publishers, (Shippensburg, PA) 1997 page 267

[239] Ibid 251

[240] Op Cit Enlow page 24

[241] Joyner, Rick The Harvest, 128-129

[242] Shultz, Steve along with Mickey and Sandi Freed, Elijah List, Feb. 16, 2007

[243] Anonymous . This statement can be found at the IHOP website on the page entitled "Affirmations and Denials"

[244] Blueprint Prophecy found at the IHOP website at http://ihop-intl.org/EnglishP2/Blueprint_Prophecy%5B1%5D.pdf

[245] Blueprint Prophecy 2009 version. Found at the IHOP website at http://www.ihop.org/Publisher/File.aspx?ID=1000014262

246 Bob Jones and Mike Bickle New Breed transcript. This transcript can be found in its entirety at http://herescope.blogspot.com/2006/02/new-breed-defined.html
247 Bickle, Mike Our Prophetic History CD #6 "An Interview with Paul Cain". 2002 Friends of the Bridegroom
248 Op Cit Hamon, "Apostles, Prophets and the Coming Moves of God" page 22
249 Hamon, Bill p. 385 The Eternal Church
250 Ibid page 349
251 Wyatt, Ryan Elijah List, March 7, 2007
252 Ibid
253 Frangipane, Francis Weekly newsletter 9/7/2006
254 Joyner, Rick Morningstar Journal Volume 2, No. 1
255 Op Cit Enlow page 24
256 Wyatt, Ryan posted on the Elijah List on August 24th, 2006
257 Ibid

Chapter 11

258 Joyner, Rick "The Final Quest", 1996 Whitaker House (New Kensington, PA) page 13
259 Ibid page 20-21
260 Bolz, Shawn "The Keys to Heaven's Economy" 2005 Streams Publishing House (North Sutton, NH) page 28. Bolz receives this revelation after coming to understand that he is to receive an inheritance left by his brother whose life was cut short by leukemia.
261 "It's Supernatural" TV show May 15, 2006 with Sid Roth see http://www.sidroth.org/site/News2?abbr=tv_&page=NewsArticle&id=5209&security=1041&news_iv_ctrl=1190
262 Ibid page 123
263 Cox, Paul Elijah List February 7, 2005
264 Jackson, John Paul "Spiritual Portals" Elijah List February 11, 2006
265 Ibid
266 Pierce, Chuck "The Worship Warrior" 2002 Regal Books (Ventura, CA) page 136
267 Walters, Kathy "God is Coming Like Niagara Falls" Elijah List
268 Steyne, Denny Elijah List November 23,
269 Boyson, Victoria "The Unclean Spirit Whose Purpose is to Convince Us He is God!" Elijah list Aug. 18, 2004 See also "Warriors of Truth" April 9, 2005 by the same author
270 Davis, Paul Keith This is found in a message delivered at Christ Triumphant Church in Lee's Summit , MO. I have this message on tape but the tape is undated.
271 Goll, Jim "A New Intercessory Assignment: Judicial Intercession" Elijah List, May 2nd, 2004
272 Malone, Henry "How to Cleanse Your House and the Land it Sits On", Elijah List October 17, 2005. this ritual 3 or 4 occasions at his home with noticeable changes.
273 Op Cit Pierce, Worship Warrior page 176
274 Bentley, Todd "Making Decrees to Activate the Heavenly Court" Elijah List October 31, 2004 All repetition and exclamation marks appear in the original. Much of Todd Bentley's material has been removed from the website since his moral failure has become widely known.
275 Davis, Paul Keith and Bob Jones "The Season of the Basilisk" Elijah List, June 21, 2007

[276] Jones, Bob "We're in the Year of the Lion-We're Coming to Authority" Elijah List, February 23, 2011

Chapter 12

[277] Clement, Kim June 16th, 2007 Published by Elijah list
[278] Hawkins, Cedric "God's Lightening Rod" April 2001 Charisma Magazine. To be clear, the article is about Rick Joyner. Frangipane is interviewed about one of Joyner's failed prophecies.
[279] Bob Jones and Mike Bickle "The Shepherd's Rod"
[280] Clement, Kim Jan 13, 2004 Elijah List (The prophecy was given on TBN 1/12/04)
[281] Ibid
[282] Ibid
[283] Jones, Bob "Bob Jones Weighs in on March 11" Elijah List 4/17/2004 On can look at articles around the same time period to see the gymnastics that were being attempted to dig Kim Clement out of his prophecies concerning Osama Bin Laden.
[284] Clement, Kim published on Elijah List Nov. 19, 2006 emphasis in the original
[285] Yount, Bill "I Heard the Father say...'I am Beginning to Prophesy Through Commercials, Candy and Clothing—Especially Over the Holidays!"
[286] Ibid
[287] Ibid
[288] Harmon, Cedric, "God's Lightening Rod" www.harvestnet.org/lookback/god'slightningrod.htm
[289] Brown, Catherine "There will be a Seven Year Period of Plenty Followed by a Seven Year Period of Famine." Elijah List.com 3/27/07
[290] Brown, Catherine "A Word about Revival in Sweden" published on Elijah List on 6/22/2007.
[291] Conner, Bobby "We Stand on the Verge of the Largest Healing Movement in the History of the Church" Elijah List July 28th, 2007
[292] Wagner, Peter "Peter Wagner Points to Accurate Prophecy by Chuck Pierce Over Colorado" Elijah List July 2nd, 2004
[292] Ibid. This prophecy by Chuck Pierce was actually given October 10, 2003

Chapter 13

[293] Bickle, Mike "Growing in the Prophetic" page 101
[294] Ibid 117-118
[295] Bolz, Shawn "The Keys to Heaven's Economy" Streams Publishing House (North Sutton, New Hampshire) 2005 page 43
[296] Ibid page 77
[297] Ibid page 102
[298] Joyner, Rick "The Final Quest" Whitaker House (New Kensington, PA) 1996 page 58
[299] Ibid page 86-87
[300] Ibid page 115
[301] Ibid page 81
[302] Joyner, Rick "The Prophetic Ministry" Morningstar Publications (Charlotte, NC) 1997 page 53

[303] Hamon, Bill "Prophets and the Prophetic Movement" Destiny Image Publishers (Shippensburg, PA) 1990 page 57

[304] Ibid page 59

[305] Wagner, CBN interview January 3, 2000

[306] International Coalition of Apostles "What is an Apostle" PDF document available at http://www.apostlesnet.net/What%20Is%20An%20Apostle.pdf

[307] Davis, Paul Keith "Engaging the Revelatory Realm of Heaven" Streams Publications 2003 (North Sutton, NH) page 29

[308] Ibid page 37-38

[309] Ibid page 55

[310] Ibid page 56

[311] Op Cit Bickle page 171

Appendix A

[312] Liardon, Roberts "God's Generals" 1996 Robert's Liardon Publishing (Laguna Hills, CA) chapter 10 page 309 "William Branham, A Man of Notable Signs and Wonders"

[313] Ibid page 332

[314] Ibid page 324

[315] Ibid page 325

[316] Liardon, Roberts "God's Generals" 1996 Albury Publishing (Tulsa, OK) pages 333; 339-341

[317] Lake, John G. "John G. Lake: His Life, His Sermons, His Boldness of Faith", 1994 Kenneth Copeland Publications (Ft. Worth, TX) page 13

[318] Ibid 196

[319] Ibid page 304

[320] Ibid page 510

[321] Ibid page 122

[322] Ibid page 133

[323] Ibid page 404

[324] Ibid page 124

Appendix B

[325] Mark I. Bubeck, *Spiritual Warfare Basics.* Sioux City, Iowa: self-published conference booklet, no date, pg. 23 Quoted in an article by Richard G. Fisher "Demons, Demons, Where are the Demons?" Published by Personal Freedom Outreach and accessed at: http://www.pfo.org/wdemons.htm

[326] Bubeck, Mark, "The Adversary" 1975 Moody Press (Chicago, IL) page 124

Other Titles by Solid Ground

In addition *Wandering Stars* by Keith Gibson, we are delighted to offer several titles that place a premium on the written Word of God.

Notes on Galatians by Machen is a reprint that is long overdue, especially in light of the present-day battle of the doctrine articulated in Galatians.

The Origin of Paul's Religion by Machen penetrates to the heart of the matter and speaks to many of the contemporary attacks upon the purity of the Gospel of Christ.

Biblical and Theological Studies by the professors of Princeton in 1912, at the centenary celebration of the Seminary. Articles are by men like Allis, Vos, Warfield, Machen, Wilson and others.

Theology on Fire: Vols. 1 & 2 by J.A. Alexander is the two volumes of sermons by this brilliant scholar from Princeton Seminary.

A Shepherd's Heart by J.W. Alexander is a volume of outstanding expository sermons from the pastoral ministry of one of the leading preachers of the 19th century.

Evangelical Truth by Archibald Alexander is a volume of practical sermons intended to be used for Family Worship.

The Lord of Glory by B.B. Warfield is one of the best treatments of the doctrine of the Deity of Christ ever written. Warfield is simply masterful.

The Power of God unto Salvation by B.B. Warfield is the first book of sermons ever published of this master-theologian. Several of these are found nowhere else.

The Person & Work of the Holy Spirit by B.B. Warfield is a compilation of all the sermons, articles and book reviews by a master-theologian on a theme that should interest every child of God. Brilliant in every way!

Grace & Glory by Geerhardus Vos is a series of addresses delivered in the chapel to the students at Princeton. John Murray said of him, "Dr. Vos is, in my judgment, the most penetrating exegete it has been my privilege to know, and I believe, the most incisive exegete that has appeared in the English-speaking world in this century."

Princeton Sermons: *Chapel Addresses from 1891-92* by B.B. Warfield, W.H. Green, C.W. Hodge, John D. Davis and More. According to Joel Beeke, this is "a treasure-trove of practical Christianity delivered by some of the greatest preachers and seminary teachers America has ever known."

Call us at **1-205-443-0311**
Send us an e-mail at **mike.sgcb@gmail.com**
Visit us on line at **www.solid-ground-books.com**